The Same but Different

Language Use and Attitudes in Four Communities of Burkina Faso

SIL International
Publications in Sociolinguistics

Publication 5

Publications in Sociolinguistics is a series published by SIL International. The series is a venue for works covering a broad range of topics in sociolinguistics. While most volumes are authored by members of SIL, suitable works by others will also form part of the series.

Series Editor

M. Paul Lewis

Volume Editor

Rhonda L. Hartell

Production Staff

Bonnie Brown, Managing Editor
Bonnie Brown, Production Manager
Karoline Fisher, Compositor
Hazel Shorey, Graphic Artist

The Same but Different

Language Use and Attitudes in Four Communities of Burkina Faso

Stuart Showalter

SIL International
Dallas, Texas

© 2001 by SIL International
Library of Congress Catalog No: 00-110258
ISBN: 1-55671-092-5
ISSN: 1091-9074

Printed in the United States of America

All Rights Reserved

07 06 05 04 03 02 01   10 9 8 7 6 5 4 3 2 1

No part of this publication may be reproduced, stored in a retrieval system, or transmitted in any form or by any means—electronic, mechanical, photocopy, recording, or otherwise—without the express permission of SIL International, with the exception of brief excerpts in journal articles or reviews.

Copies of this and other publications of SIL International may be obtained from

International Academic Bookstore
SIL International
7500 W. Camp Wisdom Road
Dallas TX 75236-5699

Voice: 972-708-7404
Fax: 972-708-7363
Email: academic_books@sil.org
Internet: http://www.sil.org

Acknowledgments

A work of this nature owes so much to so many that it seems ludicrous to sign only my name to it. Many who made this research possible will have to go unnamed for want of space on the page or of recollection of their names on my part.

Among the people of Loropéni, the Prefect, Joseph Zoungrana deserves special mention, along with other town officials, for their support of our presence among them, even though I never explained very well what a linguist actually does. The Kaan Iya, Dabla Farma, was also gracious in allowing our research to proceed in the Kaan community. I owe deep gratitude to more than 140 Kaan, Kpatogo, Dogo, and Khi who took time to voice their opinions and share their experiences with the curious *tafira* who, more often than not, showed up unannounced in their villages. Our Kaan and Lobi neighbors in Loropéni did their part by letting us observe their daily lives. The people of the Mission Protestante Evangélique and the church in Loropéni gave us companionship and spiritual support when it was sorely needed. In particular, I thank Mady Vaillant, Liselotte Liniger, Pastor André Dolli, Hans and Monique Lehmann, the Goertzens, the Fischers....

Many people helped us with language learning and surveying, even though some did not know it at the time. Philippe Farma, Misa Jean-Baptiste Suwa, Koffi Farma, Jean-Gabriel Farma, Philemon Farma, Tiole Tilkar, and Bayaba Ouattara all made invaluable contributions to our knowledge of Kaansa and our understanding of Lobiri and Jula bilingualism. Arjuma Louis-Marie Farma confirmed some of my observations in an informal chat one Sunday afternoon. Dr. Madeleine Père deserves much recognition for her own foundational research on the Kaan and the Lobi, from which this work has benefited tremendously.

Ralph Fasold, my mentor for the dissertation on which this book is based, was a willing sounding board for my ideas, and offered solid advice from his experience and knowledge of the field. Dick Tucker gave a lot of encouragement along with his insightful suggestions. Simon Battestini and Pascal Kokora, with their long experience in West Africa, added depth and realism to this work. Dorry Kenyon helped fine-tune the analysis by contributing his expertise in educational statistics. I deeply appreciate the help of these scholars, but since, in the end, the words, ideas, and statistics presented here are mine, so are the mistakes and errors that remain.

To those who have faithfully supported us from Burkina Faso to Burtonsville, we offer thanks and a promise to continue work among the Kaan people *ná Yékíri pí ya*. Fred and Kathy Kuhl are due special mention for their unflagging friendship and generosity.

Cathie, my wife, and our children, Nathanael, Esther, and Jesse, have put up with a lot to see me through; their love has provided welcome relief from too many books, papers, and numbers. Finally, I thank God for His grace and love, which are new every morning.

Contents

Acknowledgments. v
1 Introduction 1
2 Sociolinguistic Issues in West Africa 5
   Multilingualism 6
      General patterns in West Africa 6
      Multilingualism and colonialism 10
      The current situation. 11
   The spread of lingua francas. 12
      Language spread framework 13
      Pidgins and koinés. 15
      Mandé and Jula 16
      Jula 17
   Dialect continua 18
3 Language Issues in Burkina Faso 21
   Introduction to the country 21
   Multilingualism 24
   Language policy 27
   The Kaan, Kpatogo, Dogo, and Khi 29
      A synchronic description 32
      A diachronic description 43

Contents

4 Literature Review 47
   Linguistic results of interethnic contact 47
      Bilingualism 47
      Language variation and change 53
      Language shift 58
   Social-psychological results of interethnic contact:
   Language attitudes 63
      Measuring language attitudes 64
      The semantic differential and the matched guise 65
      Some language attitude studies in Africa 67

5 Research Methods 73
   Sociolinguistic survey methodology 73
      Theoretical background and general approaches 74
      Research techniques 76
   Broad survey of the Kaan, Kpatogo, Dogo, and Khi 80
      Survey design 81
      Validity 89
      Observations 91
   Specific survey of the Kaan of Loropéni 92

6 The Language Attitude Survey 97
   The samples 97
   The evaluation procedures 101
      Scoring responses 102
      Computing attitude dimension scores 103
   The results 110
      Statistical tests and the nature of the data 110
      Attitudes toward ethnic identity 112
      Attitudes toward ethnic contact 122
      Attitudes toward language awareness 135
      Attitudes toward personal character 144
      Attitudes toward social status 151

7 Language Proficiency and Use in the Kaan Community 163
      Background and approach 164

Contents

Profile of the sample	165
Language proficiency	165
Initial estimate	166
Can-do scales	166
Results compared	168
Self-comparison of Lobiri and Jula proficiency	169
Validity of can-do scales	170
Language use in six domains	171
8 Integration of the Research	**187**
Dialect and attitude issues	187
Bilingualism and language use issues	194
Mackey's bilingualism model	194
Urban and rural models of language use in Burkina Faso	196
Pervasiveness, dominance, and the lingua franca	197
Types of bilingual communities	200
The communicative economy	201
The Khi and the Dogo	202
The Kaan and the Kpatogo	204
9 Summary and Conclusion	**207**
Summary of research results	207
Chapter 6: The language attitude survey	207
Chapter 7: The language proficiency and use survey	209
Chapter 8: The analysis of integrated data	210
Chapter 5: Methodology	212
Conclusion	213
Appendix 1	**215**
Village Data	215
Appendix 2	**223**
Language Attitude Survey Data	223
Appendix 3	**245**
Language Proficiency and Use Survey Data	245
References	**253**

1
Introduction

> The existence of 'dialects', or even of 'languages' in their own right will be affirmed or denied for political, ethical, religious, or other reasons, without much actual reference to resemblances or differences in phonology, morphology, lexicon or any other linguistic system. A systematic study of attitudes in this field would be highly interesting. (Alexandre 1971:655)

Alexandre wrote this in reference to the extensive language variation he had observed in years of research in sub-Saharan Africa. This book is an attempt at such a systematic study as Alexandre suggests, focusing on the language attitudes, proficiency, and use of a small rural community in southwest Burkina Faso in West Africa. The people at the center of this research are the Kaan people, their ethnolinguistic family made up of the Kpatogo, Dogo, and Khi peoples (also known as the Gan, Gbadogo, Dogosé, and Komono), and their ethnic neighbors in the region surrounding Loropéni, the Lobi and the Jula. The first aspect of this study is a survey of the social attitudes that the Kaan, Kpatogo, Dogo and Khi hold toward their own language varieties as well as toward Lobiri and Jula, two of the regional languages of contact. The second aspect focuses on the community of the Kaan people living in and around the town of Loropéni by surveying their patterns of multilingualism and language use.

The methods employed to investigate the sociolinguistic situation were drawn from those developed by Labov, Gumperz, Hymes, Fishman, Lambert, the U. S. Foreign Service Institute (FSI), and SIL International, and were adapted in form and application for the rural, nonliterate, West African setting where this research took place.

The particular questions this study investigates concern language attitudes and multilingualism.

What attitudes and stereotypes do the Kaan, Kpatogo, Dogo, and Khi hold toward the language varieties they speak? Given the relatively high lexical similarity and intelligibility between these dialects, do they see themselves as speaking the same language or different languages? Do they see themselves as a unified ethnic group or as four different groups with separate ethnic identities? How much contact do they have with each other on a regular basis? What kind of personal character judgments do they make of each other based on dialect differences? How do their attitudes toward each other compare with their attitudes toward the Lobi and the Jula, two other ethnic groups of the region with whom they are likely to have frequent contact? What relationship can be found between measures of linguistic similarity and measures of language attitudes? How can cases of nonreciprocal intelligibility be explained in terms of dialect prestige, attitudes toward shared ethnic identity, geographical isolation, language contact, and ethnic history? What attitudes accompany other signs of language shift toward the regional trade language?

As for multilingualism, to what extent is proficiency in Jula, the regional trade language, spread throughout the Kaan community? How proficient is the Kaan community in Lobiri, the language of the Lobi people, the largest ethnic group in the region? How do the Kaan people use Jula and Lobiri in different domains of everyday life, and what do these patterns of proficiency and use tell us about the roles, dominance, and pervasiveness of Jula, Lobiri, and Kaansa in the Kaan community? Is there evidence of a language shift by the Kaan toward Jula or Lobiri?

Can methods for sociolinguistic investigation developed in European and North American urban, literate settings be adapted for accurate, valid, and informative research in rural, nonliterate, West African settings? More specifically, can the "matched guise" developed by Lambert, the subjective reaction interview developed by Labov, and the language proficiency scales developed by the U. S. Foreign Service Institute be modified and used for investigating the language attitudes and language proficiency of rural subsistence farmers in Burkina Faso? In doing so, do these methods retain reliability and validity? What are the limitations of these methods in this setting and in this adapted form?

The historical, geographical, and intellectual backgrounds for this study are established in chapters 2–5. The results of the language attitude survey of the Kaan, Kpatogo, Dogo, and Khi communities and the survey of language proficiency and use within the Kaan community around Loropéni are presented in chapters 6 and 7.

Introduction

Chapter 8 is an attempt to integrate the data from the two surveys with the historical and linguistic data presented in chapters 2–5; chapter 9 is a summary of the findings and conclusions.

The research for this study was carried out from June 1987 to November 1988 in Burkina Faso, and through March 1991 in the US. Since that time the population of Burkina has continued to grow and the government has made some administrative changes in the provincial divisions. Thes changes are reflected in the footnotes in chapter 3.

2

Sociolinguistic Issues in West Africa

Since the development of sociolinguistics as a field of research in the 1960s, African, European, and North American linguists have begun to apply the research paradigms developed by Labov, Hymes, Gumperz, and others to the daunting and yet fascinating problems of language in Africa. Though modern linguistic research in sub-Saharan Africa began in the colonial era, it has concentrated on lexical, grammatical, and comparative studies, with passing attention paid to the rich variation of form and use which we are now discovering pervades all levels of indigenous African societies. Researchers have encountered incipient multilingualism of kinds not familiar in the West. To cope with linguistic diversity and interethnic contact, indigenous peoples have adopted lingua francas for trade, travel, disputes, alliances, domination, and survival. Sometimes a lingua franca is needed to communicate even to members of one's own ethnic group, so great and yet subtle is the variation in what researchers sometimes consider a single language. To govern these diverse populations, African governments have struggled to formulate language policies which promote their aims of modernization and political independence. Yet most of these policies are reformulations of colonial legacies, which were designed to create a ruling elite using a European language. The challenge they face now, forty years after independence, is to develop systems of government and education that meet the authentic needs of their citizens, and this must necessarily include recognizing the linguistic diversity that is so much a part of indigenous culture.

Three of the many sociolinguistic issues that weigh heavily on the pace of development in Africa, and which are most relevant to the research reported here, are (1) urban and rural multilingualism, (2) the spread of lingua francas, and (3) the nature of dialect continua.

Multilingualism

Multilingualism has been a part of urban and rural African life for centuries, well before the European colonists added a new dimension by creating artificial borders and new networks of interethnic contact. Alexandre (1971, 1972) has suggested that as communication networks improve in modern Africa, multilingualism increases: it is most common where few communication barriers exist, less common in mountainous regions, forests, and isolated areas.

The ethnic diversity in nations such as Nigeria and Cameroon is staggering to the Western observer: Cameroon has over two hundred language varieties, and Nigeria over four hundred (Grimes 1984). Though one often hears the phrases "English-speaking" or "French-speaking" Africa, Alexandre (1972) estimated in the 1960s that probably not more than ten percent of the total population of the countries formed from French and British colonies could effectively speak these languages. While this percentage has obviously increased in forty years of increasingly available French- or English-based education, especially in major cities, it remains true that the vast majority of Africans maintain their indigenous languages in daily life.

General patterns in West Africa

Broad patterns of multilingualism, though infinitely detailed, are similar enough between modern nations that Alexandre (1971, 1972) has drawn up a macrosociolinguistic profile typical of most African nations.

Linguistically, populations can be classed into three different groups:

1. A small multilingual, modern-oriented group using a European (or "colonial") language.
2. A fairly large multilingual group using vernaculars plus an African vehicular language of national or regional extension.
3. A traditionally oriented group either monolingual or multilingual at a strictly local (as opposed to national) level. (1971:660)

(1) Map of West Africa

Contemporary African class structure seems to be based on control of linguistic resources. Those in the first of Alexandre's three groups usually hold much of the political and economic power and have become a separate social class in and of themselves. This minority elite is ethnically heterogeneous, but nonetheless unified by shared knowledge of French or English, and through this knowledge controls the modern sector of the nation's economy. The former colonial languages are now seen as international languages, and the regional trade languages can be called "cross-border" languages (1971:661), used for communication in groups two and three above.

The majority of the population exists divided into ethnolinguistic groups whose territory often straddles national borders. They have only African languages at their disposal for communication, and thus must go through the elite minority for interaction with the modern world. The figure in (2) illustrates a typical sociolinguistic division of a modern African country (from Alexandre 1972:85; used by permission).

(2)

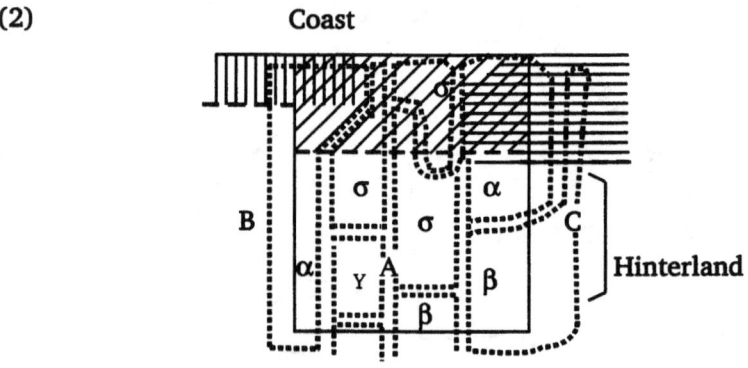

.... Tribal limit
———— Political boundaries between country A and its neighbors, B and C
– – – – Break in communication with the outside world
⧚ ⧜ Sociological zone of use of the "colonial" language

The cross-hatched zone represents the minority in country A which has a monopoly on the instrument of international communication.

The coast is a sociological rather than a geographical zone: it is the zone of maximum schooling and of maximum contact with the outside world. The tribes of this region are favored by their situation, particularly those (α) inhabiting a frontier position, which gives them access to two languages of wide communication. The tribes of the hinterland (β, σ) are less favored, especially those which, like Y, live in enclaves.

Lafage (1979, 1986) has drawn up a framework of shared African social structures to serve as a background for sociolinguistic analyses. It is obvious from her diagram, shown in (3), that class interrelationships and

Multilingualism

divisions are more complex than what we are used to in urbanized Europe and the U.S. In West Africa, ethnolinguistic diversity and the residual effects of colonialism add a new layer of complexity to familiar Western class distinctions such as occupation, education, and urbanness. The tension between modern and traditional forces permeates every layer of society and leads to expedient alliances between groups which differ from country to country and region to region.

(3) Class alliances in different West African nations (Lafage 1986:45)

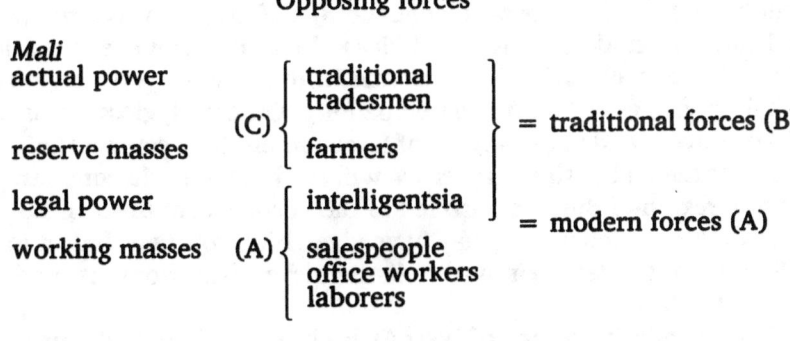

Mali
actual power
     (C) { traditional tradesmen
reserve masses   farmers } = traditional forces (B)

legal power
       intelligentsia
working masses (A) { salespeople
       office workers
       laborers } = modern forces (A)

Ivory Coast
       (C) { customary chiefs
         farmers
  (D) {
         plantation owners
         intelligentsia
      (A) { salespeople, office workers
         laborers } (B)

Senegal
       (C) { religious chiefs
         farmers } (B)
  (D) [
         Senegalese capitalists
         intelligentisia
      (A) { salespeople, office workers
         laborers } (E)

Guinea
      traditional chiefs (nonexistent)
      farmers
      intelligentsia
  (A) { salespeople, office workers
      laborers } (B)

A = Modern forces;
C = Traditional forces;
B, D, E = Expedient alliances, variable according to country

Multilingualism and colonialism

Before the advent of the European colonists, multilingualism existed in West Africa as a result of indigenous empires and multiethnic states. In these states (for example, the empires of Mali and Ghana and the Mossi and Fulani states), some of the multilingualism and diglossia was due to ritualized uses of superstrate languages (as of Arabic for Islamic worship and law and trade with North Africa) alongside languages used for regional trade (such as Jula,[1] Hausa, and Fulfulde) and layered on top of the tribal languages of the subjugated peoples. Other polyglossia was the result of slavery and various types of forced interethnic contact (i.e., migration). At the end of this chapter we will see how the Jula conquest of the Comoë region of Burkina Faso led to the enslavement of some Dogo and Khi villages, which in turn may have given birth to a new dialect in those villages. To this day their dialect distinguishes them from the other Dogo and Khi villages.

Colonial administration of West Africa brought about both quantitative and qualitative changes in patterns of multilingualism. Vehicular languages of regional origin grew in importance and in number of speakers, and Arabic, imported from North Africa, was used less as a lingua franca while continuing its more specialized function as the language of the transmission of Islam through Koranic education and Muslim worship. The colonists established their own schools to teach European culture and languages, and missionaries and linguists began using modified Roman scripts to write previously unwritten local languages or, in some cases, to retranscribe languages like Fulfulde, Hausa, and Efik that had already been written in Ajami or other indigenous scripts (Alexandre 1972, Battestini to appear). As the result of new settlement patterns, new vehicular languages sprang up (town languages: Lingala, Town Bemba, etc.); minor languages or dialects were sometimes promoted for Bible translation or Christian evangelism (Efile of Calabar, Nigeria) or as official languages (Zanzibar dialect of Swahili). The most important change to the linguistic landscape was the imposition of European languages, which after independence created exoglossic states. The European languages of the colonizers had no ties to any one ethnic group in the country, and

---

[1]This traders' dialect has been spelled Dioula (in French), Dyula (in English), and more recently Jula. This last spelling is the one used in the most recently developed written form of the language itself: *Julakan* 'Jula language' (Dumestre and Retord 1981).

consequently, colonial interpreters and the European-educated elite formed a new power group which controlled the new nations. Yet the vernacular/traditional elites (chiefs and elders) also maintained some power and control over this governing elite from prior historical, ethnic, or traditional ties. The modern tension between the two power bases is played out in the political rhetoric surrounding the formation of national language policies and in the debate over the role of vernacular languages in modern West African states.

After independence in the late 1950s and early 60s, new West African nations found themselves left with erratic national boundaries that cut through traditional ethnic networks and trade routes. But, because these borders had already begun to take on a political reality of their own, it was deemed unwise to change them. Likewise, French and English, the languages of colonial administration, had considerable power: the whole nexus of vestigial administrative forms and systems were linked to and by them, making a drastic shift to indigenous languages impractical and destabilizing.

The current situation

Modern African nations are overwhelmingly rural and agricultural. Rural life is associated with ethnic loyalties and traditional activities, whereas city life is subject to time and space constraints now common in Western culture. French and English also play a much larger role in everyday life in the city than they do in rural villages. Thus, the kinds of bilingualism researchers find in each setting spring from very different social needs. An East African example of this is given by Polomé (1982), who found that in the cities and major towns of Tanzania, Tribal language-Swahili-English (TSE) multilingualism prevailed. However, in rural areas, language use patterns fell into six categories:

a. Tribal language monolinguals (mainly inland)
b. Swahili monolinguals (mainly coastal)
c. Tribal-Swahili/Swahili-Tribal bilinguals (mainly coastal)
d. Tribal-Tribal bilinguals (only inland)
e. Tribal-Tribal-Swahili trilinguals
f. Tribal-Swahili-Arabic (Muslims) (1982:176)

While we cannot expect these same six categories to exist in West Africa, the important point to grasp is that assessing bilingualism in many African settings requires new models which take into account the kind of sociocultural language variation which is not found in the industrialized Western world. Polomé's creative approach to this task is one example of how this can be done.

Studying both urban and rural multilingualism involves a taxonomy of the factors which influence an individual to learn and retain a second language. Polomé (1982:175) found six factors which play a dominant role in multilingualism in Tanzania: (1) distance of residence from the coast (the farther away, the less exposure to Swahili); (2) amount of education (primary school = Swahili, secondary school = English); (3) mobility (length of residence in tribal area, frequency of intertribal contacts); (4) religion (Islam or Christianity); (5) profession (English or Swahili for urban or government jobs, other languages depending on language of personnel); (6) parental background (mixed marriages). Polomé concluded:

> It is obvious...that ethnic and family background, social environment, professional activity, education, and religion, as well as the regional linguistic spectrum, largely determine the individual's language choice and behavior in a multilingual environment in Tanzania as elsewhere. (p. 179)

The spread of lingua francas

Calvet (1981:7) has called trade languages and lingua francas "concrete responses" to the "challenge of Babel". Lingua francas have been given various names based on different criteria, such as the scope of a language's function (trade language, langue de traite, langue commerciale, Handelssprache, vehicular language, langue véhiculaire, Verkehrssprache), individual functions themselves (contact language, langue de relations, langue 'passe-partout', Kontaktsprache), or structural characteristics of the language (pidgin language, creole) (Heine 1970).

Languages become vehicular as a result of social and political forces tied directly to the language and not because of any inherent quality the language possesses. For example, a language does not spread because it has a 'simple' grammatical structure, but once it starts spreading and is used widely by non-native speakers, its structure goes through a simplifying process to meet immediate communicative needs, which in turn makes it easier for others to learn and encourages its spread.

Understanding the spread of lingua francas is important to this study of the Kaan community because Jula, the trade language of the region, is in the process of spreading. In addition, there is an impression among some expatriate researchers that small ethnic groups in southwest Burkina Faso are abandoning their mother tongues in favor of Jula (Solomiac 1988, Burdon 1987). It is, therefore, important to understand the framework of research on language spread and African lingua francas in order to interpret the results of the bilingualism, language use, and attitude data for the Kaan, Dogo, Kpatogo, and Khi.

Heine (1970) has attempted to classify lingua francas by distinguishing between "A type" and "B type" languages. Type A lingua francas developed, he believes, as a result of the expansion of pre-colonial empires (Mandé, Song'ai, Kanuri, Twi), as a result of their use in pre-colonial trade (Hausa, Jula), or through the spread of religion (Twi, Jula, Arabic). Essentially, these lingua francas functioned as communication systems in West Africa before the period of colonization.

Type B lingua francas grew as a result of European colonization and its concomitant improvement of communications and travel. Thus, these languages spread along roadways, rail lines, and through labor migrations to industrial centers (Wolof, Ganda). Colonial and mission schools also strengthened and spread some languages (Bulu, Kituba). Some languages are clearly one type or the other, while others share characteristics from both types (Swahili, Hausa, Mandé).

Language spread framework

Language spread has been defined as "an increase, over time, in the proportion of a communication network that adopts a given language or language variety for a given communicative function" (Cooper 1982b:6). Thus, on the microsociolinguistic level, the study of language spread is the study of language adoption. Bender, Cooper, and Ferguson (1972), on the other hand, propose a framework for the study of language diffusion based on the means by which language can spread: as a lingua franca, as a mother tongue (language shift), and as a superposed variety (a situation of diglossia).

The spread of language behavior in a community can be studied through (1) its linguistic structures (form), such as the adoption of new terms, the presence of code-switching, or the process of pidginization; (2) its roles (functions) in the community speech repertoire; and (3) its dispersion (pervasiveness) throughout different strata of the community (Cooper 1982b). The study of the Kaan community in this book focuses on the latter two aspects: the function of Jula in the community repertoire and its pervasiveness within the ethnic network. According to Cooper, the pervasiveness of a certain language behavior can be seen as a set of scaled criterion variables: awareness, evaluation, proficiency, and usage. We shall see how each of these variables is manifested in the spread of Jula in the Kaan community.

Scotton (1982) attempts to explain the interrelationship of the spread of lingua francas and elements of the societies in which they are used by advancing three general hypotheses:

> 1. Language spread can be best explained in a framework which treats both a person's linguistic repertoire and the individual linguistic varieties it includes as societal elements, alongside other societal elements such as educational attainment, educational systems, political cultures, political parties, ethnic group membership, etc.
> 2. The acquisition of the same lingua franca performs different roles for different persons, depending on the specific configuration of societal elements a person already controls before that acquisition.
> 3. At any time, there is the possibility of change in a societal element in three areas: change in the content, or change in the power of a particular element, or change in the interrelationship of that element with other elements. (Scotton 1982:63–64)

She goes on to suggest a set of values to assign to different kinds of lingua francas in Africa. For official languages (usually European languages) these are:

+ education
+ authority
+ formal

For secondary official languages or nonofficial lingua francas, she proposes these values:

~education (neutral value; learned informally, does not make a statement about education level)
+ spatial mobility
− socioeconomic status evaluation (no apparent link between how a person speaks a lingua franca and his/her profession)
− formal
− authority [though may have higher authority over local ethnic languages in some employment situations]

+national [or +regional]
~ethnicity [e.g., Hausa and Jula, though Moore in central Burkina Faso and Fulse in Cameroon may be +ethnicity]

Finally, she considers the values attached to minor locally based lingua francas:

+ethnicity
+dominance/authority relationship [i.e., master/apprentice; also may be a pattern in an interethnic marriage] (1982:74)

Pidgins and koinés

While pidgin languages are lingua francas, lingua francas are not necessarily pidgins. Manessy claims that, while elsewhere it has been shown that pidginization (especially the simplification of the outer form of a language, see Hymes 1971) is the result of interethnic contact and bilingualism, "the totality of the interference phenomena that usually result from language contact, does not appear to me, in Africa at least, to be necessarily related to the process of pidginization nor entailed by it" (1977:129). He cites the example of Senufo languages in Mali borrowing features from Bambara, the dominant language, without showing any other signs of pidginization. The same is true of Kaansa, one of the languages under investigation in this book, which shows no sign of pidginization in spite of the many words it borrows from Jula.

Perhaps a more useful concept for understanding the spread of Jula is that of a KOINÉ. Nida and Fehderau (1970) have distinguished between koinés (vehicular varieties of common, "ethnic" language), and pidgins (varieties independent of any particular vernacular language). Manessy considers Ivoirian Jula to be a koiné of the vernacular Bambara, and Pidgin English of Ghana and Cameroon to be pidgins. He also cites examples of borrowing from French and consequent syntactic and morphological change in Dagara to show pidginization processes in a vernacular, local, ethnically-bound language.

Partmann (1973) believes that koiné is the best term to describe the type of Jula used as a lingua franca in Côte d'Ivoire, Burkina Faso, and Mali. She explored the linguistic competence of L1 and L2 Jula speakers as well as their total linguistic repertoires and attitudes toward the languages they spoke. She found that the language of L2 Jula speakers (vehicular Jula) in Côte d'Ivoire has a reduced lexicon and some grammatical innovations. It is similar to pidgin languages but has experienced less change from the native variety because of regular contact with native speakers through trade. In addition, regional dialect forms are now found outside the dialect area, due to increased urban interethnic contact. Native speakers also expressed a lack of desire to maintain dialectal distinctions.

So, while Jula cannot be considered a pidgin, it is still undergoing pidginization processes which make the vehicular variety a koiné. This gives it a kind of practical efficiency which Manessy attributes to three correlative properties:

> their simplicity, or more exactly, their narrow adaptation to the referential function; their neutrality, that is to say, the fact that their use does not habitually evoke any categorization or any value judgment; and finally, their conformity to what might turn out to be the elementary structures of human language. (1977:149)

When there is a wide variation in forms and structures in a dialect continuum or cluster, it is likely that speakers of the various dialects will adopt a single variety for interdialectal communication. Such dialects have many of the properties of lingua francas, and which variety is used as a koiné depends sometimes on numerical superiority, sometimes on which dialects are written for government or church use, or sometimes on ease of comprehension (Heine 1970).

Mandé and Jula

Mandé is a general term for a large dialect chain of which three varieties are used as lingua francas in at least four countries in West Africa: Malinké is used in Guinea, Bambara in Mali, and Jula in Burkina Faso and Côte d'Ivoire. Calvet (1982) claims that in spite of their phonological differentiation, these three varieties are mutually intelligible.

War, religion, and trade are the three media which have spread Mandé throughout the centuries. Mandé speakers held economic and political power in the Mali empire from the eleventh to the fifteenth century and spread the use of Mandé throughout its territory. When the French colonizers arrived in the nineteenth century, they found Bambara useful as a lingua franca within the colonial army, whose ranks were largely made up of Bambara speakers from Mali.

South of Mali, Jula traders controlled the north-south trade routes in which Saharan salt was exchanged for Sudanian (West African) gold.

Mandé was also spread through the process of Islamicization of West African animist peoples. When traders established residence in a town, they married local women, who were necessarily converted to Islam. After two or three generations, these communities of Muslim traders controlled most of the important trade in the town and played an important role in local politics, wielding enormous social influence.

Mandé was well established as a lingua franca in West Africa before the colonial period, and the French policy toward it after colonization reinforced its position as go-between language. In spite of their best efforts to establish their language as the only language of administration and education in their colonies, the French colonists were forced to accept Mandé as the intermediate language for rural administration. It was not unusual for a French administrator to learn the local variety of Mandé. Also, by appointing Mandé speakers as local cantonal chiefs and by employing mostly Malinké and Bambara speakers in the colonial army, the colonists reinforced and expanded the social influence of the language. Thus, without ever officially recognizing Mandé, without ever allowing it to threaten French as a written language, the colonists tacitly accepted it as a way of practically governing its ethnically diverse West African colonies. Since independence, however, it is only in Mali and perhaps Côte d'Ivoire that varieties of Mandé have the potential of becoming a unifying national language.

Jula

The tribal origins of the Jula traders in Burkina Faso lie in a community of Mandé traders from the Mali empire who settled in Kong (in northern Côte d'Ivoire) as the power of Mali was waning and its empire disintegrating. There they prospered, married local tribal women, and spread Islam and their language within the newly established communities. While the number of Jula in West Africa is relatively small, their communities occupy important social positions in the trading towns throughout their region of influence. Thus, their language is used as a lingua franca by a far greater number of people than as a mother tongue.

These small communities of traders were generally well respected and valued by local traditional chiefs as an important means of contact with the outside world and as a channel of economic activity. They were respected for their adherence to Islam, which gave them access to literacy (in Arabic) and to special ritual practices that promised enhanced magical powers. *Marabouts* or *karamokos* '(itinerant) Muslim clerics' were often given official roles in the power circles of the traditional chiefs.

Thus, with Jula communities in the major towns and villages of the ethnically diverse Western Volta region, the Jula became the vital economic and linguistic link between diverse peoples.

The Jula had established themselves in this region before colonialization to such a degree that Binger, the French explorer commented:

> In looking back over the route which I have followed from Kong, one notices that the majority of peoples call themselves by Mandé [Jula] names even though most are certainly from ethnic groups such as the Komono, Dokhosié, Tiéfo, and Bobo who, originally, had names based upon an indigenous etymology. (1892:380, quoted in Griffeth 1971:174)

Yet these indigenous populations had not adopted Islam. Two of the groups (Dogo and Khi) studied in this book have adopted Islam (the Khi completely, the Dogo partially) and have taken Jula family names (e.g., Wattara and Coulibaly). The other two (Kpatogo and Kaan) have held to their traditional animist religion and their ethnic names, while a small minority of Kaan have become Christians and taken Christian names at the same time maintaining their traditional clan (family) names

Dialect continua

A geographical dialect continuum is an area or region where many very similar dialects exist.

> At no point is there a complete break such that geographically adjacent dialects are not mutually intelligible, but the cumulative effect of the linguistic differences will be such that the greater the geographical separation, the greater the difficulty of comprehension. (Chambers and Trudgill 1980:6)

In Europe, there are several well-known dialect continua: Scandinavian, West Germanic, West Romance, South Slavic, and North Slavic. Within these continua exist several standard languages such as Danish, Swedish, and Norwegian in the Scandinavian group. On a popular level, the continuous nature of language variation within these areas is obscured by the national political associations with the standardized varieties. In West Africa, however, there has been very little standardization of dialects and no association of a standard written form with national aspirations. Consequently, it is difficult to talk of any major indigenous language that is not a dialect continuum. Mandé is a very important dialect continuum in the region that concerns us. Attempts have been made, and are currently underway, to develop a standard written form for Jula, Bambara, and Malinké, but linguists engaged in these tasks inevitably make orthography choices that elevate aspects of local varieties to the level of standard. Only time and social development of the Mandé-speaking region will determine if standard dialects emerge from the Mandé continuum.

A nuclear dialect is one in which communication is always "first rate" (Grimes 1989:252), where individuals share linguistic and communicative norms to such an extent that lapses of understanding are exceedingly rare. A DIALECT CLUSTER is a nuclear dialect having a constellation of dialects associated with it between which communication is "pretty good" for most purposes (p. 256). Within a cluster, dialects are distinct yet widely recognized as closely related. Clusters can be found within a continuum, and boundaries between clusters are found by considering not just lexical similarity of one dialect to the other, but degree of communication between a nuclear dialect and its cluster. Consequently, two dialects may be very similar to each other, yet belong to two different clusters with regard to major nuclear dialects. Likewise, two dialects may be intelligible to each other at some level, yet remain clustered around two different nuclear dialects based on superior intelligibility with it, status relationships with it (as a standard for one dialect but not the other), or other classifying factors. A simple fact may be that speakers of one peripheral dialect do not readily understand the nuclear dialect of the other nearby peripheral variety (which they do understand). Intelligibility between a nuclear dialect and its clustered dialects is often assymetric, favoring the nuclear dialect. Outside of the cluster lie dialects for which communication with the nuclear dialect is just "so-so" (p. 257), where lapses of communication occur more frequently and in a wider range of situations.

While Grimes' main criterion for establishing dialect clusters is degree of intelligibility, clusters may also correspond to political or geographical boundaries. Alternatively, dialect clusters may be crisscrossed by political or other social boundaries which would force the drawing of more clusters than linguistically necessary.

What we need for a better understanding of dialect variation in West Africa is a term which refers to a group of varieties which are closely related but not unified under a linguistic standard. They may be unified under attitudinal or cultural norms (their speakers seeing themselves as the same group), or under a nominal form (the same glossonym for their varieties), or they may not be unified at all except by a vague assertion that "yes, we speak the same language, but it comes out differently," yet without a unifying glossonym or social structure.

The clustering relationship described by Grimes is very similar to what Chambers and Trudgill (1980) call HETERONOMY among dialects. Heteronomy is the dependence or relationship of certain varieties to a widely accepted standard variety. In the German dialect continuum, there are German and Dutch standard varieties. Hence, some varieties are considered dialects of Dutch and some dialects of German, even though varieties on either side of the Dutch-German political boundary may differ very little in structure. Heteronomy is a political or cultural (or perhaps, attitudinal) grouping of varieties rather than a linguistic one.

This is important for our study, because attitude studies of dialect continua in West Africa may reveal heteronomous relationships in the system, which would allow researchers and those interested in classification and standardization to group dialects differently than on the basis of linguistic similarity or intelligibility alone.

The tremendous variation within a language makes it difficult to draw lines of dialect boundaries. Even intelligibility tests only offer a special kind of data on the comprehension of specific texts. Many dialect surveys in West Africa, and specifically those done in Burkina Faso, give only cursory attention to local attitudes and opinions about the dialect situation under investigation (Hartell n.d.). Some current classifications of West African languages may be erroneous due to the fact that a given language may have several appellations, GLOSSONYMS, depending on whom the investigator talks to. Tiendrebeogo and Yago (1983) offer the examples of the Bwamu language which has ten different glossonyms, Kasim with six glossonyms, and Kurumfe with seven glossonyms.

3

Language Issues in Burkina Faso

Introduction to the country

The modern nation of Burkina Faso, formerly Upper Volta (Haute Volta), was carved out of the central West African savanna below the Sahara desert and above the coastal forests. It is a landlocked country of 274,000 square kilometers surrounded by Mali, Niger, Benin, Togo, Ghana, and Côte d'Ivoire. First designated as the territory of Upper Volta in 1919, it had been a part of the French Sudan colony from 1904. After a reshuffling of borders in 1932, when part of the territory was attached to Ivory Coast, it finally was given its present borders in 1947. Like so many other modern African states, Burkina Faso's borders were established without regard to the traditional ethnic boundaries already in place, though the old Mossi empire boundaries fall mostly within the modern boundaries of Burkina Faso. Independence from France came on August 5, 1960, and, after a series of both civilian and military rulers, a notable political upheaval took place in 1983 with the popular "revolution" led by army captain Thomas Sankara. The current leader, Captain Blaise Compaoré, took power in October, 1988.

"Terre ingrate au climat sévère..." is how one atlas sums up the geography of Burkina Faso (Jeune Afrique 1975:3). Most of the country is a flat lateritic plain at approximately 300 meters above sea level. The thin layer of arable soil is poor in quality and is often washed away by seasonal rains. These rains dump up to 1300 mm of water on the land every year, more than the annual rainfall of France. All of the rain, however, falls in a period of four to six months between May and October, leaving the rest of the year almost completely dry. Four main rivers collect the rainfall and channel it towards the coast: the three northern branches of the Volta, now named the Mouhoun, the Nazinon, and the Nakambe (formerly the Black, Red, and White Voltas, from which Upper Volta drew its name), and the Comoë. Only the Comoë and the Mouhoun hold water year round.

(4)   Map of Burkina Faso

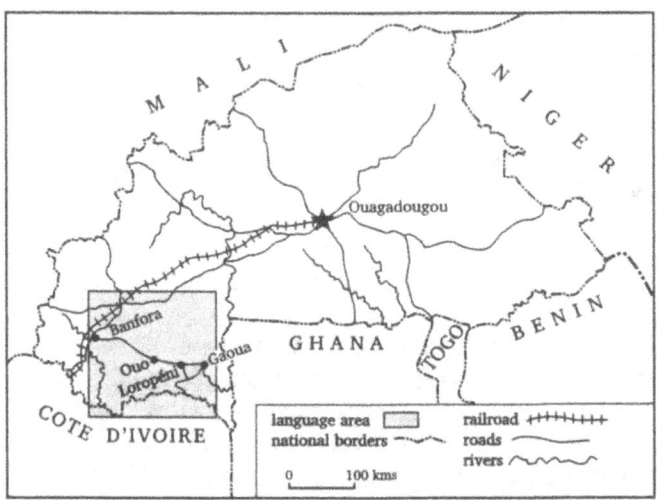

The northern tier of the country lies in the Sahel which is the hottest, driest, most desertified region; the central tier is savanna grassland with occasional clusters of trees in pockets of good soil; the southern tier is best described as forested savanna where the high grasses mix more frequently with trees and bushes (with some densely forested areas around water sources).

All of West Africa is affected by the Harmattan winds which sweep down from the Sahara from December to February each year, bringing high altitude clouds of dust thick enough to block the sun and significantly lower the temperature. This is the coldest time of the year when temperatures can dip to 15° C (60° F) at night. Normal high and low temperatures in the shade vary between 40° and 25° C (104° and 77° F) during the year.

The total population in 1985 was 8.8 million, with more than 1.1 million people living outside of the country (INSD 1986).[2] Annual population growth is projected at 2.68 percent per year according to 1991 census

---

[2]As of mid-2000, the population is 11.9 million (PRB 2000).

Introduction to the country

figures, and population density averages twenty-nine inhabitants per square kilometer.

To govern this population, the current administration has divided the country into thirty reorganized provinces based on the original colonial division of the country into ten *départements* as shown on the map in (5).[3]

These 8.8 million people are divided into some sixty ethnolinguistic groups[4] of which the Mossi are numerically dominant, comprising about forty percent of the population. Two languages serve as lingua francas for the majority of the population: Moore, the language of the Mossi is used in the central plateau and in Ouagadougou, and Jula, the trade language of the western provinces. The Jula are numerically small (approx. 45,000 in 1990) but their language has found widespread use throughout the ethnically diverse southwest.

The history of the savanna region which stretches across modern Mali, Burkina Faso, and Niger is adequately presented in a number of works, including Ki-Zerbo (1972) and Fage (1969); a short summary is found in Claessens (1981).

Much of the central plateau region now incorporated into Burkina Faso was ruled by the Mossi kingdom between the twelfth and the fifteenth centuries, and their domination of the social and economic life of that region has its residual effects even today. The western part of the country has been inhabited by a diverse patchwork of ethnic minorities, of which the Kaan, Dogo, Kpatogo, and Khi seem to be among the most ancient. The region just west of the Mouhoun (Black Volta) River was controlled by the Lobi-Birifor, a warlike group who pillaged the residents when the group arrived in the area from the east in the late eighteenth century (Labouret 1958). The Ouattara Jula from Kong dominated other parts of the region south of Bobo Dioulasso (they were never able to control Lobi territory) from the seventeenth century until the beginning of the twentieth century and French colonization. The first French incursion into Mossi territory occurred in 1884, and the entire area now within Burkina Faso was "pacified" by French troops by 1901, though the Lobi and other groups in the southwest region continued to offer resistance periodically.

---

[3]These thirty provinces have now been subdivided even further into forty-five provinces.
[4]According to a recent linguistic map, published by the Institut Géographique du Burkina (1988), there are sixty-one language varieties in the country. This map seems to be based on the study by Tiendrebeogo (1983), which also lists sixty-one language varieties. An atlas published in 1975 by Editions Jeune Afrique lists thirty-four distinct varieties. *The Ethnologue* (Grimes 2000) records sixty-six varieties.

Multilingualism

In 1983, Tiendrebeogo and Yago published a sociolinguistic survey of the country which included a nationwide study of multilingualism patterns. The graph in (5) shows the results of a question on reported multilingualism listed by the original departments shown on the map.

(5) Percentage of multilingualism

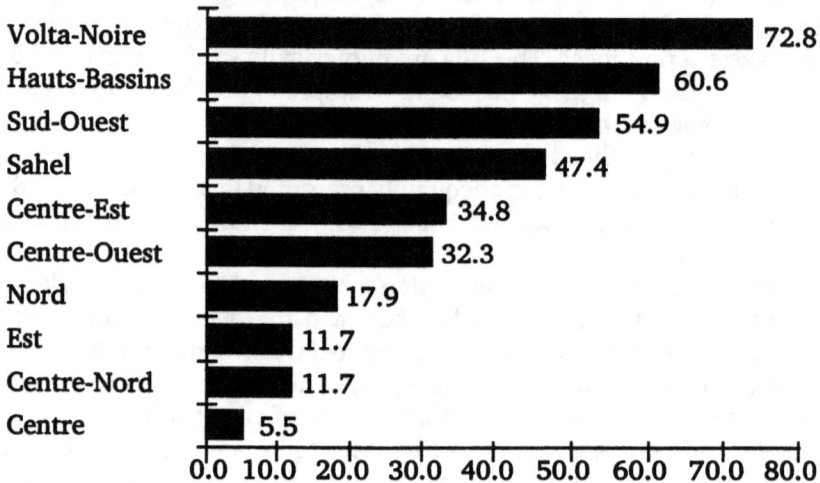

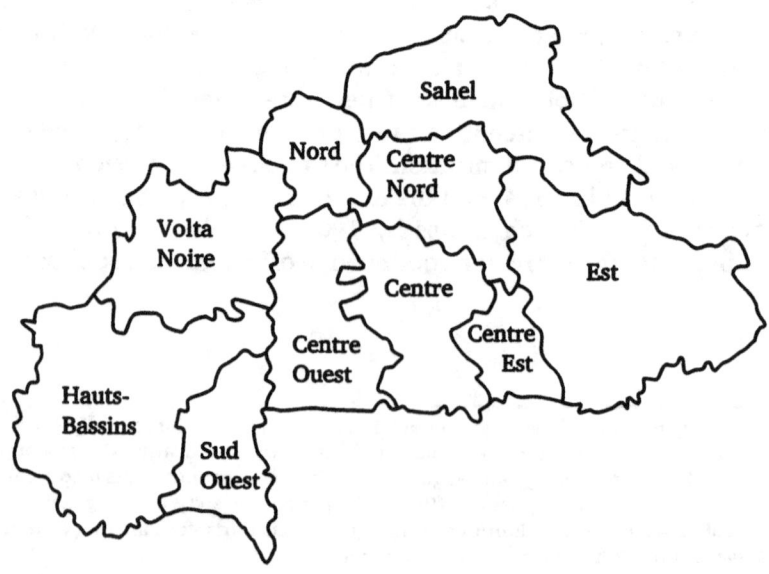

Tiendrebeogo and Yago (1983:35) conclude from these data that the (level) of multilingualism varies greatly according to the region (higher in the west than in the east) and, in a general way, according to sex and age (higher for men than women and for adults than children). The level of multilingualism is proprotionate to the linguistic complexity of a given region, to the number of important languages in contact with each other.

Not surprisingly, Tiendrebeogo and Yago also found that, in general, migrants are much more likely to be multilingual than non-migrants (1983:42-43). Seasonal migration outside of the country for work is very much a part of rural life, and since the droughts and famines of the 1970s, and because of the increasing deforestation of the northern Sahel regions, there has been an increase in internal migration and resettlement as well, particularly to the sparsely populated southwest.

Tiendrebeogo and Yago's (1983:46) conclusion about the distribution of multilingualism among the people of Burkina Faso is that population movement plays a primary role and that the level of multilingualism is proportionate to the level of migration and the complexity of the linguistic situation in a given region.

According to Fishman's (1968) distinctions between multinational states and multiethnic nations, both the former Upper Volta and the current Burkina Faso would be considered multiethnic nations. In the past, the diverse ethnic groups within its borders have taken little interest in affairs of the state; they have been neither loyal to the government nor explicitly against it. Most people in rural areas (ninety percent of the population, Claessens 1981) primarily concern themselves with survival from one season to the next, and between one-eighth and one-quarter of the population work for most of the year outside the country.

The ethnic groups in Burkina Faso almost universally advocate the maintenance of their own languages (Tiendrebéogo and Yago 1983), which for Fishman indicates a sense of "nationalism" instead of locally-based "ethnicity". However, all small ethnic groups in the country also recognize the need for and practice bilingualism in the regional vehicular languages. Stable bilingualism and polyglossia seem to be the norm in Burkina Faso, with a few exceptional cases of language shift toward the regional languages. This seems to be especially true in the southwest where Jula seems to be gaining at the expense of some islamicized smaller ethnic populations. Yet these small ethnic populations can hardly be called nationalistic in the sense that Fishman defines the concept (Fasold 1984:4).

Another indication of Burkina Faso's classification as a multiethnic nation is that the government has largely been controlled by the Mossi, not in any officially recognized manner, but perhaps more by their numerical advantage over any other group in the country and their territorial dominance over the central plateau, where the capital, Ouagadougou, is located. Ouagadougou is also the seat of the Mogo Naba, the traditional leader of the Mossi people.

With the 1983 revolution, however, and the change of name a year later, national political consciousness began to change. The new president, Captain Thomas Sankara, instituted wide-ranging changes in the political and economic life of the country, which reached out to the rural villages in all regions. He focused political and developmental attention on the rural peasants, who previously had had little real loyalty to the national government. It is possible that in contemporary Burkina Faso feelings of national identity are growing among the diverse rural populations alongside each person's local ethnic identity. This was clearly one goal of the 1983 revolution: to develop a sense of national pride and belonging that would override purely local and ethnic concerns.

Fasold (1984) categorizes the various ways in which nations and states become multilingual into four general processes: migration, imperialism, federation, and border areas. The independent state of Upper Volta, formed from the French colony of the same name in 1960, had an ethnically diverse population grouped together as the result of forced federation under French colonial rule. Yet the combination of ethnic groups and nationalities (e.g., the Mossi, the Fulani, and the Ouattara Jula of Kong) now within its borders have co-existed for centuries, due to numerous migrations and conquests. Hence, multilingualism has been a part of the social fabric for as long as there are historical records, both oral and written. It is therefore difficult to say that multilingualism in Burkina Faso is the result of one process alone; rather, it is a combination of migration, imperialism, and forced federation.

Let us focus on a specific region of Burkina Faso, the central Mossi plateau, and on a particular ethnic group, the Lyela, who live north of Koudougou, the third-largest city in Burkina Faso. Batiana (1985) studied multilingualism, dialect variation, and attitudes among this group, of which he himself is a native. The table in (6) shows language use in three loosely defined domains: the market, the workplace, and the home (p. 16).

(6) Multilingualism in urban settings

Place	Local vehicular language (Moore/Jula)	Language Official vehicular language (French)	Mother tongue (Lyele)
Market	+	+	−
Work	−	+	−
Home	−	−	+

This is obviously a simplification, since one often uses one's mother tongue in the marketplace, especially in Ouagadougou where Moore is both mother tongue and trade language. Similarly, it is very common in Bobo Dioulasso to hear Jula, the trade language and mother tongue for some, being spoken at the workplace, even in official settings such as the post office or the bank. This is still a helpful chart, and does cover the majority of situations. But language use in rural settings can be much more complex, as we will see later in chapter 7.

Concerning the use of different languages within the Lyela community, Batiana (1985:184–185) summarizes that Lyele is the main language for communicating with outsiders. Moore is used to communicate with those who speak neither Lyele nor French. French is used for technical and modern terms; it symbolizes the law, power, and knowledge; and it serves to draw people together in unity.

Batiana concludes that societal bilingualism among the Lyela carries benefits and risks. The Lyela benefit from a greater access to goods, services, and people outside their own community, yet they also face social changes that come as a result of this access. The traditional social structure is breaking down as those who control the effects of modernism through proficiency in French do not recognize or adhere to the traditional values associated with the Lyele language and the older generation.

Language policy

From independence, Burkina Faso has followed a language policy common to the former French colonies in West Africa:

> Influenced by the European model of nation state, the black elites of post-colonial Africa believed that nation building could

be best achieved through the adoption of a single national language. Ironically, the adoption of the colonial language as the official language of these emerging nation-states had the double advantage of avoiding potential inter-ethnic conflict while facilitating modernization through technology and international communication. (Bourhis 1982:48)

Thus, French was used for all levels of education and government, creating a ruling educated, literate elite while effectively blocking with the language barrier the majority of the population of rural peasants from significant participation in national affairs and development.

An attempt to introduce national languages into education in Burkina Faso began in 1979. Briefly, the initial proposal was to introduce national languages, namely Moore, Jula, and Fulfulde, into the curriculum as languages of education for the early primary years. However, Ouedraogo (1983) reports that this restructuring met with strong opposition from the country's elites. These felt that indigenous national languages were not appropriate as languages of instruction and that the new emphasis of national education on productive instruction (i.e., agriculture and animal husbandry) would obstruct a child's upward mobility through education. Other difficulties this reform program encountered were the recruiting and (re)training of teachers and the very different educational needs of rural and urban dwellers. Due to these difficulties and because of political upheaval and instability in recent years, this reform program has been put aside for the time being.

In spite of initial failure to introduce national languages into the school system, the government, non-governmental development organizations, and Christian missions (both Protestant and Catholic) have for some time been using regional lingua francas and local languages in nonformal, rural education programs such as the government-sponsored Centres de Formation de Jeunes Agriculteurs (CFJA: Training Centers for Young Farmers); more recently the government sponsored mass literacy programs in French and local languages called "Alpha-commando". The current language promotion efforts of the government are focused on teaching basic literacy at the village level under the direction of the Ministry of Education and several subsidiary organizations, primarily the *Institut de l'Alphabétisation*, the *Direction Provinciale de l'Agriculture et de l'Elevage*, and the *Direction Provinciale de l'Action Coöpérative*. These rural programs are intense (fifty-six days) and are usually carried out in one of the three national languages, though if materials are available in local languages, they are used as well.

In addition, local languages like Lobiri or Kaansa are broadcast occasionally on radio stations in provincial capitals like Gaoua and Koudougou. Batiana (1985) reports that the use of the Réo dialect of Lyele in some radio broadcasts from Koudougou has contributed to that dialect's status as local standard among the Lyela community.

How does the national language policy work out in the lives of local ethnolinguistic groups in rural towns like Loropéni? Mostly, people do what they must to get by, using a combination of languages as Alexandre (1972) suggests. Chapter 7 addresses this issue in relation to observations of practical language use in official settings. For example, at official gatherings in Loropéni (the national holiday celebration, formation of local civic assemblies, announcements, etc.) French announcements and speeches were translated simultaneously into Lobiri and Jula by officially designated translators. Occasionally, this was informally translated into Kaansa by bilingual Kaan in the audience.

The Kaan, Kpatogo, Dogo, and Khi

This study primarily concerns itself with the language habits of four small closely related ethnolinguistic groups in southwest Burkina Faso: the Kaan, the Kpatogo, the Dogo, and the Khi. Only in the last twenty years has any formal linguistic study of their language varieties been attempted (Prost 1972, Vaillant n.d., Solomiac 1983, and Showalter 1990). While these are important contributions, they remain on the level of structural sketches and preliminary, exploratory surveys. The remainder of this chapter summarizes what is known about these four groups.

(7a)

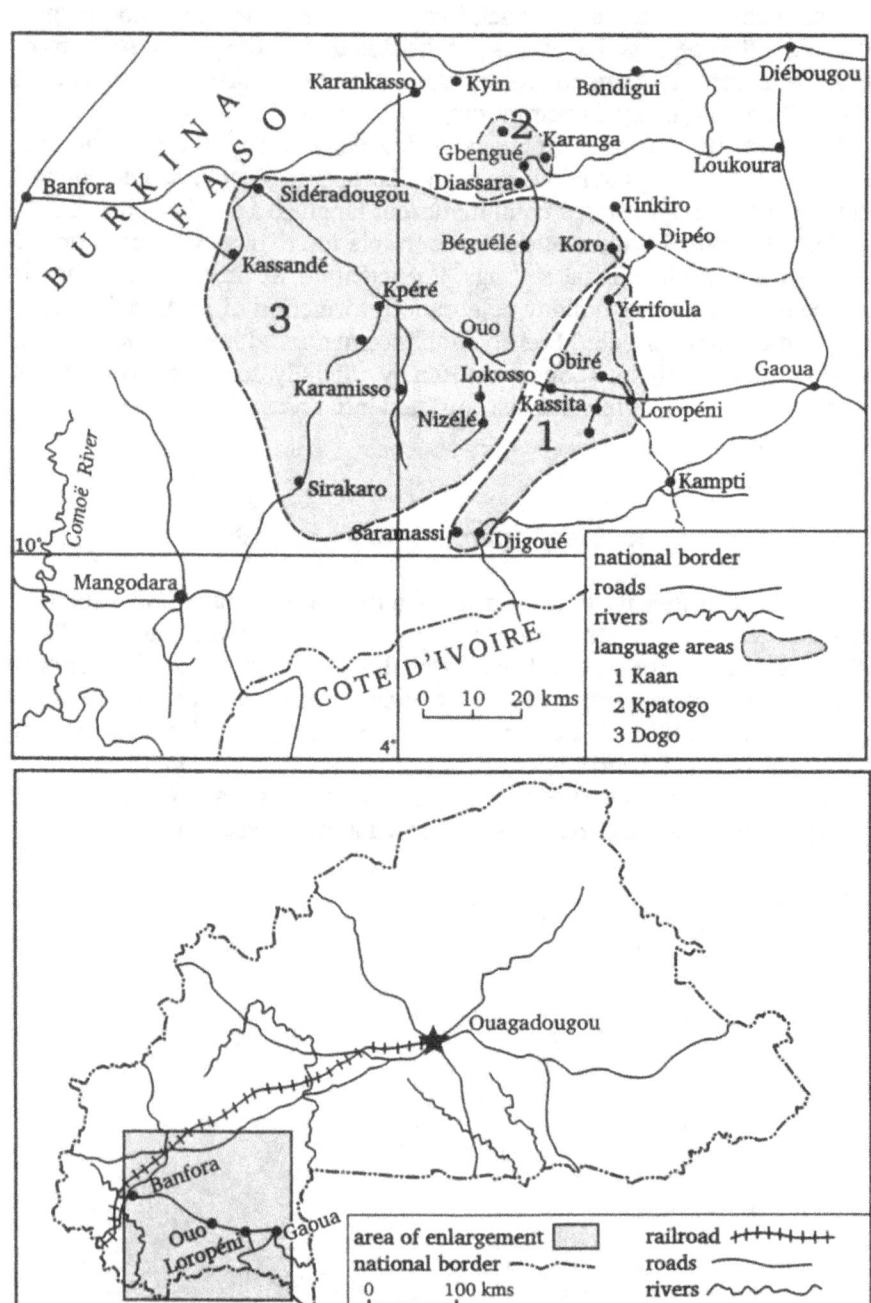

The Kaan, Kpatogo, Dogo, and Khi 31

(7b)

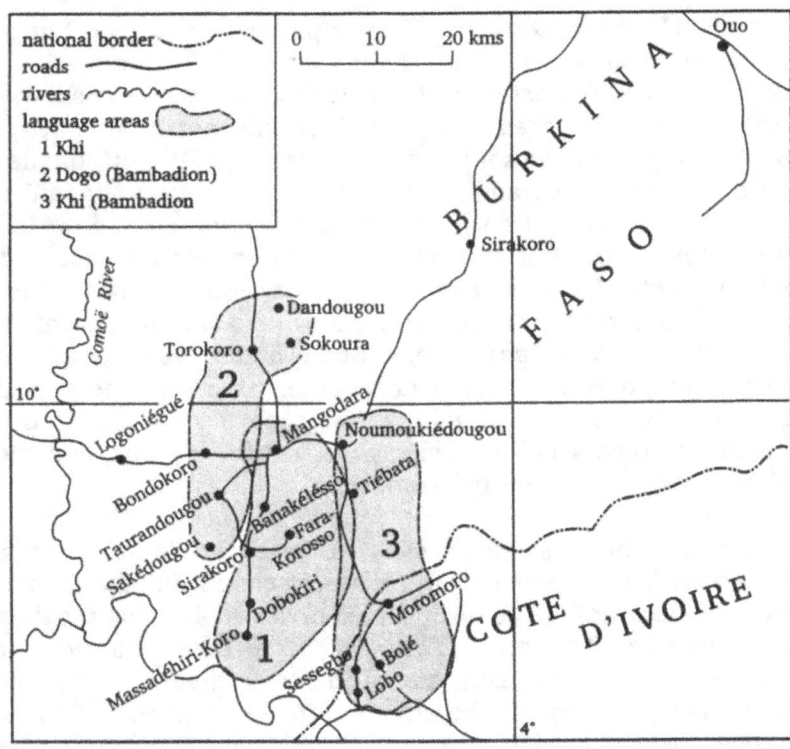

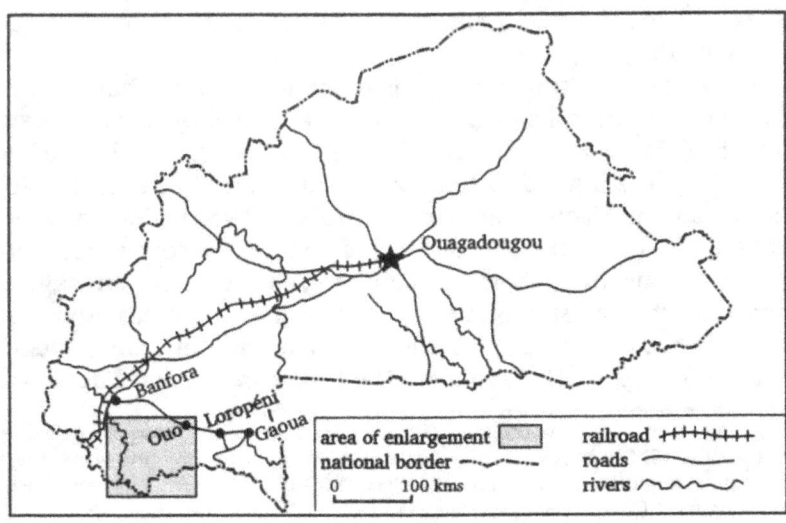

A synchronic description

General information. The Kaan, Kpatogo, Dogo, and Khi live in a rural, undeveloped area of 11,000 square kilometers in southwest Burkina Faso. The extent of their various territories is shown on the map in (7). The area is bounded on the north by Gbengué and Sidéradougou, on the south by Mangodara and Djigoué, on the east by Loropéni, Yérifoula, and Koro, and on the west by Logoniégué, and Touroukoro. This area is forested savanna with low hills and outcroppings of laterite rock. The soil is generally poor and sandy with pockets of good soil around marshes and river beds. The people of these four groups are subsistence farmers of millet, corn, and various kinds of beans and greens. Some among each group cultivate yams, though the Khi seem to do this more than the others because the soil and the climate where they live is more conducive to that crop. Small livestock such as chickens, guinea fowl, goats, and sheep are also a part of each family's resources.

The Kaan. The Kaan people (Káa, pl. Káabà, lg. Káasà) currently number about 7,000.[5] In most of the literature concerning the Kaan, they are called the Gan or Gã. The spelling used in this book is closer to the way the Kaan refer to themselves. They live in an area bounded loosely by Loropéni on the west, Lorhosso on the east, Djigoué on the south, and Yérifoula on the north. The table in (76) in appendix 1 lists all of the known Kaan villages in this area. Obiré, ten kilometers northwest of Loropéni, is their cultural center where the Kaan Iya [káa ɟjà], or chief, lives and governs the community. The map in (7a) shows the extent of Kaan territory.

Knowledge of Kaan culture, history, and traditions has been very limited until recently. Though they were mentioned by name in previous colonial works (Binger 1892, Delafosse 1912, Tauxier 1921), the Kaan were described in a limited fashion by Labouret (1931, 1958), a colonial administrator in Gaoua. Parenko and Hébert (1962) added a great deal to Labouret's sketch of their culture and history and corrected several of his mistakes concerning their clan structure, customs, and language. Parenko and Hébert also established definitively the strong ethnolinguistic relationship between the Kaan, Kpatogo, Dogo, and Khi, calling them "an ethnic family" (p. 414). Savonnet (1963) adds some notes about traditions

---

[5]The current (1990) population estimates for these four groups are calculated on the basis of the 1975 census figures (the last in which ethnic information was gathered), using the annual population growth rate of 2.68% (INSD 1986) over fifteen years. The equation is 1975 figure X (1 + annual growth rate)$^{\text{number of growth years}}$

surrounding the transfer of power from one chief or king to another, and Père (1982) provides a summary of the historical and ethnological knowledge of the Kaan up to the present. She is currently finishing a major study of the history and traditions of the Kaan tentatively entitled *Les gans de Loropéni ou des akan au Burkina Faso?* in which she explores the historical and cultural evidence that the Kaan may be a separated group of the Akan peoples which presently inhabit the coastal forests of Ghana and Côte d'Ivoire. This promises to be a fascinating study with implications for understanding the origins, customs, and languages of all four groups.

The Kaan people have a reputation for strong community spirit and social ties, especially compared to the individualistic and traditionally warlike Lobi, their ethnic neighbors. While Lobi villages are loose collections of individual farms located at least 150 meters from each other, Kaan villages are agglomerations of straw-roofed mud-brick huts built closely together. Sometimes the passage between huts is so narrow only one person can pass between them. Villages consist of round and rectangular houses and granaries grouped around an open space with cooking fires and places to sit in the shade. There are no walls around the courtyards, and pathways pass through the middle of the courtyards rather than around the outside. Like most rural Burkinabè, the Kaan people live outdoors, using their houses only for sleeping, shade, shelter from the rain, and storage.

The Kaan people are divided into four clans: Farma, Sua, Khama, and Thaama. The Farma clan comprises several subclans, one of which is a royal clan from which the Iya is chosen when the old Iya dies. There is no segregation by clan in their villages (one finds members of each clan in larger Kaan villages), though from my survey it appears that the Farma are the most numerous of the clans.

Loropéni is the largest and most important market for the Kaan people. Their traditional week is counted on the basis of the Loropéni market in a five-day cycle. Market day is [yáb dìrè], followed by a small market day in another village called [tógó dìrè]. Next comes the traditional day of rest, [yab pɛrgɛ], then two days of preparation for the next market day, [yab taka] and [yab karka]. Other markets frequented by the Kaan are held in Yérifoula, Lorhosso, and Djigoué.

Five primary schools are available to the Kaan people in Loropéni, Yérifoula, Lorhosso, Obiré, and Djigoué. However, there appears to be very little interest in formal education among the Kaan. In the school year 1987–88, only 132 Kaan children were enrolled in the schools in Loropéni, Obiré, and Yérifoula,[6] and sadly only two Kaan

---

[6]These figures were provided by Bayaba Wattara in Loropéni, Souleymane Koné in Yérifoula, and Justin Somé in Obiré. I was not able to obtain school enrollment figures from Lorhosso or Djigoué.

children actually passed their exams to receive the CEPE from these three schools in 1988.[7] I estimate that only 8 percent of all Kaan children are ever enrolled, and a negligible number ever graduate. There are a few Kaan adults, however, who have been educated up to the post-secondary level and hold important functions in government service in Gaoua, Bobo Dioulasso, and Ouagadougou. Others received some secondary education, usually while they were living with their families in Côte d'Ivoire.

The Kpatogo. The Kpatogo (Kpatɔgɔ, pl. Kpatɔgɔbɔ, lg. Kpatɔgɔsɔ) are a very small group of about 700, also known in the literature as Gbadogo, Padoro, Padorho, or Bodoro. They live in five to ten villages in the extreme southwest corner of the Bougouriba Province, a sparsely populated area of low rolling hills and light forests. Their current cultural center is in Diassara, though the traditional center is Gbengué. In addition to these two villages, most of the population can be found in Kamilidaga, Karanga, and Ouérin. The table in (77) in appendix 1 lists all of the known Kpatogo villages, and the map in (7a) shows the extent of their territory.

Several of their "villages" are in fact temporary, seasonal campgrounds called *campements* in French. During the planting season the Kpatogo leave their home villages to work in their fields, and since these may be some distance from their homes, they often live in temporary habitations nearer their fields for most of the months of May and June when preparing and planting fields is so important. Massamo and Danyini (or Dahinkorosso) are two of these "campements".

The Kpatogo have their own Iya, or chief, who traditionally is installed by the Kaan Iya in a ceremony in Obiré (Parenko and Hébert 1962); however, I do not know if this tradition is still followed. The Kpatogo have maintained the four-clan division of families similar to the Kaan. The Kpatogo Iya now lives in Diassara which has become the center of cultural activity and contact with other peoples. A medical clinic was built there in 1987, and a primary school was planned for the fall of 1988. For several years there has been a rural FJA school run by Mr. Achille Pooda, a Dagari who lives in Diassara and who supplied much of the information on the Kpatogos presented in these paragraphs. He teaches basic agricultural techniques in Jula and serves as a liaison between the Kpatogo and the local governing authorities in Loukoura.

Kpatogo villages are very reminiscent of Kaan villages, with a few architectural variations, such as flat mud roofs on men's houses rather than straw. There is no market in town or in any Kpatogo village; they reported

---

[7]Certificat des Etudes Primaires Elémentaires. It is required to successfully complete primary school in Burkina Faso. The school in Obiré did not offer the final two years of instruction, so the two children who received the CEPE were in Loropéni and Yérifoula.

trading at the Lobi market in Kousséra and in a market they called [tiyẽ] located along the Bobo-Diébougou road (which may be Kyin, seven kilometers northwest of Diassara, near Karankasso). Occasionally, Jula traders come to Diassara to display their wares, but leave after a few hours.

The Kpatogo profess to have little contact with the Lobi who live south and east of them and claim no proficiency in Lobiri; this in spite of the fact that they occasionally trade at a Lobi market. They do interact with the Dogo south of them in a village called Lorokama [nɔrɔkámba]. The Kpatogo call these Dogo [sʊkɔrɔbɛ].

According to Solomiac (1983), many Kpatogo have migrated to Côte d'Ivoire to find work, leaving only a small group in Burkina Faso; those who migrate seldom return to their home villages. Mr. Pooda reported, however, that fewer and fewer Kpatogo leave now due to economic stagnation in the coastal countries and fewer available jobs.

The Dogo. The Dogo (Dɔgɔ, pl. Dɔgɔbɛ, lg. Dɔgɔsɛ), also known in the literature as Dorhossié, Dorossé, Dogosé, or Doghosié, are the largest of the four groups with approximately 14,500 people spread out between Koro on the east, Sidéradougou on the west, Lorokama on the north, and Sirakoro on the south. Their primary population centers are Koro and Ouo, but they lack a single cultural center and an Iya[8] as the head of a well organized hierarchy, which are common to the Kaan and Kpatogo. The table in (78) in appendix 1 lists all of the known Dogo villages, and the map in (7a) shows the extent of their territory.

Virtually all of the Dogo have taken on the clan name Ouattara or Coulibaly because of their past subjugation to the Ouattara Jula of Kong. Parenko and Hébert (1962:429) note that Tauxier (1931:74) recorded only the clan name Taraore (or Traoré as it is written in French) among the Dogo, and that he was puzzled by it due to the Dogo's long allegiance to Kong. In the five Dogo villages I surveyed, I encountered no members of the Traoré clan.

Dogo villages are very similar in style and setting to Kaan and Kpatogo villages: round and square mud huts with straw roofs built closely together around open courtyards. The Dogo frequent markets in Koro, Ouo, Kouéré, Lorhosso, Yérifoula, Sidéradougou, and Mangodara. They have access to medical facilities and primary schools in these same towns except Koro, which has a village health worker but no facilities. National government presence is primarily in Ouo and Sidéradougou. The road connecting Banfora with Gaoua cuts through Sidéradougou, Kouéré, and

---

[8]Parenko and Hébert (1962:429–433) report that in 1954 the Dogo had an official chief named Komi Wattara, who traced his lineage to the first Dogo, Salangalé, who settled on the west side of the Black Volta.

Ouo, the heart of Dogo territory. It is a main route but in very poor condition; even so, merchants and taxi drivers ply the road regularly between Banfora and Loropéni, making it a primary avenue for local commerce and interethnic contact. Since the road is in such poor shape, however, few people unfamiliar with the region ever travel it.

Many Dogo have become Muslim over the last century, though no one knows how many or what percentage of the total population. From my own survey visits, I can say that the Dogo in Ouo and Sidéradougou are all Muslims, those in Béguélé, Flélélo, and Bangbara are all animist, and the populations of Koro and Nizélé are mixed.

The Khi. The Khi (Khı, pl. Khıpa, lg. Khısa),[9] also known in the literature as Komono, are a small group of approximately 3,000 people living in the southernmost corner of the Comoë Province in about ten villages between Mangodara on the north and Massadéhirikoro on the south. Their economic center is Mangodara, but like the Dogo, they seem to lack a single cultural center and an Iya. However, there is an elder in Mangodara, El Hadj Wattara Kologobo, who is considered the chief or head of the community there, and each village has its elder chief as well. The table in (79) in appendix 1 lists all of the known Khi villages, and the map in (7b) shows the extent of their territory.

Khi villages resemble those of the Kaan, Kpatogo, and Dogo in architecture and layout. The primary market for the Khi is in Mangodara, where there is also a medical clinic. They have a secondary local market in Sirakoro. The Khi have regular and frequent contact with the significant populations of Jula, Mossi, and Karaboro in Mangodara. Solomiac reported in 1983 that there were about thirty "Komono" students in the primary school there.

In 1988 the national government improved the road between Mangodara and Banfora which had fallen into disrepair. This should increase the commerce between the two population centers, since the territory around Mangodara has prime soil and adequate rainfall. The national government has also started harvesting the nearby forested area for its wood, which has contributed to the development of Mangodara as a multiethnic local commercial center using Jula as the language of wider communication. Reports gathered during my visit in 1988 indicate that all Khi speak Jula, and that at least one village (Dabokiri) has shifted from using Khisa to Jula. Another strong force contributing to an eventual shift to Jula among the Khi is their adherence to Islam: all Khi have been Muslim since 1935 when a Guinean *marabout* (itinerant preacher) preached Islam to them. Thus, not only is Jula

---

[9]See the next section on the Bambadion for an explanation of the different groups referred to as the Komono.

reinforced in their community by economic necessity and interethnic contact, but also by religious allegiance.

The Bambadion. Binger passed through the region inhabited by the Dogo and Khi, which he called Dokhosié and Komono. In one village he encountered a subgroup of Dogo called "Bambadion". "En quittant Lokhognilé...on atteint Sakédougou, petit village habité par des Mandé-Dioula, et des Dokhosié qui portent le nom de Bambadion-Dokhosié" (1892:281).

Four decades later Tauxier (1931:72, 79) described a subgroup of Dogo which lived south of the Dogo in Sidéradougou and which he called "Dorhosié-Finng"[10] or "Dorhosié-Noirs". Later, Parenko and Hébert (1962:430) mention the existence of the "Dorossié-Fing" as a separate group of Dogo and speculates as to their origin. In addition, Parenko and Hébert note the existence of a subgroup of Komono called "Bambadian" while tracing their history:

> En 1714, Famagan Wattara montant vers Bobo-Dioulasso traverse sans grande résistance tout le pays Komono...Bamba, fils de Sékou[11]...se distingua par son ardeur guerrière. Il commença par des expéditions en pays komono où il combattit un chef nommé Bambana...Dans le bas Komono, on désigne encore sous le nom de Bambadian les anciens captifs de Bamba.[12] (1962:439)

More recently Solomiac reported the existence of two subgroups of Dogo and Khi calling themselves by the same name yet speaking very different languages, in spite of the fact that their language names are very similar to Dogose and Khisa:

> Dogoso et kheso: Ces deux parlers restent pour nous une énigme. Ils portent les noms d'autres langues mais ne leur ressemblent presque pas. Les locuteurs vivent au milieu ou tout près de leurs homonymes mais ne leur parlent qu'en dioula, car ils ne se comprennent pas, témoin le score de 0% au test dogose passé à Taurandougou. Bien que le pourcentage de mots partagés entre les deux ne soit très élevé, les scores obtenus au test d'intelligibilité semblent prouver que la communication entre les deux groupes se fait sans problème. (1983:19)

---

[10][fĩ] or [fiŋ] is Jula for 'black' or 'dark'.
[11]The Jula ruler in Kong.
[12]*-dion/-dian* or [djõ] means 'slave, captive' in Jula.

The map in (7b) shows the villages where, according to Solomiac, these two groups live and the extent of their territory.

Later in his report, Solomiac (1983:21) mentions that the Dogo subgroup who live in Taurandougou are called "Dogose Noirs" or "Black Dogose" by other groups around them, and that this distinguishes them from the "Dogose Blancs" or "White Dogose" farther north, around Ouo. This is the strongest evidence I could find in the literature that the Bambadion mentioned by Binger and Parenko and Hébert are the same as the Black Dogose mentioned by Tauxier. That the Bambadion speak varieties which are dissimilar to Dogose or Khisa, yet have essentially the same name, may indicate that the Bambadion during their slavery developed some kind of distinct variety which they have preserved ever since.

Since Solomiac has demonstrated the dissimilarity of the Bambadion varieties to Dogose and Khisa through intelligibility tests (see the following section), I chose to leave these two enigmatic groups out of the language attitude research presented here. However, the Bambadion will be the subject of future research in the Mangodara region (Showalter n.d.)

Language classification. Greenberg (1966) classified "Gan", "Doghosie", and "Doghosie-Fing" in a Lobi-Dogon subgroup of the Gur languages in the Niger-Congo language family of West Africa. Another current classification of "Gan", "Padorho", "Doghosye", and "Komono" is found in Manessy (1981:105), where he puts these four groups together as a subgroup of Gurunsi languages but mentions that this is based only on "the current state of our knowledge", which was very limited. The most recent attempt, which builds on Manessy's work, is by Naden (1989:144-149) who puts Kaanse and Dogose in their own sub-branch of southern Gur languages. Past attempts at classifying these languages have been made by Tauxier (1921, 1931), Delafosse (1912, 1924), Labouret (1931, 1958), Lavergne de Tressan (1958), and Prost (1972). In the introduction to his sketch of the Dogose variety, Prost (1972:2) comments that while Kaansa, Dogose, Kpatogoso, and Khisa share the characteristics of Voltaic languages (as they had been defined by Manessy (1963), such as a complete system of nominal classes with agreement in the qualifiers, demonstratives, numerals, and personal, relative, and interrogative pronouns), the lexical roots seem very different from the most ancient and best-known languages in the Voltaic group, such as Moore, Dagomba, and Gurunsi. In addition, he comments that Lobiri does not have a nominal class structure, which casts doubt upon Labouret's (1931) classification of the "Gan" and "Dorhossie" into the "Lobi Branch". In addition, our own research into the phonology of Kaansa (C. Showalter n.d.), as well as Vaillant's studies of both Kaansa (n.d.) and Lobiri (1967), show very different phonological systems in the two languages, as well as different morphology and lexical roots. Needless to say, more study must be done before these four varieties can be classified with any certainty.

Lexicostatistics. A comparison of word lists recorded by Solomiac and his colleague Ole Kristensen among the Kaan, Kpatogo, Dogo, Khi, and the two groups of Bambadion revealed a high percentage of shared cognates between the first four groups. Shared cognate percentages were calculated following the method described in Sanders (1977), and the results are presented in (8) from Solomiac (1983:17).

(8)

	Kaansa	Kpatogoso	Dogose	Khisa	Bambadion/Kheso
Kpatogoso	81		69	72	
Dogose	68	69		82	
Khisa	71	72	82		
Bambadion/Dogoso			15	16	56
Bambadion/Kheso			14	13	

Solomiac concluded from this comparison that the Bambadion varieties could easily be classed as different languages, though related to each other with a divergence of about forty percent of the lexical roots between the two. With regard to the four varieties of interest to us, Solomiac postulated two subgroups, Kaansa/Kpatogo and Dogose/Khisa, with a thirty percent divergence between the two groups. Within each pair of varieties there is about twenty percent divergence. These divergences between dialects are represented in (9) after Solomiac (1983:18).

(9)

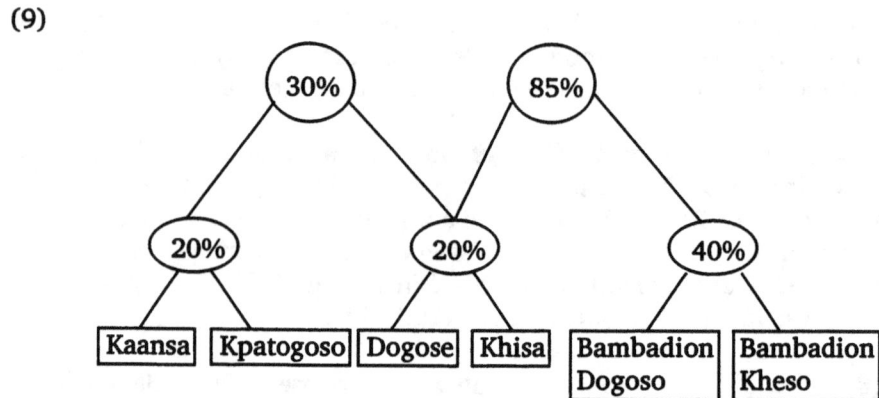

Intelligibility. The natural question arising out of this analysis is how well each group understands the others in normal interaction: To test comprehension Solomiac and Kristensen employed a recorded text testing method described in Casad (1974) and discussed later under "Intelligibility" in chapter 4. The tables in (10) and (11) from Solomiac (1983:15) provide the average adjusted scores of these intelligibility tests, adjusted to eliminate possible error introduced by the testing situation (see Casad 1974:31).

(10)

Texts	Villages tested		
	Kpatogo	Dogo	Khi
Kaansa	90	79	76
Kpatogoso	100		
Dogose	95	100	99.5
Khisa		77	100

It is clear that the Kaansa text was understood the best by the Kpatogo, less so by the Dogo, and the least by the Khi. The Dogose text, on the other hand, was understood quite well by both the Khi and the Kpatogo. It is interesting to note, however, that while the Khi understand Dogose very well (average intelligibility score of 99.5/100), the Dogo were less able to understand Khisa (average intelligibility score of 77/100). This is a clear case of non-reciprocal intelligibility, and in chapter 6 we will examine the social attitudes within these two groups which accompany this phenomenon.

In (11) the two groups of Bambadion understood each other quite well, but did not at all understand the Dogose text. After testing three people in Taurandougou (Dogoso), it became clear that the subjects did not understand Dogose. Apparently, Solomiac and Kristensen deemed it unnecessary to play the Dogose test tape among the Khe in Tiébatta.

(11)

	Villages tested	
Texts	Bambadion/Dogoso	Bambadion/Kheso
Dogose	0	
Bambadion/Dogoso		97
Bambadion/Kheso	90	100

Bilingualism and attitudes. Another goal of Solomiac and Kristensen's survey was to administer tests of bilingualism in Jula, using the same recorded-text testing method recommended for intelligibility tests. They tested a total of sixty-four subjects in five villages: Diassara (Kpatogo), Ouo (Dogo), Mangodara and Sirakoro (Khi), and Taurandougou (Bambadion Dogoso); the average adjusted scores of Jula bilingualism from Solomiac (1983:14) are presented in (12).

(12)

Village	Language	Subjects	Average adjusted score
Diassara	Kpatogoso	14	81.92
Ouo	Dogose	12	93.91
Sirakoro	Khisa	12	92.26
Mangodara	Khisa	14	98.75
Taurandougou	Bambadion Kheso	12	92

It is obvious that virtually all of the subjects understood the Jula texts well and answered most, if not all of the questions correctly. If we assume that people who took this test were the best speakers of Jula in each village,[13] then these results tell us very little about how bilingualism in Jula is distributed in the community. Solomiac's report does not provide any information about the age or sex of the subjects in each village, though he does provide a graph of responses by all sixty-four subjects arranged by age (though not differentiated by village, sex, or mother tongue).

---

[13]When a European expatriate researcher visits a rural village asking to test people in their second language, it is common that, barring any random selection process on the part of the researchers, the village leaders will provide subjects who they feel will perform the best for the researchers. Hence, the assumption that test results reflect the highest level of bilingualism in the community. This is a normal assumption by SIL surveyors, and trying to work around this tendency is one of the unique challenges of rural language surveys.

In addition to these tests, Solomiac and Kristensen administered a sociolinguistic questionnaire to a group of inhabitants in five villages: Ouo (Dogo), Mangodara (Khi), Taurandougou (Bambadion Dogoso), Tiébatta (Bambadion Kheso), and Diassara (Kpatogo). Their questionnaire was based on Bendor-Samuel's (1980) "Sociolinguistic Profile" and provided important, if sketchy, background information to the text results.

Let us examine briefly a few questions and responses from this questionnaire which bear on the issues of dialect intelligibility, use of Jula in these villages, and social attitudes toward language use.

Question six asked, "Which language do you speak to neighboring villages?" The Dogo in Ouo claimed they speak Dogose when with the Kpatogo in Diassara, and the Kpatogo respond in Kpatogoso without any barrier to understanding. They claimed the same interaction pattern with the Kaan. With the Lobi and other ethnic groups, however, they reported using Jula.

The response of the Kpatogo in Diassara to this question confirmed this report; they claimed to speak to the Dogo in Kpatogoso and to understand their responses in Dogose. Equally, they talk to the Kaan in Kpatogoso and understand the responses in Kaansa. The Kpatogo speak in Jula with the Lobi, though they reported some elders who spoke Lobiri.

The Khi of Mangodara claimed to speak Khisa with the Dogo and Kaan and to understand their responses in Dogose and Kaansa. They reported, however, that they must speak Jula to the two groups of Bambadion in order to communicate.

The Bambadion Dogoso of Taurandougou reported that they speak Jula with all outsiders, including the Dogo and Khi. Though it was not stated specifically, their answer implies that they speak Jula with the Bambadion Kheso as well. The Bambadion Kheso, on the other hand, claimed they could communicate with the Bambadion Dogoso of Taurandougou when both were speaking their own varieties.

Essentially then, the Kpatogo, Dogo, and Khi claim to speak their own varieties together, but Jula to people outside of this ethnic family, whereas it is unclear from these data if the Bambadion use Jula together or if they can communicate in their own varieties.

From responses to other questions about knowledge and use of Jula, it is clear that all five of the groups interviewed spoke Jula, had learned it when they were very young through contact with other Jula speakers, and that Jula had been spoken in their communities for several generations, from before the French colonized the region. The Khi in Mangodara and the Bambadion Kheso in Tiébatta said they sometimes use Jula at home with family members, whereas the others said they never did this.

Though all five groups of subjects reported that their people travel a great deal (mostly to find seasonal labor in Côte d'Ivoire), all except the Kpatogo in Diassara said their people return after a year or so. Those in Diassara said that even those who return from Côte d'Ivoire plan to leave again after a brief stay at home.

The five groups also unanimously reported marrying within their ethnic group, that is, they claimed they did not marry people of a different ethnic background, and this seemed to include people from different dialects. According to their report, the Dogo generally do not marry Kaan, nor the Khi the Dogo, etc.

A diachronic description

The region between the Black Volta on the east and the Comoë on the west which today forms the greater part of southwest Burkina Faso has a long history of migrations, conquests, and ethnic diversity.

The Kaan and their ethnic family are probably the most ancient of the present ethnic groups living in this region. While Labouret (1958) has them migrating into the area from what is now Ghana around 1710, Parenko and Hébert (1962:417) put their immigration back two centuries to around 1540. They calculated this based on the fact that the Kaan have oral histories of thirty chiefs since their immigration, each with an average of fifteen years reign. Other historical notes place their origin around Bondoukou, Côte d'Ivoire (Delafosse 1912) or farther south along the Atlantic coast (Tauxier 1921).

The Kaan, however, were not the original occupants of the region, for their oral history affirms that upon arrival in their present territory they found large stone ruins which are still intact today. The historians of this region have speculated about the origin of these ruins, ranging from slave traders building holding pens for their human chattel to a lost indigenous civilization to a Mediterranean people who travelled across the desert (Parenko and Hébert 1962:443–448; see also Labouret 1920 and Bertho 1952).

It is unclear whether the Kpatogo, Dogo, and Khi were distinct groups that migrated shortly after the Kaan, or if they share the same ancient ancestors and have diverged since that time. Parenko and Hébert have the Kpatogo, Dogo, and Khi migrating between 1600 and 1700 as separate groups, but Père (1982, 1987) mentions a group of Kaan who split off and migrated north to live with the Dogo; these Kaan are called [kpaya-dogbo] 'travel-Dogo (plural), which sounds very similar to the name Kpatogobo.[14] In

---

[14]The name for the Dogo in Kaansa is [tɔgɔ], or the "-togo" of "Kpatogo".

addition, Parenko and Hébert (1962:429) write that Salangalé is the ancestor of the Dogobo who lived for a while in Dalo or Dalogo before moving north to their present territory, while an oral tradition of the Komono in Côte d'Ivoire (the Bambadion Kheso?) traces their origin to a chief named "Senengel" (Schmidt 1986:4). Tauxier also traces the origins of the "Dorhossié-Finng" from Ghana to Dalogo, and then north to their present villages. This convergence of oral history leads me to suspect that the Dogo and the Khi (Komono) share a common ancestor and later split up after migrating from the east.

The first recorded contact between Europeans and the Kaan, Dogo, Kpatogo, or Khi occurred in the late 1800s when Binger crossed the Comoë region on his way to and from Kong. He encountered the "Bambadion-Dokhosié" in Sakédougou and the "Komono" in Niambouanbo (modern Niabango?) and Tiébatta. His first impressions of them as a people are not complimentary. He describes them as constantly drunk from *dolo*, a local millet beer, and showing no signs of real intelligence. Binger (1892:338) believed their ethnic group, small, poor and wretched, would die out in the near future. It is interesting that one hundred years later they survive with their language intact, in spite of increasing pressure to use Jula.

In two places, Binger mentions that the Komono had prisoners ("captifs") or slaves (pp. 338, 344). Could this be a reference to the Bambadion?

Binger moved on north into Dogo territory, passing through several small villages until he reached Sidéradougou. Before entering the town he was met by the son of the chief who, Binger wrote, was insolent and insulting (p. 355), and as a result he bypassed the town to move on to another Dogo village called Dissiné. He observed that many of the Dogo were circumcised and carried the facial scarifications of the Wattara Jula in addition to their own traditional marks on the cheek and abdomen. He noted that the Dogo all seemed to speak Jula and assumed they were gradually forgetting their mother tongue (p. 356).

It is unclear how much actual contact Delafosse (1912), Tauxier (1921, 1931), and Sidibé (1927) had with the people they described in their works. The conventions of anthropological description of their day did not seem to demand explicit mention of their sources, though it is safe to assume they gathered oral histories and traditions from informants where they lived and traveled. Nevertheless, these early descriptions are invaluable historical records in spite of what strikes the modern researcher as obvious prejudices and misunderstandings that surface in their texts.

Labouret (1925, 1931, 1958) made a conscious effort to learn local languages, visit elders, and attend ceremonies of the peoples living within his jurisdiction as colonial administrator in Gaoua. Consequently, he obtained a great deal of accurate information about the ethnic groups he called the "tribes of the Lobi branch". However, he freely admits having trouble making any real, productive contact with the Kaan and Kpatogo (1958:36), which leads the researcher to suspect the accuracy of his accounts concerning their history and culture. Indeed, Labouret's classification of the Kaan and Dogo in the Lobi branch is based on shared cultural and linguistic traits (1958:21–22), and these criteria have proven erroneous for the Kaan ethnic family. Obvious differences between the Kaan and the other Lobi branch groups, which have come to light through the research of Parenko and Hébert (1962) and Père (1982, to appear), are found in their dress habits, village architecture, and social organization. My own research and that of Prost (1972) have confirmed that, structurally, Kaansa and Dogose have very little in common with Lobiri.

Griffeth (1971) and Person (1968) have chronicled the expansion of Jula influence in West Africa, which reached its zenith around the end of the nineteenth century under the control of Samori Touré and his armies. This coincided with the advent of the French colonial forces, which defeated Samori and set up their own political structures. Yet, the legacy of the Jula lies in their economic and linguistic dominance of the region which continues today. It is recorded in the clan names of the Dogo and Khi who all bear the name Wattara; it is scarred upon the faces of these two groups and many others formerly under the domination of Kong; it is alive in the oral traditions of the Kaan who fought against the raiding armies of Sarantye Mori, Samori's son (Labouret 1925, Savonnet 1963); and it is alive in the Jula bilingualism which seems to pervade the four communities under study. Indeed, the Jula influence in this region will probably increase as development increases, for it has become the language of regional access and travel, and is well poised for official acceptance and development in the future language planning of Côte d'Ivoire and Burkina Faso.

4

Literature Review

Linguistic results of interethnic contact

When two ethnolinguistic groups have prolonged contact, the effects of this contact can be found in individuals as well as in their communities. The contact affects the language varieties in their code repertoires, first by adding the necessary varieties for intergroup communication. As contact continues over generations, the codes in each community's repertoire change in structure, each affecting the other in accordance with the status relationships between them. If these status relationships are extreme, for example if one community holds a great deal more socioeconomic power over the other, the bilingualism in the dominated group is likely to shift to monolingualism in the language of the dominant group, especially if the domination persists in the extreme over several generations.

Thus, bilingualism, variation in language structure, and language shift are some of the linguistic results of interethnic contact, and these mechanisms are very much at work in modern West Africa.

Bilingualism

It is impossible to say how many people in the world are bilingual, but bilingualism is normal for more people than we in the industrialized West may suspect.

When one considers the number of languages and ethnic groups in close contact in regions like South Asia and sub-Saharan Africa, it is easy to understand that mere day-to-day survival requires that a significant number of people know how to speak at least one language other than their own.

Mackey (1968:555) defines bilingualism simply as "the alternate use of two or more languages by the same individual". Weinreich (1953) had earlier called this languages in contact, a part of a larger phenomenon of culture contact, which normally is studied by anthropologists. Weinreich's point, however, is that the contact between languages and cultures come together in the individual, thus necessitating a combination of linguistic, anthropological, and psychological research to arrive at an adequate understanding of the phenomenon.

The setting in which language contact occurs plays a major role in determining the nature of bilingualism in an individual. Thus, an investigation into the bilingual abilities of an individual or a community must include an investigation into the social context of the interethnic contact which gave rise to the bilingualism.

Bilingualism and diglossia. Fishman (1972b) has discussed the interrelationship of bilingualism and diglossia (Ferguson 1959). He presents four logically possible combinations of these two: bilingualism with and without diglossia, diglossia without bilingualism, and neither bilingualism nor diglossia. Here we will discuss only two: bilingualism with diglossia and diglossia without bilingualism.

The most stable situation is one that is characterized by diglossia and wide-spread bilingualism. In communities where interethnic contact is common, people are bilingual and the languages they speak take on distinct roles in the community.

Diglossic situations remain stable because the social roles and domains for language varieties are compartmentalized; the language associated with one territory does not trespass on the territory of another. Some have argued that such is the case for the modern West African states (Schuerkens 1983, Djité 1988), where French or English serve as the high form and indigenous languages as the low forms.

However, regional or national lingua francas do not fit neatly into this binary scheme, and so Mkilifi (1978) has proposed "triglossia" to bring the role of lingua francas into the diglossia equation for Africa. His study in Tanzania put Swahili into an intermediate level between English (H) and local languages (L). Fasold (1984:45) calls this "double overlapping diglossia".

Fishman (1972b) goes on to discuss diglossia without widespread bilingualism, that is, where elites and masses speak different languages without much interaction between the two classes. In Burkina Faso, this might be said of the urban elites in relation to the rural masses. This is suggested on the basis of the very low rates of literacy and education outside of major cities, and the fact that, until recently, rural peasants have participated very little in national political affairs. On a personal level, however, members of the educated elite certainly have not abandoned their ethnic identity nor their native language. When a bureaucrat in Ouagadougou leaves his French-language-dominated workplace, he returns home to an extended family where he most likely will speak Moore, Jula, Bisa, Lyele, Bobo, or any of several other Burkinabè languages to cousins, sisters, grandparents, or uncles of the peasant class.

Grosjean (1982) points out that being bilingual does not automatically entail biculturalism. He notes that in communities where a lingua franca is part of most people's repertoire, as in much of West Africa, individuals remain firmly established in their own ethnic group without any sense of shared ethnicity with the native speakers of the lingua franca. A particular case of this among the Kaan of Loropéni will be examined in chapter 7.

Language choice. Bilingualism in an individual necessarily entails choosing to speak one language or the other in each new circumstance. In addition, bilinguals often switch between one code and the other in the middle of a sentence or phrase. Language choice in a situation is regulated not just by knowledge of vocabulary in either language, but also by social constraints relating to the participants in the interaction, the situation or setting of the interaction, the content of the discourse, and the function or purpose of the interaction. Grosjean details these constraints as follows:

Participants
  Language proficiency
  Language preference
  Socioeconomic status
  Age
  Sex
  Occupation
  Education
  Ethnic background
  History of speakers' linguistic interaction
  Kinship relation
  Intimacy
  Power relation
  Attitude toward languages
  Outside pressure

Situation
  Location/setting
  Presence of monolinguals
  Degree of formality
  Degree of intimacy

Content of discourse
  Topic
  Type of vocabulary

Function of interaction
  To raise status
  To create social distance
  To exclude someone
  To request or command (Grosjean 1982:136)

Gumperz (1962) has pointed out that each linguistic community is made up of a communication matrix which is the intersection of the functionally related ROLES of the individuals or subgroups in the community. The communication matrix uses a CODE matrix as the linguistic correlates to its roles, though not all community roles may have a distinct linguistic correlate.

The nature of this code matrix is different for each community, and may comprehend a set of slightly varying phonological features or discourse styles, or a set of completely different and structurally unrelated languages. Roles and their linguistic codes also vary in the degree that they are distinct from each other. For example, behavior toward the peer groups is very different from behavior toward outsiders, and this may manifest itself in the use of two different languages, one indigenous, one superposed by outside forces.

In settings where multilingual communities are undergoing rapid social change, previous norms of language choice break down, and consequently, language choice must be negotiated in everyday situations.

A West African example of NEGOTIATION is reported by Yanco (1983) who studied the use of Zarma and Hausa in Niamey, Niger. Niamey is about one half native Zarma speakers, one quarter native Hausa speakers, and one quarter speakers of other African languages; neither Hausa nor Zarma serve uniquely as the lingua franca of the city. Instead, Hausa and Zarma speakers tend to learn each other's language, creating a "generalized bilingualism". Knowing both languages is seen as highly desirable when questioned about it in formal interviews. Yet, deciding which language to use in a given situation requires some negotiation.

Linguistic results of interethnic contact

Sometimes, bilinguals will refuse to accommodate to the preferred language of the interlocutor, for example, when a Zarma-speaking native will refuse to speak Hausa simply because he considers Zarma to be the local language which the other must adapt to.

This produces conversations where Hausa and Zarma speakers use their own language, thus relying on the passive control of each other's language to ensure communication. This happens because there is a failure to establish one language as the code of interaction in a particular situation.

> In contrast to situations where one group effectively imposes its language on another, this exercise of 'mutual passive bilingualism' (or the guise of it) makes for a situation of relatively peaceful coexistence between the two major linguistic groups on one level while, at the same time, allowing each group to maintain its own definition of the situation. (Yanco 1983:8)

CODE SWITCHING is very common in bilingual speech, and can range from inserting words from a second language to switching to a second language for sentences at a time. Most bilinguals feel uneasy about code switching, calling it "lazy", "embarrassing", or "not pure" (Grosjean 1982:147). Yet, in spite of negative attitudes, bilinguals everywhere do it frequently. Grosjean suggests some of the reasons for code-switching:

> Fill a linguistic need for lexical item, set phrase, discourse marker, or sentence filler
> Continue the last language used (triggering)
> Quote someone
> Specify addressee
> Qualify message: amplify or emphasize ('topper' in argument)
> Specify speaker involvement (personalize message)
> Mark and emphasize group identity (solidarity)
> Convey confidentiality, anger, annoyance
> Exclude someone from conversation
> Change role of speaker: raise status, add authority, show expertise. (1982:152)

Fishman (1972c) distinguishes between situational and metaphorical code switching. Situational switching involves a particular social setting or situation that requires a particular language to be used, such as a government office in Ouagadougou where two Mossi will converse in French rather than their native language Moore. A metaphorical switch, on the other hand, is determined by the social meanings the interlocutors want to convey through the switch. If the Mossi visiting the government office uses Moore for a plea to relax government regulations, he is metaphorically appealing to the Mossi bureaucrat's ethnic loyalty which the supplicant hopes will temporarily override the bureaucrat's loyalty to the government. The bureaucrat's cold response in French would be metaphorical appeal to law and the power of the state.

In the ethnically diverse Central Volta Region of Ghana, Ring (1987) found that in church services, when the form of worship was in focus (liturgy, readings, singing), Ewe is used; but when people focus on the content of the message (sermon, announcements, prayer) the local language is used. This kind of switching is topic-based and may also be tied to the emotional tenor (formality) of the interaction. But, Ewe is also used in a number of situationally defined ways, in what Ring calls "externally introduced activities" (literacy, school, church, etc.). The local language is used exclusively in what Ring calls "traditional rites" (funerals, marriage, enstooling of chiefs, etc.). Ewe and local languages are both used in activities of "public cultural expression" (games, arbitration, dances, public gatherings, etc.).

Description of bilingualism. An adequate description of bilingualism as both an individual and societal phenomenon involves questions of DEGREE, FUNCTION, ALTERNATION, and INTERFERENCE (Mackey 1968). Degree refers to how well one speaks language X or Y, i.e., an individual's competence in either language. Function refers to the role of each language in the individual's behavior patterns. Alternation refers to how, when, and why an individual changes from one language to another. Interference refers to the extent to which an individual mixes languages together or keeps them separate (degree and type of code-switching) (p. 555).

In order to show the connection between micro- and macrosociolinguistic studies of societal bilingualism, Fishman has formulated the concept of DOMAIN OF LANGUAGE USE. A domain is

> ...a sociocultural construct abstracted from topics of communication, relationships between communicators, and locales of communication, in accord with the institutions of a society and the spheres of activity of a speech community, in such a way that *individual behavior and social patterns can be distinguished from each other and yet related to each other.* The domain is a higher order summarization which is arrived at from a detailed study of the face-to-face interactions in which language choice is imbedded. (1972a:442, emphasis his)

Thus, the examples of code-switching in African contexts that we have discussed above can be best analyzed and described in terms of habitual, widely-accepted rules of interaction based on the combination of a specific language variety with the convergence of topic, setting, and interlocutor, in short, in terms of domains. For our hypothetical example of the two Mossi in the government office, the government or official domain is operative. Fishman points out that the social reality of domains is verified by the existence of metaphorical code-switching. If our office interaction were not governed by a shared sense of what was appropriate for this official domain, then a switch to Moore in a plea to bend the rules would not have any metaphorical appeal to traditional loyalties. Yet, this kind of metaphorical appeal does occur frequently, as evidenced by the example from Batiana, and consequently, the concept of domain of language use will be vital in our research among the Kaan.

Language variation and change

Another inevitable result of contact between language varieties is the variation and change of the form of these varieties. As speech forms change, they affect communication between groups, causing comprehension to either converge or diverge. Yet, it is also apparent from thirty years of intelligibility research that similarity in speech forms does not always correlate closely with the results of comprehension tests. The complex relationships between linguistic similarity, intelligibility, interethnic contact, and sociopolitical realities have called into question the definition of terms we all thought we understood quite well until we took a careful look at language variation.

Language and dialect. Modern sociolinguistics has had to come to terms with popular notions of "language" and "dialect". As one probes carefully into the nature of language variation, one sees less and less ground for distinguishing between these two terms in any meaningful way. Individual speech styles blend into social and regional dialects, which blend into languages. Hudson (1980:24) uses the term "variety", which he defines as "a set of linguistic items with similar social distribution". Yet after a long discussion of the problems encountered in trying to delimit languages, dialects, and registers, he concludes, "the only satisfactory way to solve these problems is to avoid the notion 'variety' altogether as an analytical or theoretical concept, and to focus instead on the individual linguistic item" (p. 71).

Alternatively, Chambers and Trudgill (1980), while acknowledging the difficulties involved, do offer working definitions of "language" and "dialect". For their purposes, a language is "a variety which is autonomous together with all those varieties which are dependent (heteronomous) upon it" (p. 11); and dialects are "varieties which are grammatically (and perhaps lexically) as well as phonologically different from other varieties" (p. 5). These will be the working definitions for this study.

The speech community. Problems defining language and dialect arise out of problems defining the elusive yet foundational concept of speech community. Gumperz' formulation of this concept is widely accepted as

> Any human aggregate characterized by regular and frequent interaction by means of a shared body of verbal signs and set off from similar aggregrates by significant differences in language usage. (1971:114)

Speech communities can be defined with two sets of criteria: linguistic and nonlinguistic. Nonlinguistic factors may be objective differences, internal values, intergroup relations, and political action. Linguistic factors, speech and language, are not always carefully distinguished. Hymes believes a speech community shares two types of rules: "rules for the conduct and interpretation of speech, and rules for the interpretation of at least one linguistic variety" (1972:54). However, patterns of speaking may be shared across a wide area, such as in a *Sprechbund* (the Germanic countries of Central Europe). The notion of language variety is equally complex and imprecise. Do multilingual members of one community also belong to two or three other communities simply because they can speak their language? Can one know the language of a community without being a member of it?

After reviewing and severely critiquing prominent definitions of a speech community advanced by Gumperz (1971), Hymes (1972), Labov (1972a), and Fishman (1972c), Raj Dua offers this synthesis of the concept:

> In order to capture the reality about the patterns of language divisions, we must view a speech community as consisting of layers of speech community within speech community, each speech community having patterns of interaction and a set of verbal signs distinct from the other and yet sharing them with another. This concept of speech community aptly describes the multilingual character of the politics involved. It shows that the term 'speech community' has a relative value and can be meaningful only when we specify the level of abstraction and interrelationship among various levels for specific purposes. For such a characterization of speech community the explication of the nature of interaction, network size, sharedness or norms for the conduct and interpretation

of speech in social interaction become critical questions in sociolinguistic research. (1981:97)

Intelligibility. Simons considers intelligibility a synonym of comprehension and understanding, and so dialect intelligibility is "the degree to which speakers of one dialect understand the speech of another dialect" (1983:2) regardless of whether that understanding comes about through lexical and grammatical similarity alone or through frequent exposure to each other's speech. Grimes, on the other hand, prefers to think of intelligibility as "a side effect of one's ability to speak one's dialect" (1985:169). Simons calls this theoretical construct of degree of understanding between two dialect speakers that have never come into contact with each other INHERENT INTELLIGIBILITY. Other kinds of comprehension that one gains through prolonged contact with another dialect Grimes (1987:35 calls BILINGUAL OVERLAY).

Karam (1979) sees intelligibility as simply the range of variation a speaker of a particular language variety finds acceptable and understandable in other speakers. Thus, saying two dialects are intelligible means for Karam that the range of variation between the two falls within the area of acceptability for each set of speakers. As the variation increases, dialects approach a threshold of intelligibility. Conceivably, the amount of variation in this range will change with the amount of contact one has with other dialects.

In a DIALECT CONTINUUM, we expect to find several possible degrees of intelligibility or interdialect comprehension. J. Grimes (1989) has described, in simple terms, four basic levels of intelligibility one expects to find in a dialect continuum, or in any grouping of similar language varieties:

1. FIRST RATE communication within the nuclear dialect: communication without difficulty due to differences in language structure;
2. PRETTY GOOD communication: outside the nuclear dialect, but with a degree of understanding based on knowledge of the nuclear dialect rather than interdialectal learning. Lapses of communication are more numerous than in the first situation, but still rare;
3. SO-SO communication: "...the forms of speech used are similar enough that the quality of the interaction is adequate for a few purposes, but inadequate for most others." (p. 257)
4. IMPOSSIBLE communication: dialects may share similar structures and vocabulary, but are ineffective for interdialectal communication.

Karam's (1979) continuum of intelligibility covers the entire range of language variation, from level one (intradialect communication) to level six (two unrelated languages with no intelligibility between them). Without considering social factors, it is at Karam's levels four and five[15] that researchers encounter the most difficulty in classing varieties as separate languages or divergent dialects.

Methods for testing intelligibility in dialect continua have been developed by SIL international in Mexico, and used all over the world as a measure of comprehension between dialects. Casad is the definitive manual of the process, which he describes as determining "for a multilingual area the smallest possible set of primary centers capable of providing adequate communication to the entire area" (1974:37). This is done by testing comprehension of simple texts in different dialects at key population centers in dialect areas. Calculations of degrees of intelligibility are based on test scores in different towns and villages, and lead to the drawing of a contour map of a dialect network, where "the number of contours that separate two points [i.e., villages or towns] is inversely proportional to the strength of association between these points" (p. 43). In short, the contour lines show the limits of communication between the various dialects in a chain, and suggest subdivisions based on language variety within the speech community. The low-level threshold of intelligibility "is the level at which two speakers of separate dialects, both bilingual in a lingua franca...would switch to that lingua franca rather than try to communicate in their own dialects" (p. 46). Or as Karam (1979) would put it, it is the threshold of their range of acceptable variation.

This, of course, is a rather simplistic understanding of the roles languages and dialects play in the repertoire of a multilingual speech community. It is quite possible that speakers from two dialect groups that understand each other quite well will still speak to each other in a lingua franca because of the social setting, the relationships of power and solidarity between the speakers, attitudes toward the varieties in question, and/or the topic of discussion, in short, because the domain requires it. So the use of a lingua franca between two dialect speakers is not necessarily a sign of low intelligibility. It is true, however, that lingua francas are often used to bridge gaps of understanding between related dialects.

Casad does recognize that communication patterns within a dialect chain are seldom uniform or reciprocal, and that where inherent intelligibility may be quite low, for socioeconomic or cultural reasons, interethnic contact and dialect understanding may yet be quite high. Certainly,

---

[15]"(4) Significant differences are perceived with a major impairment of mutual intelligibility; (5) Extensive significant differences are perceived with no mutual intelligibility but there exists a recognized similarity" (Karam 1979:120).

intelligibility in a dialect chain is influenced by more than just lexical and grammatical similarity (e.g., see Wolff 1959, 1967).

A popular distinction between language and dialect is that dialects are MUTUALLY INTELLIGIBLE while languages are not. One problem with this conception is that interdialectal comprehension seems to be an elastic rather than a two-sided phenomenon. Intelligibility is not always mutual, and Hudson (1980) points out that since intelligibility is in practice a function of relations between people (as opposed to a property of the language itself), it is determined as much by the motivation and experience of the individuals as it is by linguistic similarity. It is understandable then that these factors work differently in individuals, causing uneven intelligibility when they try to communicate.

Wolff (1959:36–38) studied three examples of nonreciprocal intelligibility in the Niger Delta region of Nigeria:

1. Nembe and Kalabari are very close linguistically and geographically. The Nembe claim close similarity to and comprehension of Kalabari, but the Kalabari deny they can understand Nembe. They say some Nembe have learned Kalabari, but the Kalabari never learn Nembe; indeed, the Kalabari seemed to despise the Nembe. The Kalabari were enjoying an economic boom through proximity to a major harbor town, while the Nembe were poor fishermen. Thus, Kalabari attitudes toward the Nembe prevent them from acknowledging any similarity between their respective dialects, even though the Nembe demonstrate good understanding of Kalabari.

2. Three language varieties in southwest Nigeria, Edo, Ishan, and Etsako, show enough linguistic differences and low intelligibility to warrant being called separate languages by that measure. Prior to Wolff's study, the Oba, the leader of the Edo had launched a plan to unite all three varieties under one called 'universal Edo', claiming that the other two groups understood Edo well. However, speakers of Ishan and Etsako denied mutual intelligibility and claimed their understanding of Edo came from frequent contact with them in Benin City. Ishan and Etsako speakers acknowledge the Oba as cultural leader, but want to preserve their linguistic and political independence.

3. Degema and Abuan are two distinct, unrelated languages in the Niger Delta. Degema fishermen sell fish in Abuan markets and communicate with them in Abuan. The Abuans have expressed the attitude that since the Degema can understand and talk to them, their two languages must be related. However, the Abuans never learn Degema.

On the basis of these three studies, Wolff concluded that "linguistic communication, involving a certain type of intelligibility (nonreciprocal), exists because cultural factors provide a basis for it. Comparability does not enter into the picture" (p. 38). Hence, Wolff calls for a deeper understanding and development of an operational model of linguistic intelligibility.

The verbal repertoire available to a community may be quite wide, and can be distinguished in terms of historical provenience, mutual intelligibility, and specialization of use. Historical provenience and mutual intelligibility may clash, however, as in the case of Hindi and Urdu, which are considered two languages though mutually intelligible. If mutual intelligibility is expressed in terms of degree (e.g., ninety percent intelligible, see Casad 1974), what is the cutoff point for considering two varieties different codes or the same? It seems that the question of defining a code as a language or a dialect is one to be answered by extralinguistic factors rather than intelligibility.

Simons (1983) feels that social attitudes affect social interaction directly and intelligibility indirectly, though attitudes have little direct effect on comprehension. I will explore the relationship between social attitudes and intelligibility in chapters 6 and 8.

Language shift

When ethnic groups come into contact, and as that contact increases, then issues of linguistic and ethnic identity become more important. Inevitably, minority communities feel pressure to increase their verbal repertoire to include the code(s) of the majority with which their contact is increasing. Some believe that modern, technology-based civilization carries with it inherent hostility towards minority languages. Edwards (1985:50) challenges this assumption and suggests that hi-tech civilization per se is not hostile, but rather, technological advancement bestows economic power and dominance on the language of those who control it, regardless of whether that language is spoken by the majority or the minority. For example, Chinese language speakers outnumber native English speakers, yet English has become the linguistic gate to science, technology, and international contact.

Edwards maintains that while hostility may be the prevalent feeling in the subjugated groups, the dominant group may simply be ignorant or ambivalent towards linguistic minorities. Even the feelings of hostility in the minorities are accompanied by admiration, pragmatism, and a desire to shift towards the dominant language and culture. For example, the shift from Irish to English in Ireland is as much a result of Gaelic speakers' desire for upward mobility and a better standard of living as it is of English hostility or hegemony toward Irish.

The practical considerations for survival which fuel a language shift may exist alongside very favorable attitudes toward the minority language being abandoned. People may feel very sentimental about their language and culture, but realize at the same time that speaking it won't get them a job. This may be what is happening among the rural peoples of southwest Burkina Faso. While there may be no negative feelings toward their own languages, the economic force of Jula requires them to learn it well for survival. This issue is examined further in chapters 7 and 8.

Edwards (1985) stresses the central importance of ECONOMIC CONSIDERATIONS to the process of language shift. His research has shown that the ethnic minority peoples he has studied have been pragmatic in their life-style choices, and that often a small group of ethnic revivalists or intellectuals have stronger sentimental attachments to their language than most of the common people do. He does note, however, that occasionally groups hold onto their language against all odds, usually for religious reasons.

Gumperz has talked of the "communicative economy" of a community as "the total set of linguistically distinguishable communicative settings accessible to residents in any one case..." (1976:86). When this communicative economy changes by means of introduction of innovations such as new roads, new business activity linked to the dominant language, the conventions of speaking must necessarily change as well if the community is to survive.

Edwards' (1985) fundamental thesis is that ethnic identities evolve, and that language is just one way to maintain identity. If a language becomes a handicap to survival, it will be abandoned, but that does not mean minorities will cease to think of themselves as different or distinct. They may just chose to maintain that distinctiveness in other ways, for example, through a dialect of the majority language, or through specialized uses of the former mother tongue in cultural or religious ceremonies (see Battestini (to appear) on Efik). Ethnic identity undergoes constant evolution, and the need for a unique, vital language variety as a support for group identity may shrink as practical needs for survival change.

After a brief survey of known cases of language shift around the world, Edwards presents some general trends that emerge from the data:

1. We note again a powerful concern for linguistic practicality, communicative efficiency, social mobility, and economic advancement.
2. Competence in more than one language is required in many, if not most, settings, but the increasing power of supra-ethnic or ethnically "neutral" varieties restricts this

competence to highly specific situations...a decline in the existence and attractions of traditional life styles also inexorably entails a decline in languages associated with them.
3. ...support for given languages becomes problematic when many exist within state boundaries. Lingua francas become important for trade and communication. They also begin to carry national or regional identity, replacing the mother tongues in those roles.
4. Standardization and modernization of internal varieties is always theoretically possible, but not always practical. Language planning is always possible, but only in the sense of adjustments to linguistic phenomena made possible themselves by forces quite outside the boundaries of conscious planning.
5. Even where indigenous varieties have achieved a developed status they are still not necessarily equal in all senses to external languages.
6. Environments change, people move, and needs and demands alter; and it is much more natural for language-use to change, or for linguistic contact to emerge and recede, than to have linguistic stasis. (1985:85–86)

Approaches to the study of language shift. How does one study a language shift, which can sometimes take place over several generations? How can a researcher in a short period of time discover with any certainty a process which was at work in a community long before the researcher arrived, and will continue long after his or her departure? Isn't it presumptuous of the researcher to say a language shift is in progress, when the outcome may not be known for another generation or two?

Gumperz (1976) studied a Slovenian-to-German language shift in a rural Slovenian community in modern Austria. His study showed that the process of language shift can be recorded through the examination of discourse features and pragmatic inferences, as well as in larger patterns of use, acquisition, and social network. Gal (1978), who also studied a language shift in a rural peasant community in Austria (Hungarian-to-German), asserts that

> Linguistic change is neither so fast nor so slow as to be unobservable; new forms which eventually replace older forms can first be located in synchronic variants in the speech of subgroups within the community; and changes observed over time are the result of the redistribution of synchronic variants

to different linguistic environments, to different social situations, and to different speakers...language use, or more specifically, the pattern of language choice in a bilingual community, also undergoes change according to these same general principles. (1978:227)

In order to illustrate the synchronic variation in language use of the community, Gal set up an implicational scale of language choice in which it was clear that one's age correlated closely with whether one chose German or Hungarian in a set of eleven different communication settings. The two factors that seemed to determine language choice most accurately were the age of the speaker and the peasantness of his or her social network. Gal concluded that "...whatever a speaker's social status, his linguistic presentation of self is constrained by his social network" (1978:233). From her ethnographic observations and personal interviews, she demonstrated that the age-graded implicational scale of language choice reflects real diachronic change, not just the pattern of language choice over a lifetime.

This code-switching (language-use variability) only occurs in a narrow range of situations for each speaker. Gal observed that it is usually the individuals caught in the middle of this language shift—the ones who no longer live in a completely peasant world, nor who have fully transferred their social and ethnic identity to German Austria—who find themselves code-switching in the critical situations she highlighted. Gal concludes that "the simultaneous use of language choice for stylistic rhetorical purposes, as well as for signaling social group membership is an indication that language change is in progress" (1978:237).

Language shift in Africa. In much of Africa, nationalism associated with the post-colonial state clashes with ethnic loyalty and pride, which is a more traditional and deeply rooted form of nationalism, and both of these sentiments clash with pragmatic concerns of survival. In the post-colonial period the decision to continue using European languages for government and education has been purely pragmatic. The use of one code for international integration, another for communication in multi-ethnic regions of a country, and another for vibrant village life and culture, has made stable trilingualism a reality in many parts of East and West Africa. Edwards (1985) feels that as long as populations are predominantly rural and immobile, this situation will continue. But as mobility and urbanization continue, the processes of language shift will gather momentum.

We must ask ourselves "Are the findings illuminating language maintenance and shift in Europe generalizable to situations in Africa?" Tabouret-Keller (1968) believes they are, with certain modifications to our understanding of the social forces involved. She defines two kinds of maintenance/shift situations: among sedentary populations and among migrants.

The pressures of social necessity leading to language shift operate differently on a community depending on whether it is in an urban or a rural setting. The ethnically diverse populations in major African towns sometimes feel pressure to shift to the tribal language of the majority of residents. This is certainly the case for Wolof in Senegal, where it is the primary language of the largest towns and cities, located in traditional Wolof areas. But Wolof has also spread outside of its traditional areas and is quite common in central towns across the country. One cause of this is intermarriage with Wolof speakers, where Wolof rather than the local language is passed on to the children.

This pattern is also found in Ouagadougou, where immigrants must learn Moore, the language of the Mossi, who historically ruled the central part of the savanna south of the Niger. A similar pattern does not obtain in Bobo Dioulasso, however, where the trade language Jula is learned, rather than the language of the Bobo, the original residents.

Tabouret-Keller asserts that in rural areas of Africa language, shift is not apparent; that in the villages, linguistic homogeneity is the norm. However, the research to be presented in chapters 7 and 8 shows that multilingualism has been the norm in southwest Burkina Faso for a long time, even in rural areas like those surrounding Loropéni.

Certainly language shift is much more of an immediate necessity among communities of immigrants in large cities such as Abidjan and Dakar. Tabouret-Keller (1968) reports that in Dakar new arrivals tend to settle in the farthest suburbs, making them the most linguistically heterogeneous. Yet, Wolof continues to expand there and is now well-entrenched in towns in the interior, in spite of different indigenous languages in surrounding villages. In fact, recent estimates of the spread of Wolof in Senegal propose that more than eighty percent of Senegalese speak Wolof (Bruhn 1984, Mansour 1980) as either a first or second language. Clearly, in Senegal Wolof is not just the language of urban migration, but has now become its de facto national language.

In Burkina Faso, seasonal migration outside of the country for work is very much a part of rural life. Not surprisingly, Tiendrebeogo and Yago (1983:42–43) found that in general, migrants are much more likely to be multilingual than nonmigrants. Yet, there is little data on language shift among these migrants. From my own experience and observations in Loropéni, I can suggest the somewhat obvious proposal that shift to Jula or popular French (Djité 1988) would be most likely among the children of those who spend many years in Côte d'Ivoire without returning regularly to their home villages. Seasonal migrants, on the other hand would maintain their mother tongues when they return home each year to work their fields.

Tabouret-Keller concludes that the factors that influence language shift in both Africa and Europe are the expansion of primary school education, urbanization, and changes in socioeconomic conditions of everyday life. What maintains traditional language patterns is the rural way of life and traditional, ethnic social structures. A synchronic comparison between language shift processes in Europe and Africa shows more differences than similarities. Until the last decade, language shift in much of Europe has moved toward monolingualism in standard national languages. Africa, she asserts, is moving from rural-based monolingualism (with many exceptions) to urban-based multilingualism. Tabouret-Keller (1968:116–117) believes, however, that a diachronic comparison between the two shows that Africa is undergoing many social changes that were prevalent in Europe during the nineteenth century.

Social-psychological results of interethnic contact: Language attitudes

Modern studies in social attitudes toward different languages and dialects trace their origins to a study by Lambert et al. (1960) at McGill University in Quebec of attitudes held by the resident French- and English-speaking communities toward their languages and toward each other.

The method they used was the now well-known matched guise, and the attitude judgments were made on semantic scales developed by Osgood et al. (1957). Since this study, language attitudes has developed as a field of research in sociolinguistics and social psychology in settings around the world.

Defining the object of language attitude studies has not been easy. Agheyisi and Fishman (1970:138) note that attitudes have been defined from a mentalist and behaviorist point of view. Mentalists see attitudes as a kind of neural state of readiness which can be called a mediating concept, a readiness to respond, or a hypothetical construct. The behaviorist position considers an attitude as simply an observable response to certain stimuli. Both of these perspectives are subject to criticism: the mentalists because their object of study is difficult to measure in concrete, objective ways; the behaviorists because their object of study is dependent on each individual situation and cannot be generalized across different research settings.

Another issue of debate that is more germane to our research is whether an attitude is unitary or multidimensional. Mentalists tend to assert that attitudes have three components: cognitive (knowledge), affective (evaluative), and conative (action). Behaviorists argue that these distinctions are artificial and impossible to demonstrate in any meaningful way, and thus feel attitudes form a single component in the psyche of the individual.

Osgood, et al. (1957) developed the semantic scale with a multidimensional model in mind having essentially three dimensions: evaluation, potency, activity. In other words, people judge things as good or bad (evaluation), weak or strong (potency), and active or passive (activity). We will briefly discuss how semantic scales measure these dimensions of attitude in one of the sections below.

Another issue discussed by Cooper and Fishman (1974) is distinguishing language attitudes from other kinds of attitudes. They suggest two defining stances: attitudes toward a particular language variety (referential) and attitudes which affect language behavior (behavioral).

My own position for this research is mentalist, multidimensional, and referential. I realize, however, that what I have observed and recorded is behavior in particular settings so that the attitudes studied here are inferences based on observations, some emanating from controlled situations (survey interviews), others from uncontrolled situations (participant observation). In the long run, those who hold to a mentalist conception of attitudes have to admit that attitudes cannot be studied directly, but must be inferred from observable data; the reasoning process of inference must be made explicit so that studies may be compared and critiqued in a scientific manner.

Measuring language attitudes

Language attitudes have been studied and "measured" in several different ways, and these are discussed in detail in Agheyisi and Fishman (1970) and Fasold (1984). Essentially, studies have used questionnaires, personal interviews, the matched guise, commitment measures, and observations. Some of these are considered direct methods (questionnaires, interviews) and others indirect (matched guise, commitment measures, observation).

Both direct and indirect methods have their advantages and disadvantages. Direct methods need little inference to record attitudes; opinions and self-reports are taken at face value and analyzed as basic data. One cannot always assume, however, that subjects are willing, objective, or dispassionate in reporting their attitudes, especially when the language issues involved are controversial, or when the interviewer is an outsider to the community. Indirect methods infer attitudes from behavior observed in response to certain stimuli. Their advantage is that such methods may reveal attitudes that individuals may not admit to in a formal situation, or which they may not consciously hold at all. The weakness of indirect methods lies in the inference process. How does one articulate or describe an attitude toward an ethnic group based on selective individual reactions to taped speech samples? Or perhaps more importantly, which attitude, the reported one or the inferred one, plays the most significant role in determining behavior of an individual or a community?

Given the rather indeterminate nature of attitudes, it is best to study them using a variety of methodological approaches, allowing the results of different methods to confirm each other; one can most accurately observe attitude phenomena from several different research perspectives rather than just one.

The semantic differential and the matched guise

The semantic differential as an attitude elicitation method was developed by Osgood et al. (1957) from psychological research into the nature of attitudes. It consists of a seven-point scale between semantic opposites (good-bad, rich-poor, etc.), a whole set of which is attached to certain concepts the researcher is investigating. Subjects mark the intensity of their feelings on the scales for each concept.

The semantic differential is a kind of closed-question questionnaire which, when combined with a matched guise, is considered to be an indirect method of investigation. It is indirect because it asks for quick evaluative judgments of specific speakers and specific texts. Common evaluations of different varieties are extracted from the entire sample of questionnaires and scales. It is through analysis of samples of individual responses to individual language stimuli that the researcher discovers the shared evaluational norms of the community, rather than through trying to elicit explicit statements of these norms.

A weakness of this approach is that the subjects may not have the opportunity or freedom to determine the evaluational scales which appropriately represent their attitudes, and thus may be asked to make a judgment they normally do not make about the language variation in their community. This can be avoided to a certain extent by careful background research in the community before the research is begun.

Agheyisi and Fishman have described concisely the matched guise technique:

> This technique requires that selected groups of judges evaluate the personality traits of speakers whose tape-recorded

voices are played to them. The recorded voices are generally those of individuals, who, because of their native-like speaking ability in the two languages or varieties represented, have each recorded translated versions of the same text. This fact is, of course, concealed from the judges who believe that each language or variety is spoken by a different speaker. In addition to this evaluation of traits of the speakers, other measures of variables such as prejudice, personal attitudes, group preference, and degree of bilingualism are also taken, and scores from these are later examined for degree of correlations with the evaluation measures derived by use of the matched guises.

The major principle underlying this technique is that if there is adequate control of every other variable in the experimental situation—such as the voice quality of speaker, content of text, and most especially, personality of speaker—other than the actual language variety, then whatever evaluations are made of the speaker must be prompted mainly by the judge's general reaction to the speakers of that particular language, rather than by his reaction to the specific speaker in the experimental situation. And so, if there is any significant uniformity in the evaluation reactions of any group of judges, such reactions are said to represent the stereotyped impressions of that group toward the speakers of the particular language or variety. (1970:146)

While the matched guise was developed for testing attitudinal reactions to the speech of bilinguals, it has been adapted for exploring attitudes toward dialectal variation as well. In these studies, the stimulus tapes are not true guises, i.e., recordings of different dialects are not done by the same individual speakers. Instead, to achieve a naturalness not present in translated, read texts, several speakers of the dialects being studied are interviewed on nonpartisan topics, such as memorable natural events (storms, earthquakes, etc.), local tourist sites, personal adventures, or "danger of death" stories (Labov 1966, 1972b). This allows the researcher to gather several natural, contextualized texts by native speakers of the dialects in question. Normally, an attempt is made to control the age, sex, and social class of the speakers selected for the text stimuli, as well as the subject of the texts.

Another variation has been to test different groups of subjects with different guises, with the assumption that the different groups of subjects are comparable for the purposes of the study. This is the technique used by

Bourhis and Giles (1976), who compared reactions to Welsh and varieties of English used in announcements in a theater in Wales. The different guises were given on different nights to different audiences. Bourhis and Giles believe, however, that for the purpose of the evaluations (which consisted in simply turning in a questionnaire or not), each audience could be considered equal. They made this modification in order to achieve naturalness in the test situation of a kind that researchers are normally not able to provide. In "Questionnaire design" in chapter 5 we will see that a similar assumption was made for a similar purpose in developing the method of question and text rotation for the language attitude study.

The validity of language attitude studies is summed up by Agheyisi and Fishman: "Validation of attitude studies is particularly problematic because of the very nature of attitudes as properties of the psychological or mental process" (1970:150).

While studies with commitment measures can be validated by comparing results with one kind of actual behavior,

> studies which focus on either the cognitive or affective components of attitudes, or which define attitude as consisting of only an affective dimension, need as criteria behavior of a rather subjective nature. In actual research practice, the use of special operational definitions (which in many cases turn out to be highly simplified versions of conceptual ones) seems to overlook or underrate the problem of validity. This practice has no doubt increased and perpetuated the familiar problem of the low degree of consistency between attitude measures and overt behavior.... (1970:150)

The validity of a study is improved by the use of several methods of research and through building cross-checks into the methods chosen.

Some language attitude studies in Africa

Particular studies of language attitudes in West Africa, while still few and far between, have yielded some surprising results; how generalizable these results are remains to be seen in further research. Due to the variety of unique cultures living in contact with each other, some researchers have found traditional European and American methods of investigation such as the matched guise and semantic scales to be inappropriate for their particular research setting. Most seem to rely on closed- or open-question questionnaires or interviews to gather their data, though a few have tried the methods discussed above (Djité 1988, Lafage n.d.,

Mgbo-Elue 1988, Scotton 1977) with limited success. We will discuss only a few representative studies.

Attitudes toward European languages and national language policy. Djité (1988) recorded attitudes of a sample of residents in Abidjan, Côte d'Ivoire toward a wide range of issues including the current language policy, trade languages in the country, and regional dialect variation. Concerning the matter of language policy, he found that the colonial policy of using only French in education and administration has led to present attitudes that "...local languages cannot express scientific concepts and that the development of those local languages can only lead to divisiveness among Ivorians" (p. 18). He reports that some previous studies have shown that even well after independence from France, a majority of Ivoirians would choose French as the national, official language of Côte d'Ivoire over any indigenous language. French carries a great deal of status as the language of progress, modernity, and socioeconomic mobility. It was also seen by a few as ethnically neutral (that is, with regard to African ethnic groups), even though it is clearly associated with European culture.

In essence, Djité (1988:22–23) perceives three trends in attitudes toward language policy in Côte d'Ivoire: passive, integrative, and prospective. The passive attitude accepts the current situation and thinks the language problem will work itself out. The integrative attitude wants popular French to be promoted as an indigenous, national variety of a world language. The prospective attitude claims realism, asserting that while learning French is necessary, it should not exclude promoting indigenous languages; exoglossic education is elitist and should be infused with the promotion of local languages.

In Ghana, Saah (1986:372) investigated general attitudes toward English and the national language policy. Local varieties of English have developed in Ghana, which Ghanaians call 'Pidgin', 'Kru English', 'Broken English', and 'Harbour English'. There is also a sort of standard Ghanaian pronunciation of English learned in school, and those who have studied outside the country and who speak with American and British accents are often disdained for "putting on airs".

Some Ghanaians (often educators) are very concerned over the development of an indigenous style of English and attribute it to falling standards. They see correct English as an essential ingredient in the proper functioning of the political and economic process. Others disdain English as a colonial remnant and tolerate it only as a necessary evil. They don't seem to mind if the language is "butchered" and, in fact, interpret it as a kind of social protest.

Attitudes toward bilingualism. We saw in chapter 2 how the occurrence of societal bilingualism is common in West Africa; let us now examine three studies on attitudes toward this phenomenon. Mgbo-Elue (1988) used both direct and indirect methods to explore attitudes toward Yoruba/Igbo bilinguals in Nigeria. The direct study (interviews) showed that the Igbo subjects generally expressed positive attitudes toward learning Yoruba and other Nigerian languages. Yoruba subjects, on the other hand, held negative views toward learning Igbo and other Nigerian languages. Related to these attitudes is the fact that fewer Yoruba reported knowing Igbo than did Igbo who reported knowing Yoruba. Mgbo-Elue tentatively suggested that these results indicate that those who had learned another language were more tolerant of other Nigerian languages in general.

However, the indirect study of attitudes (using a matched guise)

> indicated that the Yoruba and Igbo hold biased and stereotyped impressions about speakers of the other group's language....In terms of basic personality traits such as dependability, intelligence, competence and ambitiousness, both groups view the other group as clearly inferior. (1988:160)

Mgbo-Elue concluded that though people may recognize the need and importance of learning another Nigerian language, they do not always have positive attitudes toward the second languages they are able to speak.

In Ghana's Central Volta Region, Ring (1987) found that the ethnic groups with the highest overall second-language comprehension in Ewe seemed the least concerned that Ewe would replace their own language, while the group with the lowest overall comprehension of Ewe feared loss of their mother tongue the most. They cited teaching Ewe in the schools and using many Ewe words in their own language as evidence of this attitude. Ring (1987:156) also asked about local support for mother-tongue literacy programs, and found that "those communities who feel most confident in their use of spoken Ewe feel the least need for a literature program in their own language".

In Niamey, Niger, Yanco (1983) reports that in formal interviews, Hausa/Zarma bilinguals stressed the solidarity of these two ethnic groups, but in informal comments people identified with their own ethnolinguistic group. Informal comments indicated that the Hausa do not value Zarma and do not like to learn it. The Zarma, on the other hand, thought Hausa was a difficult language which they had to learn because the Hausa didn't learn theirs. Yanco's translation task results, however, showed a wide understanding and control of both languages in both groups. Yanco reconciles these conflicting attitudes by considering the nature of the bilingualism in Niamey:

> The actual practice of mutual passive bilingualism is in fact compatible with either position: The Hausa don't have to know Zarma (in the sense of speaking it), but the Zarma do have to know Hausa (in the sense of understanding it). What is more or less the same behavior can be explained or justified in different ways depending on the self-image one wishes to maintain. (1983:6)

Attitudes toward dialect variation. It has been the tendency for expatriate linguists in Africa to divide large language varieties into small dialects, each with its own name, cognate percentage, and intelligibility estimate based on word lists and recorded text tests. All too often this is done without a serious attempt to discover how the speakers of these "dialects" see themselves in relation to the similar dialects around them; in other words, what their attitudes are toward the local language variation. One of the implications of this state of affairs, argues Djité (1988) is that such linguistic diversity is viewed as a major obstacle to national unity in the post-colonial era. In his study in Abidjan, Côte d'Ivoire, he heard many people assert that without French as the national language, the country would fall into intertribal war. Djité claims, however, that his research in identifying accented speech demonstrated that his judges were unable to correctly identify the ethnic origin of the speakers; accented speech should not be a divisive factor in the nation. He also points out that in at least one case, the same language (Wèɛ) was given two names (Wobé and Guéré) and treated as two diverse dialects by colonial administrators, and the erroneous distinction has endured in linguistic research since then. Overall, Djité reports much more tolerance toward language variation than is commonly thought and wonders if one would find similar results in rural settings.

Kanyoro (1989) expresses a similar sentiment with regards to his investigation into the Luyia dialect cluster in Western Kenya. He reviews the history of political and social change among Luyia-speaking peoples, and concludes that as a result of social factors, people will be more or less willing to tolerate language variation for the purposes of unity or division. The more reason people have to unify, the more efforts they will make to understand other dialects.

A negative example of this view of attitudes toward language variation is supplied by Akere (1982). In Ikorodu, a suburb of Lagos, Nigeria, residents speak a local dialect of Ijebu, which is itself a variety of Yoruba. In spite of very few phonological differences between their local dialect and Ijebu-Remo (the regional variety of Yoruba), some residents of Ikorodu insisted their dialect, Ijebu-Ikorodu, was distinctly different from the Remo dialect, and that their local variety is much closer to the Lagos variety, Eko. Akere reports that this sentiment is shared by most of the residents of Ikorodu, and reflects their desire to identify as a part of the community of Lagos rather than as part of the regional ethnolinguistic subgroup (Ijebu). This attitude was demonstrated in responses to questions about intelligibility and speaking competence of the local varieties. While almost ninety percent claimed Ijebu was intelligible for them, only twenty-seven percent claimed to be able to speak it. However, one hundred percent of the subjects said they understood Eko, and ninety-four percent claimed speaking proficiency in it as well.

The residents of Ikorodu show a clear preference for their mother tongue and reject Ijebu regional identity because it "represents the dimensions of parochialism, regionalism, conservatism, all of which are negatively evaluated" in the Ikorodu speech community (1982:357).

> On the other hand, Lagos Yoruba is associated with the modern progressive socioeconomic values of the city. Its acquisition and use will enhance the suburban status of the Ikorudu community. Ijebu-Ikorodu is desirable because it guarantees that the community has a mother tongue dialect and that the members of the Ikorodu community do have an ethnic identity albeit one deliberately restricted to hometown identity. (1982:357)

5

Research Methods

Sociolinguistic survey methodology

The nature of survey research is to explore unknown territory, to discover social and linguistic variables relevant to the theme and purpose of the research. Survey research is distinguished from experimental research in the degree to which one tries to control variables, and what one hopes to accomplish, demonstrate, or "prove". While experiments attempt to confirm or refute hypotheses, or show causal relationships between variables, surveys are largely correlational. These distinctions do not always hold for sociolinguistic surveys, however; often, a great deal of background research on the relevant variables is done before a survey is carried out, making surveys as much confirmatory as exploratory. In the research for this book, we used a method designed for experimental use (the matched guise) and adapted it for exploratory use. In another part of the study, a survey of language use was designed primarily to confirm observations rather than discover what was previously unknown.

Social science methods have been carefully refined over a long period, but sociolinguistic survey methods are relatively new. Cooper (1980) explains that sociolinguistic surveys are different from social science surveys in four ways: (1) sociolinguistics is a separate field with different aims; (2) sociolinguistic techniques are developed specifically for the language orientation of the surveys; (3) their practitioners are basically self-taught in methods; and, (4) interest in sociolinguistic surveys is fairly recent. Within SIL International, probably doing the most language-oriented surveying around the world, a specific focus on gathering sociolinguistic data did not emerge until the decade of the 1980s (Bendor-Samuel 1980, Huttar 1982).

Survey research is done with respect to a certain population, drawing a carefully planned sample from that population, so that results can be generalized.

Of course, survey research has its weaknesses, especially when dealing with complex issues of language shift in multilingual communities. As Gumperz has pointed out:

> The sampling procedures of surveys, moreover, assume that community or group boundaries exist, that they are generally recognized, and can easily be determined. In cases of language shift, where alterations in verbal behavior go hand in hand with radical alterations in values and group identification, such assumptions of stability clearly don't hold. Here notions of group boundaries and ethnic identity and standards of evaluation vary with context, and interview data on social attitudes is of doubtful validity. To make one's analytical premises dependent on a priori assumptions of social stability, therefore would be begging the question. (1976:85)

Theoretical background and general approaches

In his landmark article laying out the theoretical background for the methodology of sociolinguistic research, Labov discusses the "observer's paradox" which all research in secular linguistics must grapple with:

> We are then left with THE OBSERVER'S PARADOX: To obtain the data most important for linguistic theory, we have to observe how people speak when they are not being observed. The various solutions to this paradox define the methodology for the study of language in context. (1972b:113)

The way around this, Labov proposes, is to investigate sociolinguistic phenomena through several complementary research methods, such as combining elicitations with naturally occurring texts, observed language behavior, and carefully controlled experiments. This leads to what he calls "the principle of convergence" where "the value of new data for confirming and interpreting old data is directly proportional to the differences in the methods used to gather it" (1972b:118–119).

Convergent data leads to interpretations that are more accurate and defensible than those based on data from one research perspective alone.

In considering general approaches to sociolinguistic surveys, Cooper (1980) points out that the goal of surveys is to assess both language behavior and behavior toward language. Language behavior includes proficiency, acquisition, and usage. At the microsociolinguistic level, a study of this type concerns the features of language or language variety, while at the macrosociolinguistic level, these surveys study the characteristics of groups. Behavior toward language includes attitudinal or implementational studies. Attitudinal data must be inferred from individual responses or actions, but implementational data are observable actions related to language. The table in (13) shows Cooper's ten-celled taxonomy of behaviors assessed by sociolinguistic surveys, with an "X" in the cells indicating the survey research in this book. It is quite common, of course, for individual surveys to cover more than one cell of the matrix.

(13)
Behavior	Level of observation	
	micro	macro
Language behavior		
Proficiency		x
Acquisition		
Usage		x
Behavior toward language		
Attitudinal		x
Implementational		

Surveys have been carried out for several different purposes such as to inform language policy decisions, to prepare for the implementation of these decisions, or to evaluate their effects. They may also test hypotheses of linguistic theory or variation analysis. The surveys in this study were motivated by the need for information to inform language planning efforts by SIL International and the Kaan people, in preparation for the introduction of literacy among the Kaan, Dogo, Kpatogo, and Khi of southwest Burkina Faso. It was also motivated by a concern for improving our understanding of the nature of the interaction of dialect variation, intelligibility, interdialectal contact, and social attitudes in rural West Africa. In addition, I wanted to investigate, on a local, community level, issues pertaining to the spread of the regional lingua franca, Jula.

Techniques for collecting data for sociolinguistic surveys vary according to the needs of the survey. Various techniques used in past surveys have been interviews, various kinds of formal testing (language proficiency, intelligibility, comprehension), attitude scales, nonreactive observations, and content analyses of written material (Cooper 1980).

Research techniques

The process of SAMPLING a population for a survey should be done as randomly as possible to assure that the results represent as closely as possible the actual trends and processes to be found there. Such social research, however, is always less exact than other kinds of scientific sampling research because of the simple fact that individuals chosen as part of a random sample may choose not to participate in the survey. Good preparation and public relations can minimize this to some extent, but it remains a constant source of error. In addition, physical limitations of the researchers (lack of financing, poor access to the population, political barriers, etc.) can make random samples difficult, if not impossible to obtain. Consequently, one may resort to the best estimation of a representative sample. For this, researchers consider the social and geographical characteristics they deem important to the survey, and on the basis of these variables choose certain individuals or groups of individuals who are accessible and willing to participate in the survey. The sample is not random, but should represent the population in a way that is accurate enough for the purposes of the research.

A problem frequently encountered in surveys of language change or shift is how to project diachronic change on the basis of a synchronic sample. When there are differences between age cohorts in the sample, are they the result of historical change in the community's patterns, or of normal personal change in the cycle of life?

One way to explore historical change is with retrospective questions, asking about past use and proficiency. Answers to these kinds of questions can be useful, even though their accuracy cannot always be cross-checked. Even so, the retrospective answers of the older generation can be compared to the current answers of the younger generation to see if community norms have shifted. Another way of verifying changes in cross-sectional data is to try to correlate apparent changes with known societal changes (such as the building of a road or school in the community, political or economic upheaval which brought about language changes, etc.). A third way concerns the nature of the changes being investigated. If the nature of the linguistic change is such that it does not normally occur in a lifetime in stable individuals (such as a complete language shift in the home domain), any significant manifestation of this change in cross-sectional data may very well indicate a historical change in progress (Gal 1978).

Demonstrating historical change in progress in synchronic data requires rigorous research of a kind sociolinguistic surveys are not always able to deliver. Lieberson aptly comments that "one must weigh the obstacle of partially invalid data with the alternative of completely ignoring any inferences about either change or the consequences of societal events on language behavior" (1980:16).

DIRECT METHODS of sociolinguistic inquiry are those which make the subject aware of the researcher's purpose of the interaction and which take the subject's responses as face-value indicators of the variable being studied. Some examples of direct methods are formal interviews, some kinds of questionnaires, and various tests of language abilities.

Interviews. The use of interviews and questionnaires is discussed at length in Agheyisi and Fishman (1970). They point out that, though interviews allow for great flexibility and a certain amount of naturalness of setting and interaction, the large, diffuse body of data they generate is difficult to codify and analyze. It takes a great deal of time and preparation to conduct a good interview and, therefore, it is not a practical method for surveys of anything but small populations using small samples. A skillful interviewer, however, can elicit highly reliable, detailed, and specific information from a subject. This kind of information can rarely be obtained by any other method.

Questionnaires are probably used most frequently in sociolinguistic surveys. They usually contain a mixture of open- and closed-ended questions which probe the subject's situation in life, his or her abilities, and attitudes. Agheyisi and Fishman mention that responses to open-ended questions are more difficult to record and score than responses to closed-ended questions, though closed-ended questions may seem boring and perfunctory to the subjects. Closed-ended questions have the danger of being irrelevant and misleading if they have not been pretested carefully. Their advantage is in their ease and speed of administration, and in the way they focus the subject on the important issues of the survey. Agheyisi and Fishman (1970:149) feel that closed-ended questions are "among the best instruments for measuring multicomponential concepts".

Surveying second-language proficiency is one area where both questionnaires and interviews are used. Questions or "self-reports" about one's ability to speak a second language tend to produce skewed evaluations if not carefully constructed or elicited (Grimes 1987). Even well constructed "can-do" scales can only approximate true levels of proficiency (see Quakenbush 1986). Consequently, an oral interview based on techniques developed by the U. S. Foreign Service Institute (FSI) seems to be the most accurate way to assess second-language proficiency. Yet, as mentioned above, interviews are not practical for surveys of large populations, so surveyors of language proficiency often trade some accuracy for the practicality of questionnaires.

A more serious conceptual problem encountered when attempting to use FSI's five-point proficiency scale in rural situations is how to define native-like proficiency (level five) in situations where no formal education or literacy is the norm. FSI's definition of the highest level of proficiency in a second language is that equivalent to "a highly articulate, well-educated native speaker". Grimes circumvents this problem by redefining "well-educated" as "culturally relevant education or training" (1987:38) or the command of a standard dialect if it exists.

While this recognizes indigenous training in the use of language which sometimes can be quite rigorous or specialized, it still does not define it very well, nor does it deal with the very real possibility that such structured native training may not be available to those who speak the language as a second or third code in their repertoire. Yet, even without specialized training in a second language, one may obtain a high degree of proficiency through years of contact with and experience in a community which uses that language natively. In the case of Jula or other trade languages in West Africa, does the fact that a person has had no formal (Western or traditional) education in a second language eliminate the possibility of ever achieving level-five proficiency, merely by definition of that level? And what provisions can be made in our measures of proficiency to account for a high second-language proficiency which is limited to certain domains, such as work, trade, and travel? These theoretical questions have yet to be dealt with on the practical level of testing second-language proficiency in rural settings.

Tests. Intelligibility and language proficiency are most often assessed in surveys through the use of formalized "tests". These ask the subject to perform some structured task which indicates a level of ability in the area of interest to the researcher. In the case of intelligibility, this involves listening to texts of closely related dialects and then demonstrating the level of comprehension by such means as answering a set of questions or paraphrasing in the subject's own dialect what was said. For language proficiency, the test may take the same form, except that the texts are in the subject's second language instead of a related dialect, or the test may require a more rigorous translation of the texts. Another method used for testing bilingual proficiency in a survey is a sentence repetition test, where subjects are asked to repeat sentences of increasing length and complexity in the test language.

Most of these methods can be characterized generally as "recorded text tests". Grimes (1987) criticizes them as decontextualized and overly formal for surveys of rural peoples, and inaccurate and unreliable for testing language proficiency (they were designed to test intelligibility). Language proficiency, she argues, is far too complex to be evaluated with simplistic measures of comprehension.

INDIRECT METHODS of sociolinguistic inquiry do not make the purpose of the research known to the subject in the interaction, and often the subjects' responses are used as a basis for inferring values that cannot be investigated directly or for confirming self-reports or the results of tests. Four indirect methods are observations, matched guises, semantic scales, and commitment measures.

Observations. The least intrusive of any method, observation also carries with it its own sources of error. Agheyisi and Fishman criticize it for its subjectivity and privacy, and call for researchers to find ways of subjecting observational data to the same controls (scoring, counting, rating) put on more formally collected data (1970:150).

Thus, observation is an excellent tool for gathering data to complement that gathered through more direct methods, but on its own, it tends to be subjective and unverifiable. In sociolinguistic surveys, observation seems best suited for studying the domains of language use, the transactions in multilingual public settings, and for rapid anonymous surveys of the use of social markers in speech.

Guises and scales. Matched guises and semantic scales are considered indirect methods because the matched guise test reveals dimensions of one's attitude that do not appear on broad direct questionnaires. Certainly the matched guise approach is more direct than observations and less direct than questions asking specifically about attitudes. It appears from the literature that this method does tap into covert (or nonpublic) attitudes of groups. It makes no claims, however, about how the subjects will act toward speakers of other language varieties.

Commitment measures. What are the behavioral consequences of language attitude? Typically, only modest relationships are found between attitude measures and the overt behaviors which such scores are designed to predict. Can a general statement be made about the relationships between language attitudes, language behavior, and behavior toward language?

To explore this relationship between attitude and behavior, researchers in language attitudes have developed commitment measures. Essentially these are means by which subjects of an attitude study commit themselves to a certain action or personal participation in an event that is related to the interethnic attitudes they have just revealed in the survey. So for example, if a group of Anglo students shows a negative attitude toward Chicano students, they would be expected to decline an invitation to a concert of Puerto Rican music (Fishman 1969). In a survey, a commitment measure is designed to test the willingness of subjects to act in concert with their expressed attitudes (see Fishman 1968 and Agheyisi and Fishman 1970 for lengthy discussions of commitment measures).

The problem with commitment measures is finding something that the subjects are likely to be faced with rather than a hypothetical future event. In many SIL surveys of nonliterate linguistic minorities, questionnaires include some form of the question "Would you be willing to financially support a literacy project in your mother tongue?" This question makes sense to the researcher who anticipates starting such a program, but to the subject who has never read his or her language and who may not have even considered the possibility of doing so before, it probably does not seem like a real option, especially to subsistence farmers whose main concern is daily survival. Thus, this question does not seem to be a relevant commitment measure for attitudes about mother-tongue literacy.

Broad survey of the Kaan, Kpatogo, Dogo, and Khi

The goal of the first phase of my research was to investigate the attitudes each group held toward the dialects spoken by the other three, whether any one dialect was devalued or given prestige, how individuals viewed their dialects in relation to the trade language, Jula, or the language of the most numerous ethnic group of the region, Lobiri; in short, how they looked upon themselves and the other groups they had regular contact with. I also aimed to find out how much contact they actually reported having with these groups, whether they spoke their languages, intermarried with them, or traded with them. The analysis of this data would lead to an understanding of the interplay between language variation, social contact, and social attitudes.

This attitude survey was designed and prepared from November 1987 to January 1988, and carried out between February and May, 1988. From June 1987 through November 1988 my wife Catherine and I and our newborn son, Nathanael, lived in Loropéni in a mud-brick house with a tin roof which we rented from a Lobi man in town. We lived in the western part of town, beyond the marsh, across the main road from where most of the Kaan people who lived in Loropéni resided. Most of the survey visits to surrounding villages could be done in a day's trip from Loropéni by motorbike. The hand-drawn map in (14) shows the neighborhoods relevant to this research in Loropéni (Poni Province), Burkina Faso.

Survey design

The design of this survey was inspired by Lambert's matched guise and Labov's subjective reaction test (1972a). It was thus an indirect measure of shared language attitudes in these four communities.

The survey instrument itself consisted of texts of each of the four related dialects, as well as one text each in Lobiri and Jula, the common languages of contact in this region. Each subject listened to a set of these texts and was asked to make judgments about the speaker or about "people who speak like that". These judgments were usually yes/no responses to questions pertaining to the subjects' attitudes toward the ethnic identity, social status, and personal character of the text speaker. Other questions dealt with the subject's opinions about how much contact he or she had with people like the text speaker, and how familiar the subject was with the language or dialect of the text.

Sampling. To obtain a sample of each of the four ethnolinguistic communities, I chose to visit five villages located in different areas of each group's territory. Some villages were located on main routes of travel and trade, others near larger population centers, others were nestled in rural areas and accessible only by footpath. The table in (80) in appendix 1 lists the villages surveyed from each group, along with some distinguishing characteristics of each village.

I tried to interview six people in each village: an elder, an adult, and a youth of each sex. This would give me a minimal population sample of thirty individuals, but due to difficult traveling conditions over a wide area and the amount of time available to carry out these surveys, I set a goal which I felt was attainable though in only one case did I meet this goal.

My procedure for interviewing individuals in the village was to approach the village elders and, once permission to interview was granted, to ask them to designate the three men and three women to interview. Most often we interviewed the men first, then the women, according to local preference.

(14)

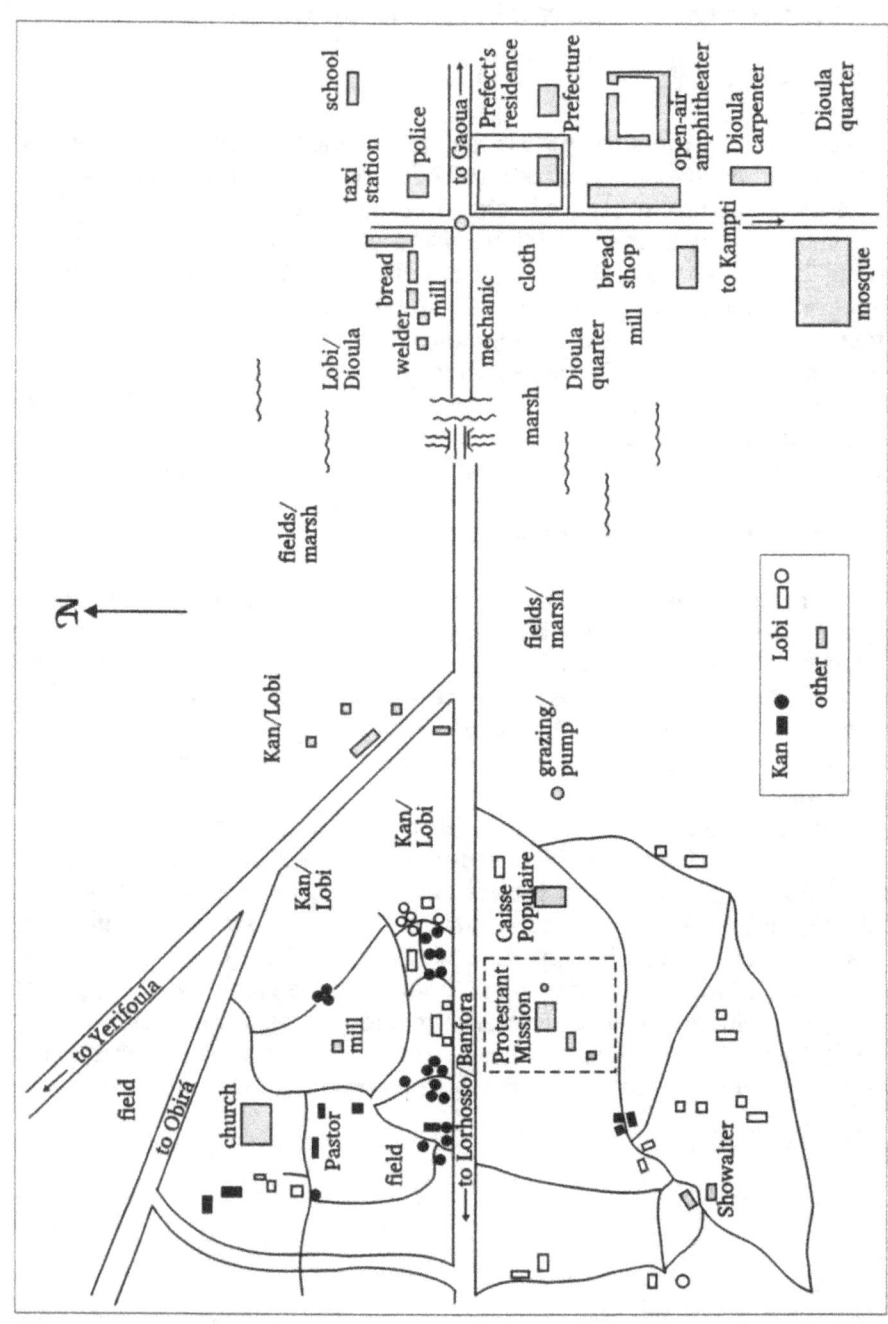

Interviews were done in public, with curious onlookers standing around. This also reflects strong local preference for group interaction with outsiders, especially with whites. This setting, which I found unavoidable in pretesting, due to a strong reluctance on the part of the Kaan to be interviewed in private, was the major factor influencing the design of the attitude questionnaire, which will be presented in the next section.

As a survey team of two, translator Misa Jean-Baptiste Suwa and I found that on day trips from Loropéni, six people were the most we could interview in one sitting. In some villages, fewer than six people were forthcoming to be interviewed. The number and type of people interviewed in each village was dependent on the general cooperation of the village elders, the willingness of each individual to participate, and our own level of fatigue. We encountered the same difficulties interviewing women as were reported by Tiendrebeogo and Yago (1983) and Djité (1988). Consequently, women are underrepresented in this sample.

Each interview took twenty minutes to a half hour. With the necessary formalities of introductions, explanations, and general discussion, a village visit could last from four to six hours.

Questionnaire design. The conventional form of a matched-guise test as described in chapter 4 needs radical adaptation in order to be used effectively in a rural nonliterate setting such as this one in Burkina Faso. To create a questionnaire for this survey I had to design innovations which compensated for not only the lack of literacy and school testing experience in the populations studied, but also for the local norms for social interaction, i.e., group interviewing versus individual interviewing.

Adaptations. The two greatest factors which influenced the design of this survey questionnaire were (1) the wholly oral nature of the language varieties and their cultures, and (2) the social norm for collective interaction with outsiders. The primacy of oral interaction (indeed, the near total absence of literacy in any language) in these communities required, naturally, that the questionnaires be administered orally in a local language the subjects understood well. For this, I formulated questions in Kaansa with the help of language assistants in Loropéni.[16] Once the first form of the questionnaire was complete, I interviewed two people in Loropéni, four in Yérifoula, and two in Obiré to test the entire design of the questionnaire as well as the form and effectiveness of the questions themselves. It was during this pretesting that I

---

[16]At this stage I worked with Philemon Farma, Gabriel Farma, Misa Jean-Baptiste Suwa, and Philippe Farma, all young Kaan men living in or near Loropéni. Philemon and Gabriel, both teenagers, had completed primary school in French, and Jean-Baptiste and Phillipe, in their mid-twenties, had learned some French informally in their travels in Côte d'Ivoire.

realized I needed to radically restructure the testing instrument to fit more naturally into the interactive norms of rural village life in these four communities. The final form of the questionnaire, that is its system of rotating questions and texts, will be described at the end of this section.

Once this restructuring was complete, I conducted each interview in Kaansa with my assistant present to repeat questions that I had not pronounced well, or that the subject had not understood for some other reason. Even when interviewing in Kpatogo, Dogo, and Khi villages, I asked questions in Kaansa first. If people could not understand at the first try, Jean-Baptiste repeated the question, first in Kaansa, and then in Jula if they still had a problem understanding.

Creating and using a semantic scale for evaluating the survey texts in this oral nonliterate setting, while not impossible, seemed to require a deeper knowledge of the language and culture than I had at the time. Thus, instead, I formulated relatively simple questions which focused the subject's judgments on the text speaker or on people like him.

Text gathering and question formulation. The stimulus texts for the survey were gathered in interviews in Loropéni (Kaansa), Béguélé (Dogose), Diassara (Kpatogoso), and Mangodara (Khisa). For these interviews, I generally followed the eliciting strategy suggested by Labov (1972c) which seeks to elicit a whole range of speech styles from formal reading or reciting style to very casual or excited styles. Labov's goal was to create a corpus of recorded text which demonstrated the change in use of certain phonological variables according to how much attention was paid to the form of speech. My own goal was less thorough: I only sought to elicit enough natural, casual speech in each dialect to use as short texts to call forth the social attitudes each group held towards the other dialects, and toward their own. Thus, I asked questions about personal experiences while traveling and when growing up, as well as stories about danger and sickness. The question about past illness struck a responsive chord in most of the interviewees and proved to be the most productive of all the questions.

In order to control as many text variables as possible, I selected from this large corpus of recorded interviews short (17–78 seconds) narratives about personal illness spoken by one elder and one younger male of each dialect group. In this way I controlled the age and sex of the text speakers and the subject of the text itself. Thus, I had eight texts to use as stimuli for the questionnaire.

In addition to these eight texts, I added a true matched guise by recording personal narratives on the same subject in Jula and Lobiri spoken by the same young Kaan man who gave me one of the Kaansa texts. This young man spoke both of these languages well, which I determined at the time through the informal evaluations of his ability by others in Loropéni. The final set of texts included eight dialect texts and two contact language texts, as shown in (82)–(91) in appendix 2.

The questions used in the survey were developed out of three sources: (1) six months of my own observations of village life and interethnic contact in the region; (2) the discussions held at the end of the text-gathering visits to the four dialect areas; and (3) informal interviews and conversations in Loropéni. In some cases I turned comments made to me into questions, e.g., "Does he 'speak in his throat'?", "Does he 'speak with his mouth closed' or 'with his mouth open'?". In others, my observations about important cultural events (e.g., "Do people like him do funerals the same way you do?") or trends (e.g., "Are people like him abandoning the traditions of the elders?") inspired questions.

The questions I formulated in French were translated into Kaansa by a language assistant. Next, I tried them out on another assistant to test for clarity, grammatical correctness, and my own pronunciation. I also asked another assistant to translate the questions back into French for me to test for conveyed meaning and accuracy. I made more adjustments to the form of the questions in Kaansa after pretesting them, and a few were fine-tuned once the surveys got underway.

Final form of the survey instrument. To vary the PRESENTATION OF THE TEXTS from one interviewee to the next I recorded two sequences of seven texts each, as is seen in (15).

(15)   Text sequences A and B

Text sequence A:[17]
1: KY 2: KpY 3: KE 4: JY 5: DE 6: KhY 7: LY
Text sequence B:
1: JY 2: KhE 3: KpE 4: LY 5: DY 6: KE 7: KY

The Dogose, Khisa, and Kpatogo texts were distributed such that one text sequence had the younger speaker and the other the elder speaker text. The KY, JY, and LY texts were included in both sets because they formed a true matched guise in that the three texts were spoken by the same young man. I wanted to be sure that each interviewee heard and judged these guises. I also included the KE text in both sets to keep the number of texts the same for

---

[17]D = Dogose, K = Kaansa, Kh = Khisa, Kp = Kpatogoso, J = Jula, L = Lobiri, Y = youth, E = elder.

both sets, and as a way to test my assumption that the age of the speaker of each text would not significantly affect the judgments given that dialect. This could only be done if each subject made judgments of both the elder and the younger speaker of any one language variety.

In the second halp of chapter 4 we saw that some social psychologists have defined attitudes as multidimensional mental filters, or states of readiness. As a proponent of this view, I attempted to set up the survey questionnaire to explore different dimensions of the subjects' attitudes toward the language varieties of their region. I decided to explore five dimensions: (1) attitudes toward shared ethnic identity, (2) attitudes concerning the nature of interethnic contact, (3) perceptions of the social status and (4) personal character of speakers of these varieties, and (5) awareness of the language varieties around them.

The final set of questions to be used in the survey were divided into sets relating to each of these five attitude dimensions. Within each dimension, questions were grouped into subdimensions which defined the semantic content of the dimension itself. For example, the dimension of shared Ethnic Identity is defined as attitudes concerning a *shared language, familial relations, shared traditions, culture maintenance,* and *arbitration* of disputes. While it is true that ethnic identity can be defined in other ways (indeed, there is no consensus on the meaning of the term), for the narrow scope of this survey this is how it will be defined here. This is also the case for the other four attitude dimensions. (Examples (92)–(96) in appendix 2 list the five attitude dimensions explored here, and their corresponding subdimensions and questions.)

With this approach we can gather data which reveals the nature of the mental filter by the shape of the responses which fall through it at specific locations in semantic space. By the way people respond to the questions concerning each subdimension we can construct a model of the shared attitudes of the group towards the language varieties in question.

The actual form and content of the questions (in Kaansa, and as they are reflected in the English translations) have been designed to cross-check and amplify each other. This is a control device which has been built into the survey and which will be discussed in further detail under "Built-in controls" in chapter 5.

The group setting of the interviews, combined with the need to interview individuals one by one led to the creation of a system of rotating texts and questions from one interview to the next. This resulted in a set of questions and texts whose sequence for each new interview was neither predictable to the group of observers, nor overly repetitive to the subjects.

Some questions were relevant to all of the texts, and others were relevant only to certain texts, such as the dialect texts or the Lobi and Jula texts. I grouped the questions into four categories:

1. base questions, which came first on the questionnaire and were asked consecutively of all seven texts in each interview;
2. dialect questions, which were asked only of the dialect texts;
3. Lobi/Jula questions, which were asked only of the Lobi and Jula texts; and
4. shared questions, which were asked of both dialect and Lobi and Jula texts, but in a rotation sequence not shared with the base questions.

Questions from the five attitude dimensions were mixed together and then distributed among these four categories according to their relevance to the texts. Then the categories were divided into subcategories to further distribute the questions and break them down into manageable groups of three to five questions.

Grouped into categories and subcategories, the questions were assigned to the texts in a rotation system which produced four different sequences of questions, and thus, essentially, four different questionnaires. An example of the final form of one of these questionnaires is found in (97) in appendix 2.

Thus, the subjects interviewed with questionnaire 1A heard the Kaansa-Youth text first and were asked the base questions (B), the third set of dialect questions (D3), and the first set of shared questions (S1). Next, the same subject listened to the Kpatogoso-Youth text and answered the base questions, the first set of dialect questions (D1), and the second set of shared questions (S2). This continued as shown in the table in (16) for a typical attitude survey interview session of six subjects in a single village.

(16)

Subject	QR[18]	Text sequence	Heard texts	Answered QS
1	1A	A	1:KY	B, D3, S1
			2:KpY	B, D1, S2
			3:KE	B, D2, S3
			4:JY	B, LJ2, S4
			5:DE	B, D2, S1
			6:KhY	B, D1, S3
			7:LY	B, LJ1, S1

[18]QR = questionnaire used; QS = answered questions (listed by question category code).

Subject	QR	Text sequence	Heard texts	Answered QS
2	2B	B	1:JY	B, LJ1, S2
			2:KhE	B, D2, S4
			3:KpE	B, D3, S1
			4:LY	B, LJ2, S3
			5:DY	B, D1, S2
			6:KE	B, D3, S1
			7:KY	B, D1, S4
3	3A	A	1:KY	B, D1, S2
			2:KpY	B, D2, S3
			3:KE	B, D3, S4
			4:JY	B, LJ2, S1
			5:DE	B, D1, S3
			6:KhY	B, D3, S2
			7:LY	B, LJ1, S4
4	4B	B	1:JY	B, LJ1, S3
			2:KhE	B, D1, S1
			3:KpE	B, D3, S4
			4:LY	B, LJ2, S2
			5:DY	B, D3, S4
			6:KE	B, D1, S2
			7:KY	B, D2, S3
5	1A	A	1:KY	B, D3, S1
			2:KpY	B, D1, S2
			3:KE	B, D2, S3
			4:JY	B, LJ2, S4
			5:DE	B, D2, S1
			6:KhY	B, D1, S3
			7:LY	B, LJ1, S1
6	2B	B	1:JY	B, LJ1, S2
			2:KhE	B, D2, S4
			3:KpE	B, D3, S1
			4:LY	B, LJ2, S3
			5:DY	B, D1, S2
			6:KE	B, D3, S1
			7:KY	B, D1, S4

This rotation system allows twelve to fifteen questions per text, only slightly fewer than in the pretest (eighteen per text). It is very much less repetitive than the pretest, however, because it is not asking exactly the same questions of each text. To the interviewee, each text seems to have different questions asked about it, even though the questions probe the same attitude dimensions and subdimensions.

This rotation system allowed me to interview up to eight people per village in a group setting without undue repetition or predictability from one interview to the next. In actual practice, however, I found I got quite tired after six interviews, and by then the group was also getting restless.

To have a more balanced sample, then, I could have administered three different questionnaires instead of four to the six people in each village (to complete the rotation sequence twice). Rotating four questionnaires among six interviewees resulted in questionnaires 1A and 2B being administered twice in each village, and 3A and 4B only once, thus creating an imbalance in the distribution of questions to interviewees.

Validity

The validity of this test design rests on certain assumptions about the functional equality of the texts and their rotation in the course of an interview, the questions themselves, and the form of the questionnaires. Some controls for internal validity, which allow us to spot sources of error introduced by the survey situation, have been built in as well.

Assumptions. It is assumed that each recorded text, whether spoken by an elder or a youth, equally represents its language variety and, therefore, calls up the same stereotypes and attitudes about the speakers of this dialect as a whole. This assumption is tested by comparing the results of the judgments of the two Kaansa texts and by comparing subjects' judgments of elder and younger speakers across dialect groups. It is also assumed that the two different sequences in which the texts are presented do not significantly affect the judgments of the texts.

It is further assumed that the system of rotating questions and texts between the four questionnaires does not elicit significantly different judgments of the same texts from the interviewees. That is, a subject judges the texts of a particular dialect the same way regardless of whether he or she receives questionnaire 1A, 2B, 3A, or 4B.

Built-in controls. Several "controls" were designed into this questionnaire which allow us to spot and isolate misunderstandings or other errors introduced by the interview situation (distractions), the researchers (poor presentation of questions), or the subjects (misunderstandings, lack of attention to responses). The first of these controls was to ask the same question twice in the interviews, once positively and once negatively. For example, under the attitude dimension Ethnic Identity and subdimension Shared Traditions, the two questions in (17) followed this positive/negative pattern.

(17) S1-2: Are the traditions of people like him different from yours?
S4-2: Are the traditions of people like him the same as yours?

Notice that in this case the negatively-phrased question was the second question asked in the Shared subcategory one (S1-2), whereas the positively-phrased question was the second question in the Shared subcategory four (S4-2). This simply indicates that the questions appeared at two different places on the questionnaires in order to elicit a fresh answer from the subjects. The net effect is that the answers to one question should confirm the answers to the other.

A second structural control was built in by phrasing some questions to clarify and inform each other in a general-specific relationship. For example, the questions in (18) on ethnic identity were related in this way. The first question asks for a general evaluation, the second asks for a more specific judgment, though one that also supplies an answer for the general question. Given that there are only two widespread religious traditions in these groups, Islam and animism, a yes or no answer to this question can easily be interpreted as confirming, informing, or contradicting the previous, more general question.

(18) LJ2-1: Is the religion of people like him different from yours?
LJ1-1: Are there more Muslims among them than there are here?

A third control in the actual administration of the survey was the way the questions were asked. As mentioned above, I always asked each question in Kaansa first. If it was not understood, Jean-Baptiste repeated it in Kaansa, and then translated it into Jula, if necessary. This is the progression we followed in each interview in order to establish reliability of administration.

Finally, the rotation sequence itself functioned as a means of controlling against unthinking responses from individuals, coaching from the group, and repeating the status quo responses others had given. Since each new subject was faced with what must have seemed a new sequence of texts and a new set of questions, he or she was more likely to pay closer attention to the questions, was less susceptible to coaching (it was new and different for the coaches as well), and found it difficult to repeat the same answers other interviewees (who were perhaps more powerful socially) had given because the questions were not exactly the same.

Observations

In the six months which preceded the development and administration of the surveys, I lived in Loropéni with my family in order to begin learning Kaansa and to observe language use among the Kaan living there. During that time I discussed with people with whom I could communicate their attitudes toward the Dogo, Kpatogo, Khi, Jula, and Lobi. In addition, I listened for casual comments people made about these ethnic neighbors, such comments often revealing attitudes which the individual may not have been aware of or would not admit to in a conversation with an outsider. I recorded these observations in several notebooks.

During the text-gathering visits to Béguélé, Diassara, and Mangodara, I asked about attitudes toward shared ethnic identity, contact, and intelligibility within the four dialect groups and recorded their responses.

The survey visits themselves also accorded many opportunities to note extended comments subjects made in response to any of the questions. Thus, in many cases, subjects would not just answer "yes" or "no", but would amplify their responses to explain them. To the extent that I understood these, or they were translated to me, I wrote them down on the subject's questionnaire and will consider them in the interpretation of the survey results.

Specific survey of the Kaan of Loropéni

The survey of the Kaan in relation to their ethnic neighbors was complemented by a survey of multilingualism in the Kaan community itself. This survey consisted of observations of language use in the Loropéni market and in other aspects of daily life, the oral administration of a questionnaire on language use which sought to verify or elaborate on the observations I had already made, and a self-rating scale for proficiency in Jula.

Language use. Early in our sojourn in Loropéni, I was struck by the apparent easy Kaansa-Lobiri-Jula trilingualism present in many of the Kaan people we could observe. Their frequent and proficient use of Lobiri and Jula did not seem to threaten the place of their own language, though it seemed that the use of Kaansa was limited to the Kaan community alone. We did observe, however, some Lobi who spoke Kaansa, and it was asserted to us by different Kaan in different villages that some Lobi who live near Kaan villages and have regular contact with them have learned to speak Kaansa. Even more surprising, on one occasion we observed a Jula who had learned Lobiri and spoke it comfortably. These observations, which ran contrary to my expectations, led me to investigate this multilingual aspect of the verbal repertoire of the Kaan community in and around Loropéni.

During the entire eighteen months of our stay, I recorded observations and reports of language use in notebook journals. I also undertook to observe, over an extended time, the interactions that took place in the Loropéni market, which was the primary marketplace for the Kaan people and the largest market in a twenty-kilometer radius area. The Loropéni market is ethnically diverse: Jula merchants live in town and also come from Gaoua and Banfora; the Lobi of the region sell their produce there; Mossi immigrants have set up small businesses; the Dogo come south from Koro and east from Ouo; and individuals from other ethnic groups who have settled nearby for one reason or another are also present.

From this body of observations I formulated direct questions which sought to explore eight common domains of language use in the community. For each of these domains I had an idea of how language was actually used, but the direct survey of the community served to elicit individuals' own perceptions of their language use. This approach filled in the gaps in my knowledge as well as revealed differences between real and perceived language use. It also supplied data for discovering attitudes among the Kaan about the role their language plays in the region.

The eight domains explored in this questionnaire were (1) the *official* domain (interaction with government and health officials in Loropéni), (2) the *market* domain (interactions in the marketplace), (3) the *friendship* domain (interaction in informal, local settings), (4) the *religion* domain (interactions at traditional rites, funerals), (5) the *travel* domain (interaction when traveling outside the area), (6) the *school* domain (interaction at school), (7) domains of *topic* (interaction about different topics), and (8) the domain of *interethnic contact* (interaction with the other ethnic groups of the region).

The questions of the survey focused on situations where I had either observed language use or where I specifically wanted to probe for self reports. Lacking the same time for preparation that I had for the attitude survey, I formulated the questions in French and asked a survey assistant[19] to translate them orally in our interviews. Naturally, we discussed how each of the questions should be translated before we started the surveys. However, the nature of these questions—direct, simple, self-reports—did not demand the same kind of precision in translation as the indirect attitude survey questions. Nor was there a need to rotate questions for the group interview, as I had done in the language attitude survey. In this case we were dealing with reports of personal language use, not opinions, judgments, or beliefs (the expression of which is often influenced by group pressure). These language use questions were less threatening; people showed no reluctance to answer and seemed unconcerned or unaffected by the responses of others. Thus, the cultural norms which necessitated a complicated rotation system for the language attitude questionnaires did not affect the group interview situation for the language use questionnaires due to the nature of the questions and the subject of the survey. The final form of the language use survey questionnaire is found in (99) in appendix 3.

To obtain a representative sample of the community, I visited five villages chosen from various locations in the Kaan region. In each village I requested the elders' permission to interview three men and three women: an elder, an adult, and a youth of each sex. This gave me a total sample of thirty subjects, five people in each age/sex subgroup. To this sample I added five more subjects whom I was able to interview individually in Loropéni. The total sample for the language use and proficiency survey is displayed in (19).

(19)	Youth		Adult		Elder		
Village	M	F	M	F	M	F	N
Bopta	1	1	1	1	1	1	6
Loropéni	3						3
Obiré	2	3	1		1	1	8
Kassita	1	1	1	1	1	1	6
Soronkina	1	1		2	1	1	6
Sandi	1	1	1	1	1	1	6
Totals	9	6	5	5	5	5	35

[19]My assistant for this survey was Koffi Farma of Obiré-Kapti. He had completed some secondary-school education in Côte d'Ivoire and had worked extensively with M. Père in her anthropological research on the Kaan. I had more confidence in his ability to translate from French to Kaanse than I had had for my assistant in the language attitude survey. In addition, my own passive knowledge of Kaansa was advanced enough by that time to understand the translations of the questions into Kaansa. In only a few instances did I ask the translator to translate the question again because I felt his original translation was not what I really wanted to ask.

Showing up unannounced and interviewing people like this did not seem to cause a problem, partly I think, because I was beginning to be known in the Kaan community by then, and because my language helper was known among many in the community from having worked previously with a French anthropologist.

Bilingualism. Of the proficiency testing methods discussed at the start of this chapter, it seemed the most advantageous trade off between accuracy and practicality was gained by using a self-rating questionnaire or "can-do" scale which could be administered orally as part of the language use survey described above.

Past research in the use of self-rating scales in rural environments has revealed the tendency of subjects to over- or under-report their abilities for a variety of reasons (Grimes 1987, Quakenbush 1986). In spite of the inherent limitations of can-do scales, I still felt they would provide me with more accurate data on the distribution of global proficiency in Jula throughout the Kaan community than a recorded-text test would, and would be much more feasible than some form of an oral interview.

For the Kaan community survey, I focused on proficiency in Jula because it is the trade language of the entire southwest region of the country. Community proficiency in Lobiri was touched on in the language use questionnaire by asking subjects which of the two languages they spoke better. Their responses to this question, combined with their more extensive self-reports of Jula proficiency would allow me to estimate a rough measure of their Lobiri ability as well.

Can-do scales. To create a locally relevant can-do scale of Jula proficiency, I developed a set of language-task statements, using the skill level descriptions in the SLOPE documents (SIL 1987) and the self-rating scale in the back of LAMP (Brewster and Brewster 1976) as a guide, adapting the specific language tasks mentioned in these sources to common local tasks and situations. In French I formulated ten language-related tasks per skill level (excluding "plus" levels), and later refined that to four or five tasks per level. I added a quick self-estimate at the beginning of the questionnaire so that I could jump to the appropriate part of the questionnaire first and then work out from there. In other words, if a person claimed at first to speak Jula well, I would start asking questions at level three. If the subject clearly had trouble at level three, I would move down to questions about level two tasks. If the subject had no trouble with level three tasks, I would move on to levels four and five. An example of the final form of the self-rating questionnaire can be found in (100) in appendix 3.

Specific survey of the Kaan of Loropéni   95

Since the tasks in a self-rating scale were hierarchically organized from the simplest to the most complex, a subject was rated at the highest level at which he or she could perform all the listed language tasks. Plus levels (3+, 4+, etc.) were given to those who could perform at least two tasks at the next level higher than their full competence. This is the scoring method used in LAMP and reflects somewhat the ranking process in the FSI test and the SLOPE adaptation.

It is proper to ask how the validity of the can-do scale can be established. External validity can be assumed to the extent that the language tasks at each skill level conform to the general skill-level descriptions of the FSI test (see Lowe and Stansfield 1988 for discussions of the validity of these descriptions) and to the extent to which one can assume these skill-level descriptions are appropriate for rural, nonliterate West African communities.

Internal validity can be judged on the basis of whether subjects' responses fall into the expected pattern for this kind of evaluation. That is, do their responses change noticeably at what could be considered their threshold of proficiency? Are they consistently unable to perform tasks after a certain level is reached? An analysis of the results in chapter 7 will tell us if the scale created for this survey has this kind of validity.

6

The Language Attitude Survey

The samples

The villages sampled from each dialect community were marked for certain characteristics which would provide data for an analysis of the extent to which each village was isolated from contact with the three dialect communities as well as from the other ethnic groups living in the region. During survey visits, information was gathered about (1) the physical access to the village, (2) the national government presence there, (3) the nearest health clinics, (4) the nearest weekly markets, and (5) the ethnic composition of the village. I quantified these indicators[20] and developed a VILLAGE ISOLATION FACTOR which would allow for a comparison by a rough measure of the extent to which village residents were likely to come into contact with other ethnic groups in the region on a regular basis.

To arrive at this village isolation factor, each of the indicators listed above was assigned a simple number based on the following criteria:

1. *Access.* The possible means of access were by path, assigned a value of (1); former road which had obviously once been graded but had not been maintained in several years and was overgrown, rutted, and fairly difficult to travel. It is wider than a path, however, and usually more heavily traveled, though only by foot, bicycle, or motorbike (2); secondary road or plowed road which is in better repair than a former road, though not necessarily regularly maintained. Heavy local traffic,

---

[20]See De Vaus (1986) for a discussion of the importance of finding specific, concrete "indicators" in the process of investigating abstract concepts such as "village isolation".

including the occasional truck or car, but very little nonlocal use (3); and main road which is a graded and regularly maintained dirt road, with regular vehicle traffic of all kinds from outside the immediate region (4).
2. *Government presence.* Every village has at least a delegate who is responsible to the local prefecture. So, every village is assigned at least a value of (1) in this category. Other government establishments include a school, police, a prefecture, a comité révolutionnaire, etc. Each government establishment was given one point, so the more government presence in a village or town, the greater number of points given that category. The maximum number given here was (7).
3. *Nearest clinic.* If no health clinic existed in the town or village, it was given the value (1) for this category. Villages with health clinics were given (2). Villages without clinics were deemed more isolated, those with them, less isolated.
4. *Nearest market.* Scored in the same way as health clinics. Villages without local markets were more isolated than those with them.
5. *Ethnic composition.* Homogeneous (1) or mixed (2). Naturally, ethnically mixed villages would have more opportunities for interethnic contact than ethnically homogeneous ones.

Some of these indicators are nominal (market, clinic) rather than additive (government presence), yet even the nominal indicators manifest a significant change in degree of exposure to social influences from outside the village. This method of assigning value to indicators provides us with the table in (20). The results suggest that the Kpatogo villages are the most isolated, the Dogo villages the least isolated. By this measure, the Dogo and Khi villages provide almost twice as much opportunity for regular interethnic contact as the Kpatogo villages do.

(20) Village isolation scores

Village	Lg	Access	Govmt presence	Clinic	Market	Ethnic composition	Village total	Group average
Karanga	Kp	1	1	1	1	1	5	
Ouérin	Kp	1	1	1	1	1	5	
Kamilidaga	Kp	1	1	1	1	1	5	
Gbengué	Kp	2	1	1	1	1	6	
Diassara	Kp	2	2	2	1	1	8	5.8

The samples

Village	Lg	Access	Govmt presence	Clinic	Market	Ethnic composition	Village total	Group average
Béguélé	Dg	1	1	1	1	1	5	
Koro	Dg	2	2	1	2	2	9	
Nizélé	Dg	2	1	1	1	1	6	
Ouo	Dg	4	4	2	2	2	14	
Sidéradougou	Dg	4	7	2	2	2	17	10.2
Massadéhirikoro	Kh	3	1	1	1	1	7	
Mangodara	Kh	4	7	2	2	2	17	
Sirakoro	Kh	3	1	1	2	2	9	
Bandakelesso	Kh	3	1	1	1	1	7	10.0
Yérifoula	K	3	3	2	2	2	12	
Loropéni	K	4	4	2	2	2	14	
Obiré	K	2	2	1	1	1	7	
Soronkina	K	1	1	1	1	1	5	
Saramassi	K	1	1	1	1	2	6	
Sandi	K	3	2	2	2	2	11	
Kerié	K	1	1	1	1	1	5	8.6

While we cannot assume that these figures fully represent the dialect communities, they do give us a means of comparison between these specific villages. In the presentation of attitude survey results to follow we shall see if the attitudes expressed by some of the inhabitants of these villages reflect their varied opportunities for interethnic contact.

From the personal information gathered from each interviewee, it is possible to construct a profile of salient characteristics of the total sample taken from each dialect group. These characteristics involve profession, religious practice, housing, family structure, personal transportation, schooling, and travel experience.

Profession. All of the subjects in all four samples were involved in subsistence farming in some way, and for the overwhelming majority, this was their only profession. These rural farmers have the traditional knowledge and skills necessary to live off the land from year to year (a formidable task), but few other marketable abilities. Other occupations mentioned by a few were soldier, interpreter, blacksmith, indigenous medicine seller, mechanic, and health worker.

Religious practice. The Kaan and the Kpatogo were nearly all traditional animists, though two Kpatogo were Muslims. Religious practice is quite mixed in the Dogo community: forty-six percent (13) of the sample were traditional animists while the slight majority (54%, 15) were Muslim.

This is nearly a half-and-half split with some villages completely animist (Béguélé), some completely Muslim (Ouo), and some mixed (Koro, Nizélé, Sidéradougou). All in the Khi sample were Muslim.

On the whole, we can see that for three of the communities, their religious practice is stable and unanimous. The Dogo community, however, seems to be either slowly becoming Muslim or informally separated into two religious subgroups. In my survey visits to mixed Dogo villages, I sensed no animosity between Muslims and traditional animists. The interview groups included both religions, and there seemed to be a general cooperation and acceptance. My observations, however, were limited to brief four- to five-hour visits and cannot be taken as determining the interactional norm.

Housing. Almost all of the Kaan, Kpatogo, and Khi sampled lived in mud-brick houses with straw or mud roofs. Only four subjects out of these three groups had tin roofs, and only one of these had a house made of cement block rather than mud brick. In the Dogo sample, four people lived in tin-roofed houses, and two others had cement-block houses with tin roofs. Inasmuch as housing is a sign of personal or family wealth, the Dogo sample showed a slightly higher proportion of such wealth than the other three groups.

Family structure. The Kaan and the Khi samples showed the highest rates of polygamy (fifty percent or more), while the Dogo and Kpatogo were approximately two-thirds monogamous. The Kaan women were the most procreative, giving birth to an average of 4.6 children each, and the Kpatogo were the least procreative averaging 2.6 each. The Dogo and Khi women averaged at about 3.8 children each.

The four traditional clan names are not evenly distributed among the Kaan and Kpatogo samples (if, indeed, they are in these populations at large). For both groups, sixty-six percent were of the Farma clan, and seventeen percent were of the Swa clan. The other two traditional clans, Kama and Thama, were not represented in the Kpatogo sample, while there were four Kpatogo who had taken on the Jula clan name of Wattara. Among the Kaan, however, five were Kama and one was a Thama. This imbalance may reflect the distribution of clans in the population, or it may result from the villages I chose to survey, or even the families which agreed to be interviewed in each village.

The Dogo and the Khi have switched entirely to the Jula clan names Wattara and Coulibaly, with the overwhelming majority (greater than ninety percent) taking the name Wattara.

Personal transportation. Nearly all the men in each sample (75–90%) had at least a bicycle for personal transportation, and surprisingly, more than half of the Khi men also owned motorbikes, compared with twenty percent or less among the other three groups. Women did not have personal transport of their own.

Education. Eighty to ninety percent of the Kaan, Kpatogo, and Dogo samples had never had any government-sponsored formal education. Ten to fifteen percent had done some formal French-language schooling, mostly primary school, and the rest had had some training either in the army or from rural FJA schools taught in Jula. None of the Khi reported having government-sponsored education.

Travel experience. Travel to Côte d'Ivoire was highest among the Kaan (81%) and lowest among the Kpatogo (41%), though among the Kaan and the Khi, the men travelled locally much more than the women did. In contrast, only one person from the Kaan and no one from the Khi had visited Kpatogo villages, and only one Khi man had ever been to a Kaan village.

Overall, the Kpatogo villages were the least visited, and the Dogo villages the most frequently visited. This coordinates well with the village isolation factors calculated in example (20). Kpatogo villages were rated most isolated and reported as least visited, while Dogo villages were rated least isolated and reported as most visited. The two factors, obtained independently through different research measures, substantiate one another.

The evaluation procedures

The large majority of questions on this survey were answered by simple yes, no,[21] or I don't know.[22] These verbal responses were recorded on the questionnaire as +, −, or 0, with additional notes and annotations when explanations or extra information were offered. These were recorded in a computerized database with an additional notation of + − or − + for "yes, but..." or "no, but..." responses that were often accompanied by brief explanations.

Careful attention was given during the survey to understanding the positive or negative intent of an interviewee's response. Yes or no responses

---

[21][íyó] and [ɔ́ʔɔ̃́], respectively, in Kaansa, [ɔ̃hɔ́] and [ɔ́ʔɔ̃́] in Jula. In Dogose and Khisa, [ìiyà?] sometimes was used for no.

[22]Kaansa: [mì tò wĩ?] or [mì tò síra wĩ?].

could not always be taken at face value due to culture-based pragmatic norms in answering this type of question. For example, in English, the natural counterfactual response to the question, "Isn't he coming?" is "Yes" [He is coming]. In other cultures, however, such a counterfactual yes may be interpreted as an affirmation of the negative suggestive intent of the questioner, e.g., "Yes" [He is not coming]. Being aware of this difference was especially important for question D2-2-SS [Does this man speak like he does not want to be a VIP?], which I often followed up with another brief question to verify that I correctly understood the intent.

In very few interviews, when subjects seemed tired or bothered by a question to which the answer was obvious to them and to me, I would skip the question and use the obvious response in compiling the results.

Scoring responses

For most questions, the responses were scored with the value 1 for yes, the value 0 for no, and the value .5 for I don't know. The reasoning behind this is that for most questions, the response of yes indicated a positive attitude with regard to the particular attitude dimension or subdimension, the response no indicated a negative attitude, and I don't know meant an uncommitted opinion or lack of knowledge about the question, in short, what I have termed a neutral attitude.

With this method of scoring, the average score of a sample indicates the strength and direction of the shared attitudes in the group. A group average approaching 1.00 indicates that a positive attitude is widely held in the group; a group average approaching 0.00 indicates a negative attitude. A group average approaching .50 indicates that either there is no consensus in the group with individual scores all across the spectrum, or that there are general neutral feelings, that is, the majority did not have an opinion or did not feel strongly enough to provide a definite yes or no. A quick glance at the distribution of the scores in a sample reveals which of these phenomena is the case.

Though the majority of questions were scored in this way, some questions, because of their content or the way they were worded, needed special attention and scoring.

Positive-negative questions. In "Built-in controls" in chapter 5, I showed how some questions were formulated both positively and negatively. Special care had to be taken in scoring responses to these. For negative counterparts to the positive questions, the method for assigning value to individual responses was reversed. For example, question S1-2 under the subdimension of Shared Traditions/Ethnic Identity asked, "Are the traditions of people like him different from yours?". A response of yes indicated a certain separation or distance felt by the interviewee. This response was scored as 0 because it represents a negative attitude with regard to shared identity. Conversely, a response of no was scored as 1 because it represents a positive attitude with regard to shared identity.

In the presentation of scores to follow, questions which were worded negatively are marked with an asterisk in the tables of results.

General-specific questions. Questions which were related to each other within a subdimension in a general/specific relationship could not always be scored in the normal way. Care had to be taken to determine if responses really indicated positive or negative attitudes. In some cases, because of the nature of the question, a response of no did not automatically indicate a negative attitude, while a response of yes did show a positive attitude. In such cases, no was scored as .5 while yes still received a value of 1. Don't know was also scored as .5 in these cases. The following examples will clarify this.

In the attitude dimension of Social Status, under the subdimension of Personal Importance, question D3-2-SS asked, "Does he speak like a village chief?". A response of yes to this questions clearly indicates personal importance and, thus, high status in the village. However, a response of no does not automatically indicate lack of importance or low status. So, no receives a neutral value of .5 while yes receives a positive value of 1.

Another example, phrased negatively, may be found in the attitude dimension of Ethnic Identity, under the subdimension of Shared Religion. Question LJ1-1-EI asked, "Are there more Muslims among them than there are here?". While an answer of yes indicated an important perceived difference between the respondent's group and the one being evaluated (and is thus scored 0), an answer of no did not mean that there were fewer Muslims in the evaluated group. There may have been fewer or there may have been the same number, but such information was not collected at this point. Therefore, the value assigned to the response no was the neutral value .5.

Computing attitude dimension scores

A typical table of raw scored responses in one attitude dimension is found in (21). The table presents each question of this dimension twice, once for each text (elder or younger speaker). For example, the first question, B-1, appears twice, once with responses from those who heard the

Kpatogo youth speaking and once with responses from those who heard the Kpatogo elder speaking. The same presentation is followed for each question; the text speaker, elder or younger, is marked above the number of each question. Reading from left to right, the subdimension groupings of questions are marked by two-letter codes: UN (understanding), SA (speaking ability), and FM (familiarity). This tells us that the subdimension Understanding comprises the questions B-1, D1-1, and D3-3, and so on for the other subdimensions. As mentioned above, the asterisk following D3-3 indicates that the question was worded negatively. The L and J questions to the far right of the table are Lobiri and Jula.

It is apparent immediately that some questions only have a few responses (D2-3 has five), and that others only have responses to either an elder or a younger text, but not to both. This is the result of the rotation system described in "Questionnaire design" in chapter 5. In one sense this was planned into the survey instrument, and the process of compiling scores discussed below compensates for it to a certain extent. In another sense, however, this somewhat awkward distribution of responses could have been made more symmetrical by better planning and execution of the rotation system. Since this was the first attempt at such a system, these irregularities will appear as we examine the results. It will be important to take into account these irregularities and design features when compiling and interpreting the attitude dimension scores, and to guard against using statistical tests that do not fit the nature of the data.

The evaluation procedures 105

(21) **Language Awareness judgments of Kpatogoso texts**

						UN						SA								FM			
						KPY	KPE	KPY	KPE	KPY	KPE	KPY	KPE	KPY	KPE	KPY	KPE	KPY	KPE	KPY	KPE	L	J
Record	A	S	MT	Village	QR	B-1	B-1	D1-1	D1-1	D3-3	D3-3*	B-4	B-4	D1-3	D1-3	D2-3*	D2-3*	D3-1	D3-1	S2-3	S2-3	LJ2-3	LJ2-3
1	A	F	Dogose	Koro	1A	1	0					1	1							1			
2	A	F		Nizélé	1A	0	0					1	0							1			
3	A	F		Sidéradougou	1A	0	0					0.5	1							0.5			
4	A	M		Béguélé	1A	1	0					1	1							1			
5	A	M		Nizélé	1A	1	1					0	1							0.5			
6	A	M		Ouo	1A	0	0					0.5	1							1			
7	A	M		Ouo	1A	0	0					1	1							1			
8	E	M		Koro	1A	1	0					1	0							0.5			
9	Y	M		Béguélé	1A	1	0.5					1	1							1			
10	Y	M		Sidéradougou	1A	0	0					0.5	0.5							1			
11	A	M		Ouo	3A	1						1	1	1									
12	A	M		Sidéradougou	3A	1						1	1	0									
13	Y	M		Béguélé	3A	0						0.5	1	0									
14	Y	M		Koro	3A	1						1	1	1									
15	Y	M		Nizélé	3A	1						1	1	1									
16	A	F		Koro	2B	1					1	1							1				
17	A	F		Nizélé	2B	1					1	1							1				
18	A	F		Béguélé	2B	1					0	1							1				
19	E	F		Béguélé	2B	1					1	1							1				
20	A	M		Koro	2B	1					1	1							1				
21	E	M		Nizélé	2B	1					1	0							1				
22	Y	M		Sidéradougou	2B	1					1	1							1				
23	Y	M		Ouo	2B	1					1	1							1				
24	A	F		Béguélé	4B	1					0	1							1				
25	A	F		Nizélé	4B	0					0	0							1				
26	A	F		Sidéradougou	4B	1					1	1							1				
27	A	M		Ouo	4B	0					0	1							1				
28	A	M		Koro	4B	1					1	1							1				

Questions and subdimensions. Attitude subdimensions, such as Understanding or Speaking Ability are simply groupings of similar questions that are intended to elicit responses which help to define the interviewee's attitude. Referring again to (21), we see that the subjects' attitudes toward their ability to understand the texts they heard were measured by questions B-1, D1-1, and D3-3, spelled out in (22).

(22) Language Awareness attitude: Understanding

B-1: Did you understand everything?
D1-1: Is it easy to understand?
D3-3: Is it difficult to understand people like him?

While three questions were asked, we see that questions D1-1 and D3-3 are positive/negative formulations of the same question, and that B-1 is also very similar. In compiling the scores for this subdimension, therefore, the responses to D1-1 and D3-3 were combined as responses to the same question, yielding question score or one Q score. Then, the responses to B-1 were combined into a Q score for the subdimension and averaged together for each subject with his or her Q score for D1-1 and D3-3. This scoring process is displayed in (23).

Two things need to be noted here. One is that those subjects with questionnaire 3A did not have an opportunity to respond to questions D1-1 or D3-3; their subdimension score is, therefore, the same as their response to question B-1. Given the similarity of the questions in a subdimension and their interamplificatory nature, it is unlikely that this kind of irregularity would skew the final results.

The second thing to notice is that those with questionnaire 1A and 3A responded to the younger text speaker and those with questionnaire 2B and 4B responded to the elder text speaker. In the second section of chapter 5 it was pointed out that a key assumption of this design is that the age of the text speaker will not make any consistent difference in the way subjects respond to questions. Yet, here there seems to be a consistent difference in the responses to each text speaker. In this particular case it seems to be the result of the quality of the recording rather than the age of the text speaker. However, a full discussion of this issue is presented later in the final section of this chapter.

(23) Sample score: Language Awareness: Understanding

Record	A	S	MT	Village	QR	UN KPY B-1	KPE B-1	Q-score	KPY D1-1	KPE D1-1	KPY D3-3*	KPE D3-3*	Q-score	Subd score
1	A	F	Dogose	Koro	1A	1.00		1.00	0.00				0.00	0.50
2	A	F		Nizélé	1A	0.00		0.00	0.00				0.00	0.00
3	A	F		Sidéradougou	1A	0.00		0.00	0.00				0.00	0.00
4	A	M		Béguélé	1A	1.00		1.00	0.00				0.00	0.50
5	A	M		Nizélé	1A	1.00		1.00	1.00				1.00	1.00
6	A	M		Ouo	1A	0.00		0.00	0.00				0.00	0.00
7	A	M		Ouo	1A	0.00		0.00	0.00				0.00	0.00
8	E	M		Koro	1A	1.00		1.00	0.00				0.00	0.50
9	Y	M		Béguélé	1A	1.00		1.00	0.50				0.50	0.75
10	Y	M		Sidéradougou	1A	0.00		0.00	0.00				0.00	0.00
11	A	M		Ouo	3A	1.00		1.00						1.00
12	A	M		Sidéradougou	3A	1.00		1.00						1.00
13	Y	M		Béguélé	3A	0.00		0.00						0.00
14	Y	M		Koro	3A	1.00		1.00						1.00
15	Y	M		Nizélé	3A	1.00		1.00						1.00
16	A	F		Koro	2B		1.00	1.00			1.00		1.00	1.00
17	A	F		Nizélé	2B		1.00	1.00			1.00		1.00	1.00
18	A	F		Béguélé	2B		1.00	1.00			0.00		0.00	0.50
19	E	F		Béguélé	2B		1.00	1.00			1.00		1.00	1.00
20	A	M		Koro	2B		1.00	1.00			1.00		1.00	1.00
21	E	M		Nizélé	2B		1.00	1.00			1.00		1.00	1.00
22	A	M		Sidéradougou	2B		1.00	1.00			1.00		1.00	1.00
23	Y	M		Ouo	2B		1.00	1.00			1.00		1.00	1.00
24	A	F		Béguélé	4B		1.00	1.00			0.00		0.00	0.50
25	A	F		Nizélé	4B		0.00	0.00			0.00		0.00	0.00
26	A	F		Sidéradougou	4B		1.00	1.00			1.00		1.00	1.00
27	A	M		Ouo	4B		0.00	0.00			0.00		0.00	0.00
28	A	M		Koro	4B		1.00	1.00			1.00		1.00	1.00
Totals						9.00	11.00	20.00	1.50		9.00		10.50	17.25
Count						15	13	28	10		13		23	28
Average						0.60	0.85	0.71	0.15		0.69		0.46	0.62

In the subdimension explained above, two of the questions were really mirror images of each other. This is not the case in all subdimensions of this questionnaire; in other subdimensions the questions are related in a general/specific relationship such as those in the Family Relations subdimension of the Ethnic Identity set. These questions are given in (24).

(24) Ethnic Identity attitude: Family Relations

S4-1: Are their families similar to your families?
S1-1: Do people like him marry girls from here?
D2-4: Are there people in your family who talk like that?

Here, question S4-1 is the general question and S1-1 and D2-4 are specific questions. In this case, if a subject believes families of two groups are similar, it may be the result of some intermarriage, and thus, it is likely that some people in the subject's extended family speak the language variety in question. If subjects answer positively to the first question, they would likely answer positively to the second and third questions as well. Likewise, positive responses to the second or third question indicate real interfamily links which would create positive attitudes toward shared family traits.

As nice as this sounds, it is really just supposition at this point in my knowledge of traditional family relations. It is entirely likely that a person will recognize the practice of intermarriage between two groups, or not have any objections to the prospect, but not know anyone in his or her extended family from another dialect group. Or, a subject may have a general feeling that the families of the two groups are similar (in language?, in authority structure?, in lineage?; a deliberately vague question), but not know of any personal links through intermarriage.

So rather than claim that a positive answer to one question is the same as a positive answer to the others (as is the case in the paired questions worded positively and negatively), let us simply count each question as contributing to defining the group attitude toward shared ethnic identity within the family. Compiling scores in subdimensions such as this one follows the same principle as was demonstrated in (23).

Dimension scores. We arrive at a composite score for an attitude dimension by averaging the component subdimension scores for each subject. This can be seen in the scores from the Language Awareness attitude dimension in (25).

The evaluation procedures 109

(25) **Sample attitude dimension score: Language Awareness**

Record	A	S	MT	Village	QR	B-1 Q-score	D1-1 D3-3 Q-score	UN Subd score	B-4 Q-score	D1-3 D2-3 D3-1 Q-score	SA Subd score	E text	Y text	LA D score
1	A	F	Dogose	Koro	1A	1.00	0.00	0.50	1.00	1.00	1.00		0.75	0.75
2	A	F		Nizélé	1A	0.00	0.00	0.00	1.00	0.00	0.50		0.25	0.25
3	A	F		Sidéradougou	1A	0.00	0.00	0.00	0.50	1.00	0.75		0.38	0.38
4	A	M		Béguélé	1A	1.00	0.00	0.50	1.00	1.00	1.00		0.75	0.75
5	A	M		Nizélé	1A	1.00	1.00	1.00	0.00	1.00	0.50		0.75	0.75
6	A	M		Ouo	1A	0.00	0.00	0.00	0.50	1.00	0.75		0.38	0.38
7	A	M		Ouo	1A	0.00	0.00	0.00	1.00	1.00	1.00		0.50	0.50
8	E	M		Koro	1A	1.00	0.00	0.50	1.00	0.00	0.50		0.50	0.50
9	Y	M		Béguélé	1A	1.00	0.50	0.75	1.00	1.00	1.00		0.88	0.88
10	Y	M		Sidéradougou	1A	0.00	0.00	0.00	0.50	0.50	0.50		0.25	0.25
11	A	M		Ouo	3A	1.00		1.00	1.00	1.00	1.00		1.00	1.00
12	A	M		Sidéradougou	3A	1.00		1.00	1.00	0.00	0.50		0.67	0.75
13	Y	M		Béguélé	3A	0.00		0.00	0.50	0.00	0.25		0.17	0.13
14	Y	M		Koro	3A	1.00		1.00	1.00	1.00	1.00		1.00	1.00
15	Y	M		Nizélé	3A	1.00		1.00	1.00	1.00	1.00		1.00	1.00
16	A	F		Koro	2B	1.00	1.00	1.00	1.00	1.00	1.00	1.00		1.00
17	A	F		Nizélé	2B	1.00	1.00	1.00	1.00	1.00	1.00	1.00		1.00
18	A	F		Béguélé	2B	1.00	0.00	0.50	1.00	1.00	1.00	0.75		0.75
19	E	F		Béguélé	2B	1.00	1.00	1.00	1.00	1.00	1.00	1.00		1.00
20	A	M		Koro	2B	1.00	1.00	1.00	1.00	1.00	1.00	1.00		1.00
21	E	M		Nizélé	2B	1.00	1.00	1.00	0.00	1.00	0.50	0.75		0.75
22	Y	M		Sidéradougou	2B	1.00	1.00	1.00	1.00	1.00	1.00	1.00		1.00
23	Y	M		Ouo	2B	1.00	1.00	1.00	1.00	1.00	1.00	1.00		1.00
24	A	F		Béguélé	4B	1.00	0.00	0.50	1.00	1.00	1.00	0.75		0.75
25	A	F		Nizélé	4B	0.00	0.00	0.00	0.00	1.00	0.50	0.25		0.25
26	A	F		Sidéradougou	4B	1.00	1.00	1.00	1.00	1.00	1.00	1.00		1.00
27	A	M		Ouo	4B	0.00	0.00	0.00	1.00	1.00	1.00	0.50		0.50
28	A	M		Koro	4B	1.00	1.00	1.00	1.00	1.00	1.00	1.00		1.00
Totals						20.00	10.50	17.25	23.00	23.50	23.25	11.00	9.21	20.25
Count						28	23	28	28	28	28	13	15	28
Average						0.71	0.46	0.62	0.82	0.84	0.83	0.85	0.61	0.72

The D scores for all of the attitude dimensions will fall between 1.00 and 0.00. We may interpret these scores by considering the midpoint (.50) and scores around it (.45–.55) as a neutral score, meaning no well-defined shared attitude or opinion in the sample. Scores from .56–.70 indicate a slightly positive attitude in the sample, .71–.85 indicate a moderately positive attitude, and .86–1.00 indicate a strongly positive attitude shared in the sample. Conversely, scores from .44–.30 show a slightly negative trend in attitudes, .29–.15 a moderately negative attitude, and .14–0.00 a strongly negative attitude shared in the sample.

Since the rotation of questions to texts is not ideally symmetrical in this survey, comparison of D scores must be done with care so that the reader understands the similarities in the process of generating the D scores within each set of comparisons that we will analyze. Generally, the four ratings of one language variety may be confidently compared to each other, since the patterned relationships of the questions to texts for each language variety were the same. So, for example, we may compare the D scores of Ethnic Identity evaluations of the Kaansa texts from each of the four samples.

The small samples in this research and the often uneven distribution of nonlinguistic variables within each sample make it unreasonable to attempt to analyze many types of within-group variation. Yet, some samples do offer enough data to compare evaluations made by the males and females in the sample. Other samples make it possible to compare the responses of adults with those of elders. In addition, I tested the assumptions of this survey design—namely, the equality of texts and equality of questions—in every case where there is enough data to do so. Most of the analysis in the rest of this chapter, however, will focus on variation between the samples, because the goal of this part of the research was to investigate shared attitudes in each dialect community towards the language varieties around them.

The results

Statistical tests and the nature of the data

The responses which make up the data for this study can be seen both as categorical and as ranks. The answers of "yes", "I don't know", and "no" are certainly categories, yet due to the types of questions asked they also reflect an attitude which can be ranked along the three-point scale as positive, neutral, or negative. While the group responses to individual

The results

questions are largely categorical, the subjects' cumulative responses which make up the dimension scores, and which can fall along several different points between 0.00 and 1.00, take on a ranking nature in relation to each other. Thus, I sought to capture this trait of the scores by using several nonparametric ranking procedures to test for significant differences among responses, as well as a categorical test (chisquare) when appropriate.

Though some statisticians relegate nonparametric tests to the "quick and dirty" category, others have found them to be very powerful when the assumption of normality cannot be held. Sawilowsky (1990:94), in a detailed discussion of the power and appropriateness of nonparametric tests, asserted that nonparametrics provide "valid analyses of educational and psychological variables that are measured as rank data obtained from judges or observers".

The nonparametric tests used here were the following:

(1) On the D scores: Kruskal-Wallis test for main effect in multiple groups (see Hays 1988:829–832 for a full description) and a rank transform of the ANOVA (see Conover and Iman 1981 for a detailed presentation of this technique). To pinpoint the source of significant results of these tests, I used a Tukey's HSD statistic on the data from the rank transform one-way ANOVA. This also is suggested by Conover and Iman (1981:128). In addition, for some D scores I used a chisquare on categories of ranges of responses in order to show significant differences that appeared only when the responses of some groups were collapsed together, for example when the responses of the Kaan and the Kpatogo as a single group were considered in opposition to those of the Dogo and Khi as a single group.

(2) On the scores of the individual difference variables of age and sex: the Mann-Whitney U test for two independent groups, described in detail in Shavelson (1981:430–439).

(3) To test the assumptions of the survey design I used a Mann-Whitney U on most tests of responses to the different elicitation texts (elder versus youth text speakers). When testing responses to the two Kaansa texts, I used a Wilcoxon t test for dependent samples. This was necessary because both text sequences, A and B, contained both Kaansa texts, and thus, each subject judged both of these texts while judging only one out of two texts for the other dialects.

(4) To test the assumption that the questionnaire rotation sequence did not add significant variation to the responses I used the Kruskal-Wallis and ranked ANOVA on the subjects' D scores grouped by questionnaire number.

In all of the tests, the null hypothesis was rejected at p < .05.

Attitudes toward ethnic identity

Attitudes toward shared ethnic identity (EI) were measured with questions pertaining to sharing a language (SL), connections in family relationships (FR), shared traditions (ST), and the maintenance of traditional culture (CM). On the charts that follow, the scores for these subdimensions are represented by their repective two-letter abbreviations on the abscissa; the ordinate axis contains the range of scores for each subdimension as well as for the combined dimension score (labeled "D score").

Dialect texts.

Kaansa texts. In (26) we see a table of the mean scores of the four groups' ethnic identity ratings of the Kaansa texts and a chart of the mean subdimension scores. As is expected, the Kaan rated the Kaansa texts significantly higher than the other three groups.[23] Conversely, the Kpatogo, Dogo, and Khi do not differ significantly in their ratings; their attitude dimension (D) scores range from neutral to slightly positive.

There is an important difference between the response of the adult and the elder Khi subjects. While the adults were neutral (.56) about shared ethnic identity with the Kaansa speakers, the elders showed a moderate to strong (.83) sense of shared ethnicity with the Kaan.[24]

Kpatogoso texts. The data in (27) shows that, as expected, the Kpatogo expressed the most positive attitudes of shared ethnic identity towards the Kpatogoso texts than did the other three groups. However, these results also show that, while the Dogo and Khi hold rather neutral attitudes towards shared identity with the Kpatogo, the Kaan differ significantly from them and from the Kpatogo as well.[25] The Kaan feel moderately positive about shared ethnic identity with the Kpatogo.

We also see again that the elder Khi showed a more positive attitude about shared identity with the Kpatogo than the younger, adult Khi subjects did, who in fact where slightly negative in their evaluation.[26]

---

[23]Analysis of variance: F obs = 35.22, df = 3, 105, p < .05.

[24]Mann-Whitney test: ASCORE: n = 11, median = 0.5800; ESCORE: n = 8, median = 0.8150; W = 69.0, p < .05

[25]Analysis of variance: F obs = 17.04, df = 3, 104, p < .05. Post-hoc analysis performed with Tukey's HSD.

[26]Mann-Whitney test: ASCORE: n = 11, median = 0.3300; ESCORE: n = 8, median = 0.7500; W = 82.0, p < .05.

The results

(26) Ethnic Identity judgments of Kaansa texts

Sample	n	Subdimensions														Age				Sex			
		SL	n	FR	n	ST	n	CM	n	D score	E texts	n	Y texts	n	A score	n	E score	n	M score	n	F score	n
Kaan	35	1.00	35	0.99	34	0.96	27	0.94	24	0.98	0.98	18	0.99	17	0.98	22	0.94	9	1.00	20	0.95	15
Kpatogo	25	0.51	25	0.40	25	0.25	25	1.00	20	0.51	0.51	15	0.46	10	0.49	12	0.61	9	—	—	—	—
Dogo	28	0.44	28	0.68	28	0.69	28	0.98	20	0.67	0.63	15	0.63	13	—	—	—	—	0.68	17	0.64	11
Khi	21	0.69	21	0.35	21	0.56	21	0.89	14	0.69	0.73	11	0.62	10	0.56	11	0.83	8	0.72	13	0.63	8

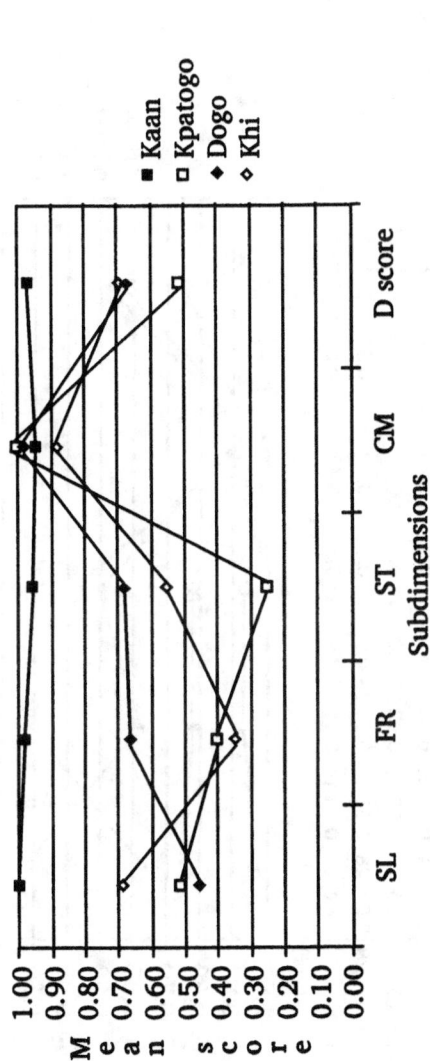

(27) **Ethnic Identity judgments of Kpatogoso texts**

Sample	n	Subdimensions												Age				Sex			
		SL	n	FR	n	ST	n	CM	n	D score	E texts	n	Y texts	n	A score	n	E score	n	M score	n	F score	n
Kaan	34	0.75	34	0.78	20	0.78	20	0.94	18	0.77	0.73	16	0.82	18	0.77	22	0.75	9	0.72	20	0.80	15
Kpatogo	25	0.96	25	0.93	15	0.93	20	1.00	15	0.95	0.98	10	0.93	15	1.00	12	0.87	9	—		—	
Dogo	28	0.29	28	0.61	18	0.50	23	0.93	15	0.53	0.52	13	0.50	15	—		—		0.59	17	0.44	11
Khi	21	0.62	21	0.29	14	0.44	17	0.95	11	0.56	0.47	10	0.64	11	0.41	11	0.77	8	0.59	13	0.50	8

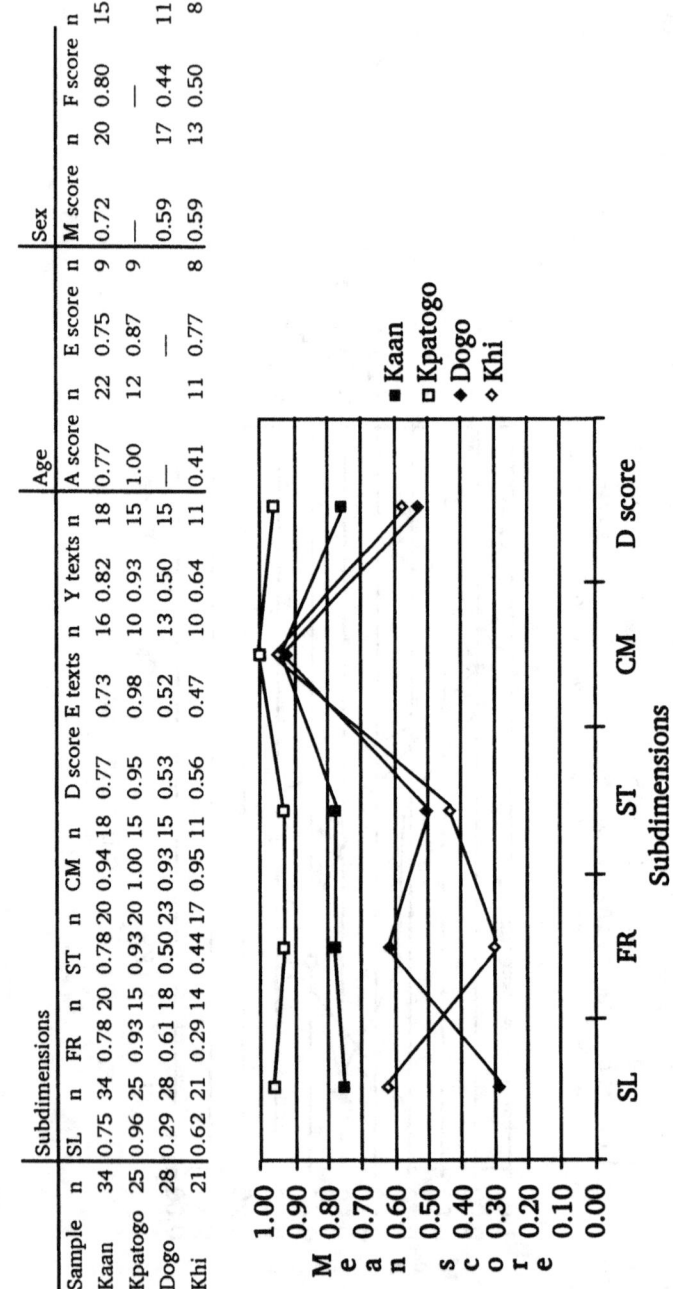

The results

(28) Ethnic Identity judgments of Dogose texts

Sample	n	Subdimensions													Age				Sex			
		SL	n	FR	n	ST	n	CM	n	D score	n	E texts	n	Y texts	n	A score	n	E score	n	M score	n	F score	n
Kaan	35	0.67	35	0.72	18	0.64	20	0.89	19	0.68		0.77	18	0.57	17	0.70	22	0.74	9	0.68	20	0.68	15
Kpatogo	25	0.34	25	0.33	15	0.20	20	0.95	10	0.40		0.42	15	0.37	10	1.00	12	0.51	9	—		—	
Dogo	28	1.00	28	1.00	15	0.90	23	1.00	13	0.97		0.99	15	0.95	13	—				1.00		0.94	17
Khi	21	0.98	21	0.80	10	0.68	17	0.82	11	0.83		0.78	11	0.87	10	0.76	11	0.96	8	0.82	13	0.85	8

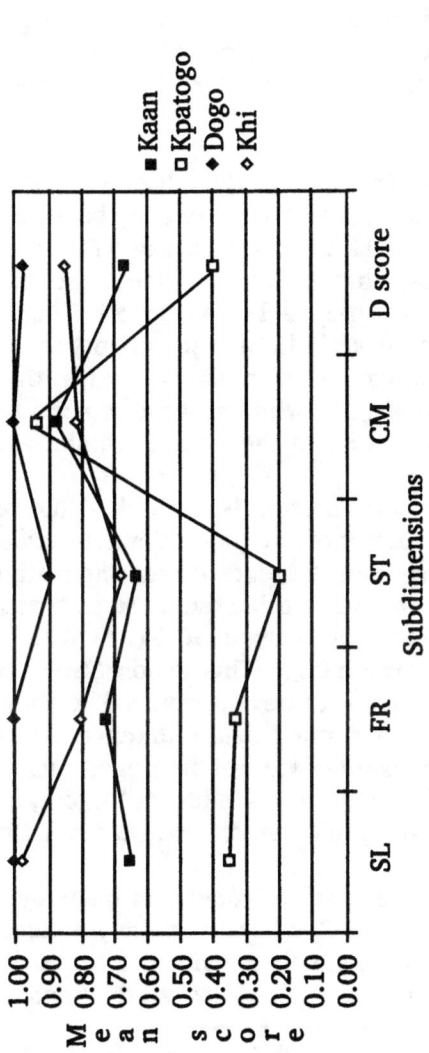

Dogose texts. The scores for the Dogose texts are given in (28). The Dogo naturally rate the Dogose speakers highest for this measure, but there are other significant results here as well. The Kpatogo rated the Dogose texts much lower than anyone else, in the slightly negative range, but the Kaan judged them significantly higher (as slightly positive) than the Kpatogo and not significantly different from how the Khi rated these texts (moderately positive).[27] It is also interesting to note that the difference between the scores of the Khi and the Dogo was not significant in testing.

Once more we see an age-group split among the Khi: the elders judged the Dogose texts significantly more positively (.96) than did the adults (.76).[28]

Khisa texts. The data in (29) displays the EI judgments of the Khisa texts. It is striking that, except for a flip between the Khi and the Dogo, the judgments for the Khisa texts are nearly identical with those of the Dogose texts. It appears that the Kaan and the Kpatogo feel about the Khisa speakers the same way they feel about Dogose. The Dogo and the Khi again did not differ significantly in their judgments of these texts, a fact which reveals a strong sense of common ethnic identity between these two communities. Indeed, one wonders if the subjects from each group perceived any difference at all in the dialect samples and if they identified them correctly.

To answer this question let us look at the responses to question B-2, which at the outset of every questionnaire asked the subjects to identify the ethnic origin of the text speaker. Interestingly, the large majority of Kaan and Kpatogo identified the Khisa texts as Dogose. Specifically, 83% (29) of the Kaan subjects and 96% (24) of the Kpatogo subjects said the Khisa speaker was a Dogo. This demonstrates a real unfamiliarity with the Khisa dialect among these two groups. There is also evidence that, perceptually, there is not much real difference between Dogose and Khisa, at least from the point of view of the Dogo. A full 64% (18) of the Dogo subjects also identified the Khisa text as Dogose, in this case claiming essentially that it was their own dialect. Only five Dogo subjects identified the text correctly.

Yet, when we consider comments made by subjects as they were answering question B-2, we see that many noticed a difference between the dialects, but were unable to name the varieties which were unfamiliar to them. For example, while almost all the Kpatogo identified the Khisa text

---

[27] Analysis of variance: F obs = 25.17, df = 3, 105, $p < .05$. Post-hoc analysis performed with Tukey's HSD.

[28] Mann-Whitney test: ASCORE: n = 11, median = 0.6700; ESCORE: n = 8, median = 1.0000; W = 83.5, $p < .05$.

as Dogose, several subjects commented at this question that the Dogose they were hearing was not the same as the Dogose that they were familiar with nearby. They said, "It's Dogose, but not the same as the Dogose near here," or, "It's Dogose, but not the same as the preceding text" (which was real Dogose). So they clearly noticed the difference but were not familiar with the name of the dialect.

The same seems to be true of the Dogo subjects. They commented that this Khisa text sounded like Dogose but was different from what they spoke. One man identified the text as Kpatogoso, then said, "It's not the same as the other text [which was Dogose]. It's like Dogose, like Kaansa, like Kpatogoso." Another subject, a young man, said, "It's Dogose, but he doesn't speak good Dogose; it's like he doesn't understand." Another said, "One would say it's Dogose, but it's different from my language."

Kpatogoso is the other dialect with which many were unfamiliar (not surprisingly since we saw earlier that the Kpatogo and the Khi were the most isolated and the least visited of the four groups). Even among the Kaan sample, the people who should have the most links with the Kpatogo because of their traditional, historical ties and similarity of dialect, only nine subjects identified the Kpatogoso text correctly. An equal number said it was Dogose, and even more (43%) identified it as their own dialect, Kaansa. The Dogo shared the same perception as the Kaan: fifteen of them (54%) identified the Kpatogoso texts as Kaansa and seven as Kpatogoso. One adult female Dogose commented about the Kpatogoso text, "It's like Kaansa; it's like Dogose." The Khi seemed to be completely unfamiliar with the Kpatogo: none identified these texts correctly, and interestingly, about the same proportion as the others thought they were Kaansa speakers (48%, 10).

From these responses and comments we see again that the subjects perceived a difference in the unfamiliar dialects but were not able to identify them correctly probably due to lack of frequent contact.

A shared language? The first question which contributed to this attitude dimension score was question D1-2, "Are his language and your language the same?"; it produced the 'SL' subdimension scores. Let us examine closely the responses to this question for each set of texts in the light of what was just discussed above.

(29) **Ethnic Identity judgments of Khisa texts**

Sample	n	Subdimensions												Age				Sex			
		SL	n	FR	n	ST	n	CM	n	D score	E texts	n	Y texts	n	A score	n	E score	n	M score	n	F score	n
Kaan	35	0.70	35	0.67	16	0.53	18	0.93	21	0.72	0.63	17	0.79	18	0.80	22	0.67	9	0.65	20	0.81	15
Kpatogo	25	0.29	24	0.20	10	0.15	15	1.00	15	0.44	0.24	10	0.55	15	0.50	12	0.44	9	—	—	—	—
Dogo	28	0.89	28	0.90	13	0.75	18	1.00	15	0.89	0.87	13	0.91	15	—	—	—	—	0.88	17	0.90	11
Khi	21	1.00	21	0.95	10	0.93	14	1.00	11	0.98	0.95	10	1.00	11	0.95	11	1.00	8	0.97	13	0.98	8

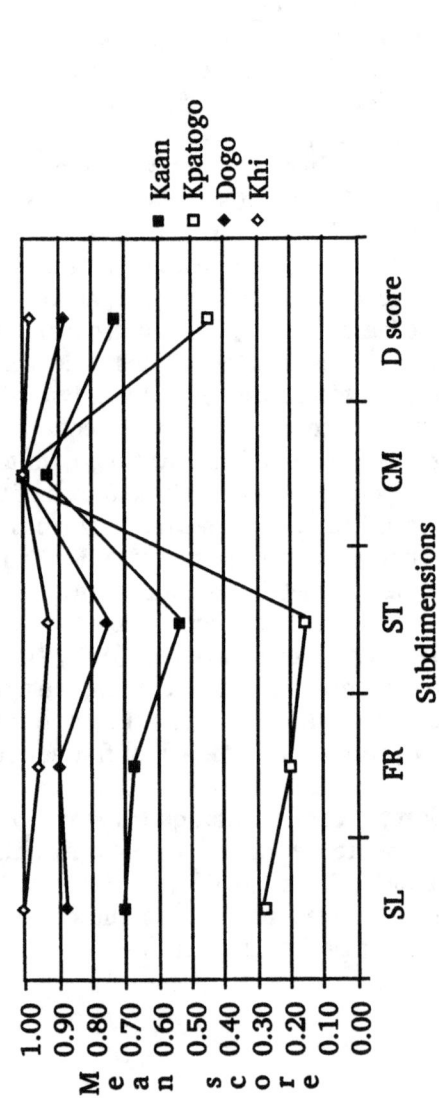

Kaansa texts. Though the mean scores of the Kpatogo, Dogo, and Khi show the Khi moderately positive and the others neutral, a chisquare run on the raw responses to this question shows that we cannot reject the null hypothesis that there is no significant difference in these scores.[29] The raw responses to this question tells us that the Kpatogo were evenly split as to whether they share the same language with the Kaan, that a slight majority of Dogo felt they did not share the same language, and that a slight majority of Khi considered Kaansa to be the same language as their own. Thus, it appears that there is no clear consensus among Kpatogo, Dogo, and Khi subjects concerning this issue.

Kpatogoso texts. It appears that the Kaan and the Khi subjects hold similar attitudes toward the Kpatogo; both groups show a slight to moderately positive opinion. The raw responses of these two groups, when collapsed together, contrast significantly,[30] however, to those of the Dogo subjects, the majority of whom felt that Kpatogoso was not the same language as their own.

Dogose texts. For these texts, the strongly positive evaluation of the Khi is very interesting. They were almost unanimous in asserting that Dogose was the same language as theirs. The Kaan and the Kpatogo, on the other hand, were much less positive, even differing significantly from each other.[31] About two-thirds of the Kaan subjects claimed that Dogose was the same language as theirs, whereas a slight majority of the Kpatogo did not consider Dogose as the same language as their own.

Khisa texts. The results for the Khisa texts are very similar for those of the Dogose. While the Dogo are not quite as unanimous about Khisa as the Khi were about Dogose, they still seemed to feel strongly that Khisa is the same language as Dogose. The Kaan and Kpatogo again are significantly different from each other,[32] many of the former claiming similarity while many of the latter see dissimilarity.

The interviewees made some very interesting comments on this question of a shared language. Many of the Dogose who said Kaansa was the same language as theirs also added, "But it's a little different." One young male said, "Yes, it's the same language, but some don't understand it." An elder Khi male said Kaansa was the same language as his but, "It's a little different...it's

---

[29] X^2 obs = 2.351, df = 2, p < .05.
[30] X^2 obs = 16.023, df = 2, p < .05. Note: 1 cell with expected count less than 5.0.
[31] X^2 obs = 11.343, df = 2, p < .05. Note: 1 cell with expected count less than 5.0.
[32] X^2 obs = 11.274, df = 2, p < .05. Note: 2 cells with expected counts less than 5.0.

only the pronunciation." Two of the Khi who said Kaansa was not their language also commented, "But one can understand it."

Some Kaan subjects pointed out that there were a few differences in Kpatogoso even though it was the same language. One young Kaan man said that it was "more similar [to Kaansa] than Dogose". Concerning Dogose, an elder male said, "One understands, but there are differences. It's just the accent." Almost all of the Kpatogo who commented on this question answered that neither Kaansa, Dogose, nor Khisa were the same language as theirs, but that they often understand each other. About Khisa one adult male said, "It's not the same, but it goes together [with our language]." Another elder male said that the Kaansa text was the same language "but the words are different. The Kaan do not always understand the Kpatogo, but the Kpatogo always understand the Kaan."

Patterns. The displays in (30) give the D scores of the four dialect texts and allow us to draw some preliminary conclusions about these four groups' attitudes toward each other concerning shared ethnic identity. First, all four groups seem to hold identical attitudes toward Dogose and Khisa. Their responses were essentially the same whether they heard the Dogose or Khisa text, except for the obvious difference that the Dogo and Khi switched places when judging their own dialect. Second, the Dogo and the Khi were virtually identical in the way they judged the Kaansa and the Kpatogoso texts, though, while they were slightly positive about sharing ethnic identity with the Kaan, they were neutral about shared identity with the Kpatogo.

There is an interesting generational split within the Khi sample. For Kaansa, Kpatogoso, and Dogose, the Khi elders judged each set of texts significantly more positively than the Khi adults did. This indicates that the older generation of Khi feels closer ethnic ties with the other dialect groups than the younger generation does, evidence that this small community is undergoing a shift in ethnic identity which would accompany a linguistic shift toward Jula.

In contrast to the close harmony of attitudes between the Dogo and Khi is the divergence of attitudes between the Kaan and Kpatogo. They differ greatly on how they feel about Kaansa, come together a bit on Kpatogoso, then diverge again in their attitudes toward Dogose and Khisa. The Kaan and Kpatogo seem to hold nonreciprocal attitudes toward each other in this dimension. The Kpatogo are neutral about sharing ethnic identity with the Kaan, but the Kaan are moderately positive about sharing ethnic ties with the Kpatogo. This may indicate a certain desire for separation on the part of the Kpatogo and conversely, a desire for unity among the Kaan.

The results   121

(30) Ethnic Identity judgments of dialect texts: Comparison of D scores

Sample	N	Kaansa	Kpatogoso	Dogose	Khisa
Kaan	35	0.98	0.77	0.68	0.72
Kpatogo	25	0.51	0.95	0.40	0.44
Dogo	28	0.67	0.53	0.97	0.89
Khi	21	0.69	0.56	0.83	0.98

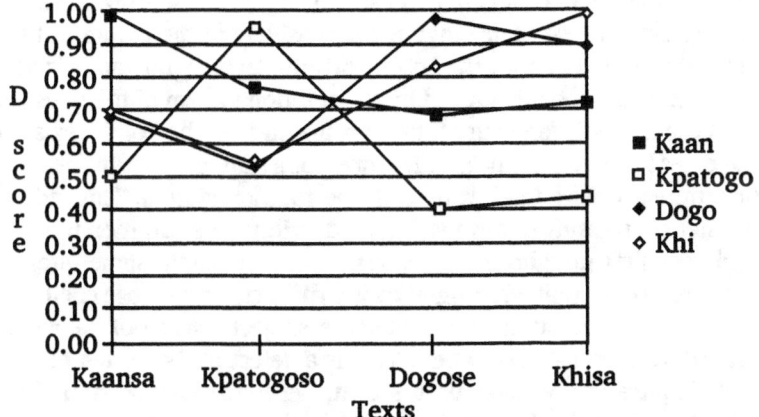

Lobiri and Jula texts. The striking information that we can draw immediately from the graph in (31) is that all four groups hold very similar attitudes toward Lobiri speakers, and that these attitudes, concerning shared ethnic identity,[33] are neutral to low. Not many feel that they share family relationships or traditions, though, interestingly enough, they are neutral about whether they share religion with them. The Lobi are strongly animistic, though a few have become Muslim or Christian. Both the Dogo and Khi groups, with sizeable populations of Muslims, were basically neutral on this issue, though the Khi, who are all Muslims, had the lowest score.

The low scores shown in (32) indicate that Labouret's (1931, 1958) classification of the Kaan and Kpatogo with the Lobi lacks empirical evidence, and is a sentiment not shared by the Kaan and Kpatogo themselves. In spite of the similarities of language and culture which Labouret tried to establish,[34] we

---

[33]Note that for the Lobiri and Jula texts, subjects answered questions in an additional subdimension named Shared Religion, represented in (31) and (32) as SR. Note also that subjects did not answer the Shared Language (SL) question for these two texts.

[34]Labouret did not adequately study the Kaansa language and admits in his 1958 treatise that the Kaan were reluctant to talk with him. Parenko and Hébert (1962) do an excellent job of correcting Labouret's misunderstandings of the Kaan.

see here a deeper attitude of separation and distinctness from the Lobi on the part of all four groups.

There is a notable difference between the attitudes of the men and the women in the Dogo sample. The men rated the Lobi overall at .39, moderately negative, whereas the women were slightly positive at .64.

In (32), judgments of the Jula text, we see that the Kaan, Dogo, and Kpatogo rated the Jula much as they did the Lobi, but that the Khi were more positive than the others in their attitudes about sharing traditions and religion with the Jula. This is not too surprising, because they are all Muslims like the Jula and use their language pervasively in the community.

It must be noted that for the Lobiri and Jula texts, significant variation in response seemed to be introduced by the rotation system of the questionnaires. This is especially true when all four groups judged the Lobiri texts. Thus, for these cases I cannot assume that D scores for a sample were uniform across the four different questionnaires used in the rotation system. This indicates that the system of rotating questions did not distribute the variation inherent in the sample evenly throughout each questionnaire, but that some questionnaires elicited responses that were significantly different from those elicited by other questionnaires. Questions asked of some subjects were not balanced out by similar questions asked of others. This is a defect in the design of the survey, and its implications will be discussed further in the final section of this chapter. Thus, the results discussed above should be seen as tentative and in need of verification.

For the Lobiri and Jula texts, as well as for the dialect texts, all four groups judged all texts as strong on maintaining cultural traditions. Judgments on this subdimension differed very little from one group to the next. While I expected the Khi in particular to be judged as abandoning their culture, they were judged the same as all the others. This indicates that if indeed a language/culture shift is occurring among the Khi, it does not seem to concern them or any of their ethnic cousins. It may be largely unnoticed, or if it is noticed, has not produced any widespread alarm in the community.

Attitudes toward ethnic contact

Attitudes toward interethnic contact (EC) were measured with questions dealing with linguistic accommodation (LA) and personal familiarity (PF). The measurement of linguistic accommodation was basically the response to a question about whether the text speaker could understand or speak the language of the subject. Personal familiarity dealt with whether the subject had frequent personal contact with people like the text speaker.

The results

(31) Ethnic Identity judgments of Lobiri texts

Sample	n	Subdimensions														Age				Sex			
		SL n	FR	n	ST	n	CM	n	SR	n	D score	E texts n	Y texts n	A score	n	E score	n	M score	n	F score	n
Kaan	33		0.21	20	0.00	18	0.73	19	0.58	30	0.44			0.46	22	0.40	9	0.42	20	0.42	15
Kpatogo	25		0.00	15	0.05	20	0.95	10	0.40	25	0.32			0.36	12	0.26	9	—	—	
Dogo	28		0.27	15	0.13	20	1.00	13	0.55	28	0.49			—		—		0.39	17	0.64	11
Khi	21		0.27	11	0.14	14	0.86	7	0.36	21	0.36			0.33	11	0.44	8	0.38	13	0.32	8

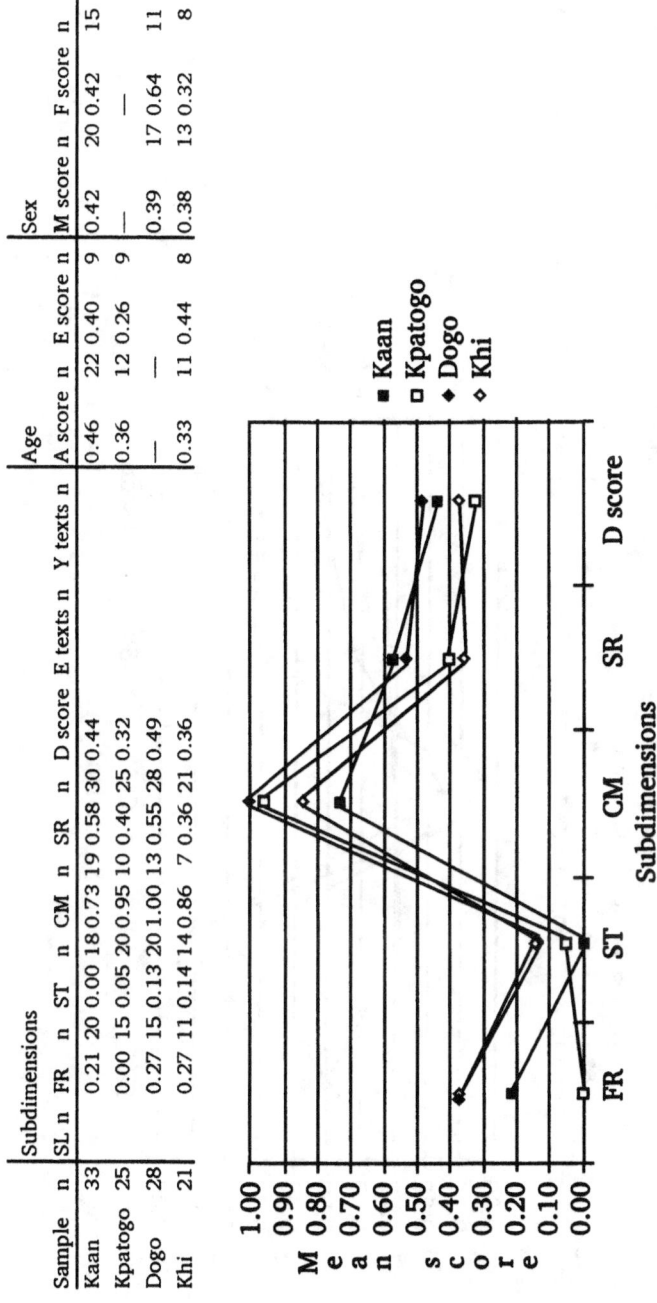

(32) Ethnic Identity judgments of Jula texts

Sample	n	Subdimensions													Age				Sex			
		SL	n	FR	n	ST	n	CM	n	SR	n	D score	E texts	n	Y texts	n	A score	n	E score	n	M score	n	F score	n
Kaan	35	0.44	22	0.07	22	0.84	19	0.58	32	0.46							0.43	22	0.5	9	0.49	20	0.43	15
Kpatogo	25	0.07	15	0.05	20	1.00	10	0.28	25	0.29							0.32	12	0.24	9	—		—	
Dogo	28	0.53	15	0.23	22	1.00	13	0.64	28	0.57							—		—		0.5	17	0.66	11
Khi	21	0.50	10	0.71	17	0.70	10	0.68	20	0.64							0.61	11	0.54	8	0.64	13	0.56	8

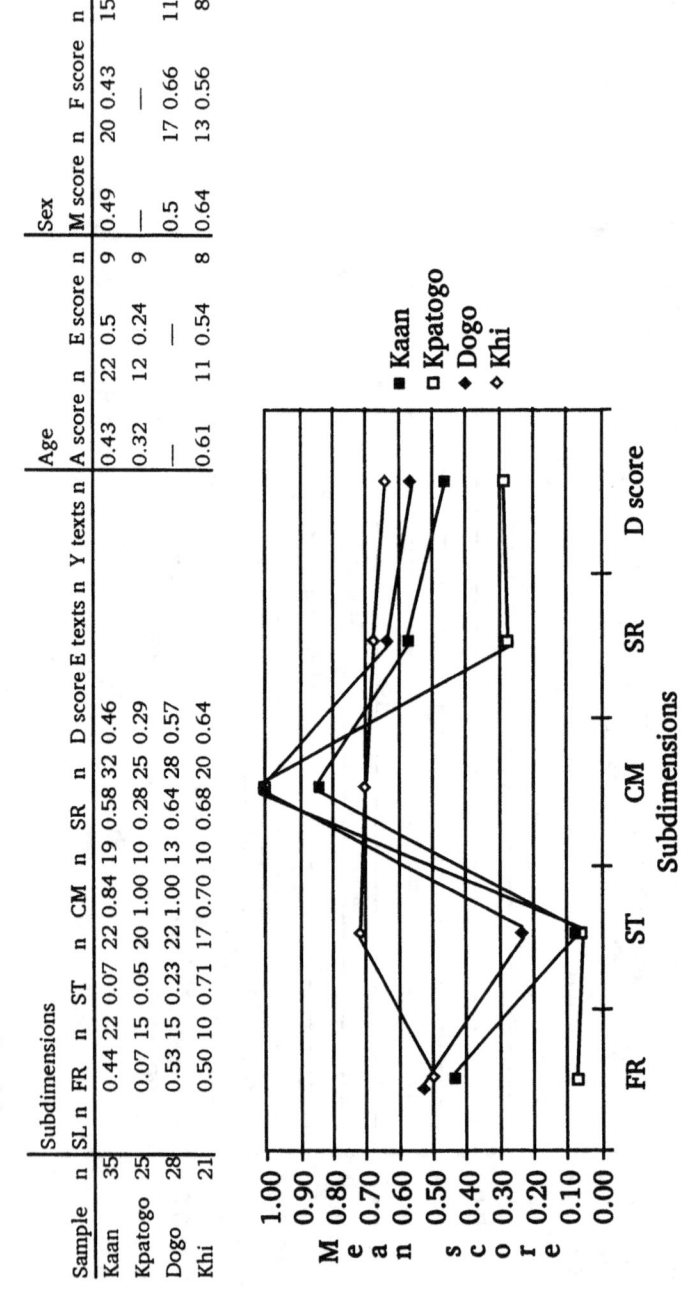

■ Kaan □ Kpatogo ♦ Dogo ◊ Khi

Subdimensions: FR ST CM SR D score

The results

Dialect texts.

Kaansa. The data in (33) show that while all four groups held relatively positive attitudes in this dimension toward the Kaansa speakers, the Kpatogo's attitudes were the lowest, in the moderately positive range. This contrasts significantly with the scores for the Kaan, as one might expect, but is not significantly different from the scores of the Dogo or Khi.[35] It is interesting that the Khi, while feeling strongly that the Kaan could understand their language, felt only moderately positive about having regular contact with the Kaan.

Kpatogoso. The graph of (34) shows an interesting grouping in attitudes toward Kpatogoso texts. In terms of personal familiarity, the Kpatogo and Dogo hold nearly identical strongly positive attitudes. The Kaan and the Khi on the other hand are similar in sharing moderately positive attitudes for this subdimension. The Dogo are the closest group to the Kpatogo in terms of physical proximity, and so it is not surprising that they are quite familiar with them. Likewise, the Kaan and the Khi are the most distant and their respective territories are not contiguous with the Kpatogo, so they feel less strongly about sharing personal relationships. There is historical evidence, however, that the Kpatogo are an offshoot group from the Kaan (Parenko and Hébert 1962 and Père 1982, 1987), and from a linguistic point of view their dialect is closer to Kaansa than it is to Dogose. Yet, in spite of these historical and linguistic ties, the Kaan and the Kpatogo do not perceive themselves to be particularly familiar with each other. It may be that for the Kaan at least, proximity has a major influence on this attitude. Some of the comments they made on this issue indicate that the only contact they have with the Kpatogo occurs when the Kpatogo come into Kaan territory for traditional observances. An adult male Kaan said that he had met some Kpatogo at funerals but that he had never traveled to their villages. Another man, a youth said he had met some Kpatogo because "when they come to make [traditional animal sacrifices], they come to Obiré."

---

[35]Analysis of variance: F obs $= 2.89$, df $= 3, 101$, $p < .05$. Post-hoc analysis performed with Tukey's HSD.

(33) Ethnic Contact judgments of Kaansa texts

Sample	n	Subdimensions									Age				Sex			
		LA	n	PF	n	D score	E texts	n	Y texts	n	A score	n	E score	n	M score	n	F score	n
Kaan	31	1.00	13	0.85	31	0.92	0.90	26	0.94	25	0.94	18	0.82	7	0.96	18	0.87	13
Kpatogo	25	0.67	15	0.76	25	0.72	0.71	20	0.86	20	0.79	12	0.81	9	—	—	—	—
Dogo	28	0.83	15	0.82	28	0.87	0.86	23	0.93	23	—	—	—	—	0.91	17	0.80	11
Khi	21	0.95	10	0.73	21	0.85	0.86	18	0.85	17	0.78	11	0.91	8	0.93	13	0.72	8

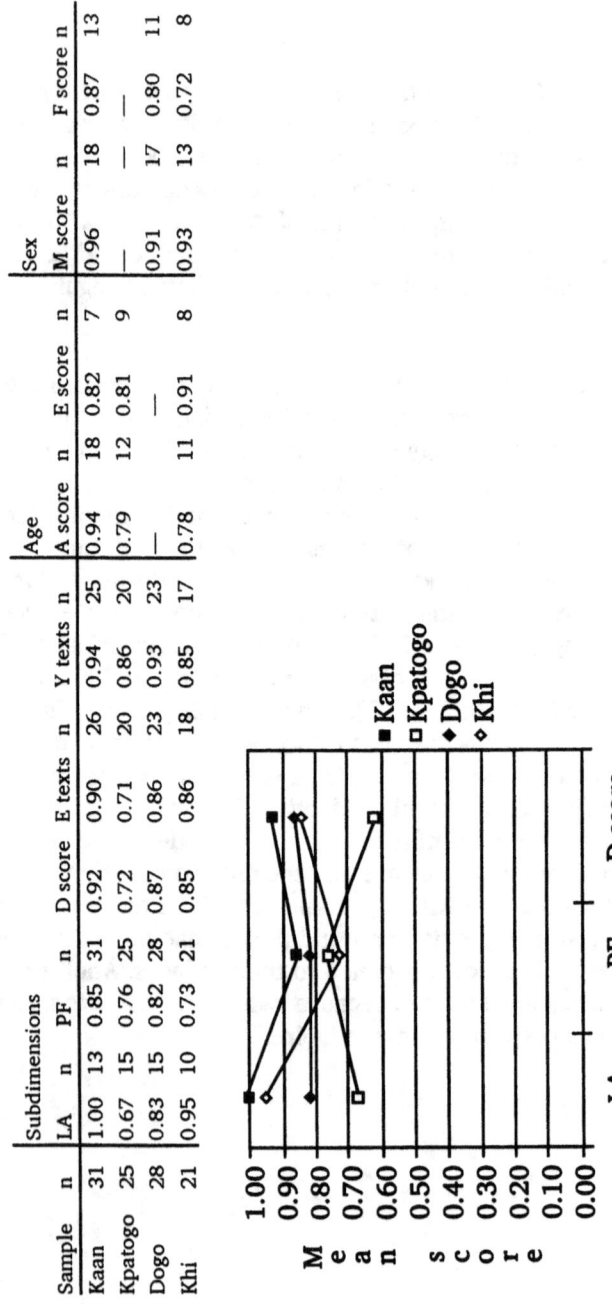

The results

(34) Ethnic Contact judgments of Kpatogoso texts

Sample	n	Subdimensions									Age				Sex			
		LA	n	PF	n	D score	E texts	n	Y texts	n	A score	n	E score	n	M score	n	F score	n
Kaan	23	0.92	6	0.63	23	0.72	0.77	15	0.63	8	0.73	13	0.71	8	0.68	14	0.78	9
Kpatogo	15	0.80	5	0.87	15	0.90	1.00	10	0.70	5	0.94	8	0.88	4	—	—	—	—
Dogo	18	0.70	5	0.86	18	0.88	0.96	13	0.65	5	—	—	—	—	0.80	10	0.94	8
Khi	14	0.75	4	0.61	14	0.68	0.75	10	0.50	4	0.50	7	1.00	5	0.67	9	0.70	5

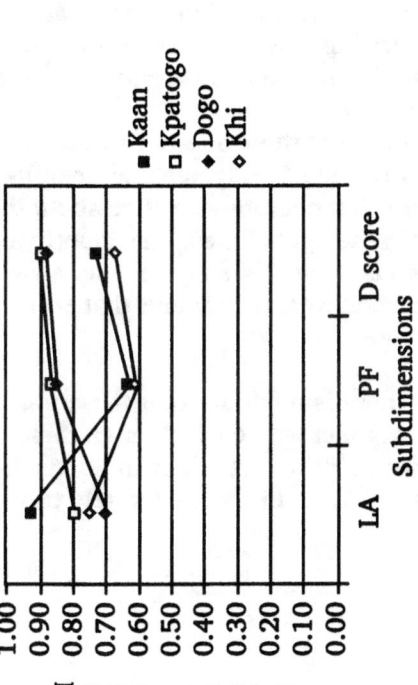

There are two crossovers here that are interesting. The Kaan subjects who were asked this question were strongly confident that the Kpatogo could understand Kaansa but, as was just mentioned, were less positive about personal familiarity. On the other hand, the Dogo were the least positive about Kpatogo accommodation to them, but very strong on personal familiarity. This is no doubt due to the facts of geographic proximity: the Dogo have more opportunity to meet and talk with the Kpatogo.

For linguistic accommodation, we see the Kaan demonstrating a strongly positive attitude about the Kpatogo understanding their language, and the Kpatogo feeling only moderately positive about the Kaan understanding theirs. It appears that there is an asymmetric intelligibility relationship between these two groups.[36]

Dogose. The distribution of responses to the Dogose texts is shown in (35). There is no significant difference between the D scores which group the Kaan, Kpatogo, and Khi in the moderately positive range. The important distinction seems to be between the Kpatogo and the other three groups in how they view linguistic accommodation. The Kaan and the Khi subjects who answered this question agreed unanimously that the Dogo could understand their languages, while the Kpatogo subjects were less sure.

Khisa. Responses to these questions concerning the Khisa texts were the most uniform of the EC judgments as seen in (36). The Dogo, Kpatogo, and Kaan were all moderately positive about their contact with the Khi. It is interesting in the light of the ethnic identity results discussed above that both the Dogo and the Khi subjects who answered the linguistic accommodation question were unanimous that each group could understand the others' language.

Patterns. There is no doubt that these four groups show positive attitudes toward contact with each other on these measures and that they differ little from each other in their evaluations. Almost all of their scores fall between .70 and 1.00, in the moderately to strongly positive range.

---

[36]The surprisingly low score of the Kpatogo in judging the linguistic accommodation of the Kpatogoso speakers is no doubt due to the low number of subjects who were asked this question (5). In fact, low numbers are a factor for all four samples with regard to this question. Therefore, the discussion above must be seen as tentative.

The results

(35) **Ethnic Contact judgments of Dogose texts**

Sample	n	Subdimensions										Age				Sex			
		LA	n	PF	n	D score	E texts	n	Y texts	n		A score	n	E score	n	M score	n	F score	n
Kaan	20	1.00	8	0.73	22	0.73	0.72	16	0.75	6		0.75	12	0.79	7	0.68	12	0.80	10
Kpatogo	20	0.70	10	0.85	20	0.78	0.77	15	0.80	5		0.72	9	0.94	8	—		—	
Dogo	20	1.00	10	0.90	20	0.90	0.87	15	1.00	5		—		—		0.85	13	1.00	7
Khi	21	1.00	7	0.79	14	0.79	0.73	11	1.00	3		0.86	7	0.80	5	0.63	8	1.00	6

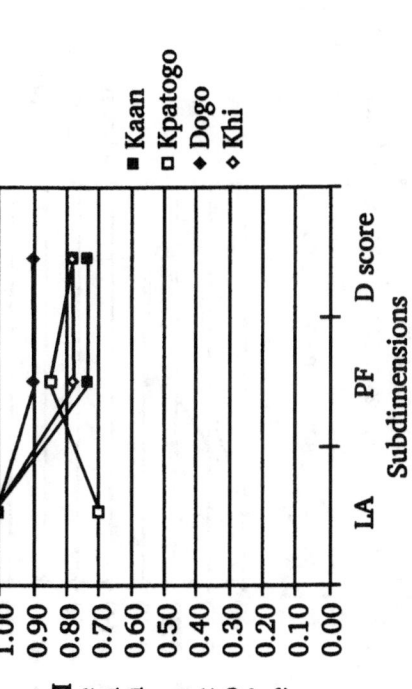

(36) **Ethnic Contact judgments of Khisa texts**

Sample	n	Subdimensions								Age				Sex			
		LA	n	PF	n	D score	E texts	n	Y texts	n	A score	n	E score	n	M score	n	F score	n
Kaan	25	0.88	8	0.70	25	0.72	0.82	14	0.55	11	0.72	16	0.57	7	0.57	15	0.80	10
Kpatogo	20	0.80	5	0.75	20	0.75	0.70	10	0.80	10	0.75	11	1.00	6	—		—	
Dogo	23	1.00	8	0.78	23	0.78	1.00	13	0.50	10	—		—		0.75	12	0.82	11
Khi	17	1.00	7	0.88	17	0.88	1.00	10	0.71	7	0.80	10	1.00	7	0.89	9	0.88	8

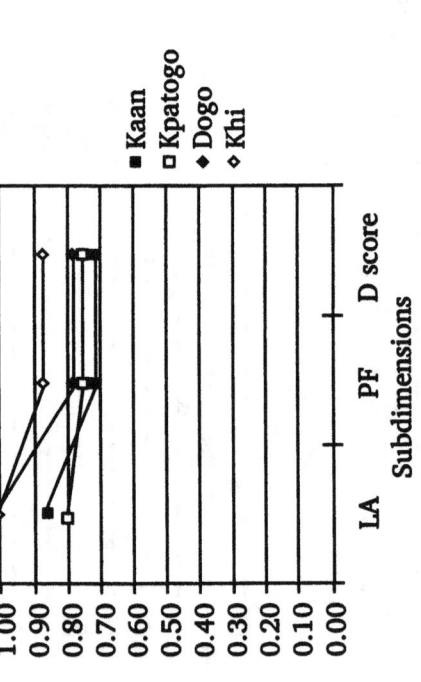

The results

In (37) we see some trends in the way these four groups judged their dialects. First, the Kaan and Khi follow a similar pattern in judging the Kaansa and Kpatogoso texts. They were both strongly positive about contact with the Kaansa speakers and borderline slightly/moderately positive about contact with Kpatogoso speakers. It is interesting that the Khi would be so positive about contact with the Kaan, since they are so distant from them. Their primary contact may come through intergroup trade of large clay jars made by the Khi. Some of the Kaan in Loropéni said they had traveled to Mangodara once to buy these jars from them.

(37) Ethnic Contact judgments of dialect texts: Comparison of D scores

Sample	N	Kaansa	Kpatogoso	Dogose	Khisa
Kaan	35	0.92	0.72	0.73	0.70
Kpatogo	25	0.72	0.90	0.78	0.75
Dogo	28	0.87	0.88	0.90	0.78
Khi	21	0.85	0.68	0.79	0.88

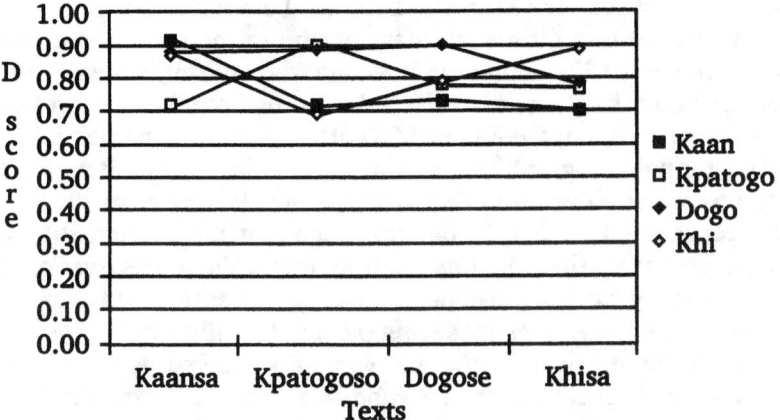

Another notable pattern is in the parallel ratings of the Dogo and Khi by the Kaan and Kpatogo. We see illustrated here the observation made above that the Kaan and Kpatogo rate the Dogo and Khi pretty much the same, whereas the Dogo and Khi do not react the same way to the Kaan and Kpatogo.

Lobiri and Jula texts. Responses to the Lobiri texts, in (38), show the Kpatogo to be slightly negative in their overall evaluation of their contact with the Lobi due largely to their strong negative opinion that the Lobi make no effort to learn their language. They were neutral about their personal familiarity with the Lobi, which means in this case that about half of those who answered these questions said they knew the Lobis and half did not.

I was surprised by the slightly positive evaluation the Khi gave the Lobi for learning to speak Khisa. Several Khi commented on this saying, "Those who live here can speak Khisa." In Massadéhirikoro I probed this question a bit and made the observation on a survey form that "Seems people believe that if you can understand a bit, then you can speak a bit, though with regard to the Lobi, they seldom if ever have actually heard them speaking Khisa."

This sentiment, though strongest in the Khi sample, was also apparent among the Kaan and Dogo, who made similar comments that those Lobi who live nearby could understand Dogose or Kaansa. The undercurrent of their comments, however, was that only individual Lobi with regular contact with their communities would learn their dialect, and that this was not true of most Lobi. During my stay with the Kaan around Loropéni, I observed a few Lobi who could speak some Kaansa, but the overwhelming choice of contact language between the Kaan and Lobi was Lobiri, not Kaansa.

The interesting difference that appears in the evaluations of the Jula text, shown in (39), is that the Dogo and the Khi subjects were unanimous in affirming that they knew the Jula and had regular contact with them. On the other hand, the Kaan and Kpatogo were only moderately positive, even though geographical proximity to Jula communities for the four groups is fairly even. In other words, they all have as much opportunity for contact with the Jula, but the Dogo and Khi evaluated this contact more positively than the Kaan and Kpatogo. These observations must be tempered by the circumstance that very few subjects in each group answered these questions regarding personal familiarity.

A chisquare run on their raw responses showed no significant difference in their scores in the PF subdimension. However, the D scores do show an interesting pattern. When the D scores of the Khi and Kpatogo are collapsed together, as well as those of the Kaan and Dogo, the difference between these two groups is significant.[37] As the graph clearly shows, this grouping is due to the similarity of their responses to the linguistic accommodation question.[38]

---

[37] X^2 obs = 5.191, df = 1, p < .05.

[38] Remember that the D scores are weighted according to how many subjects in each group answered questions in each subdimension. This is one case where the imbalance in the rotation system is evident.

The results

(38) **Ethnic Contact judgments of the Lobiri text**

Sample	n	Subdimensions									Age				Sex			
		LA	n	PF	n	D score	E texts	n	Y texts	n	A score	n	E score	n	M score	n	F score	n
Kaan	26	0.39	14	0.67	26	0.55					0.62	15	0.41	8	0.59	16	0.60	10
Kpatogo	19	0.10	15	0.63	19	0.41					0.38	8	0.56	8	—		—	
Dogo	23	0.43	15	0.76	23	0.58					—		—		0.61	16	0.50	7
Khi	18	0.64	11	0.67	18	0.61					0.50	9	0.71	7	0.62	13	0.60	5

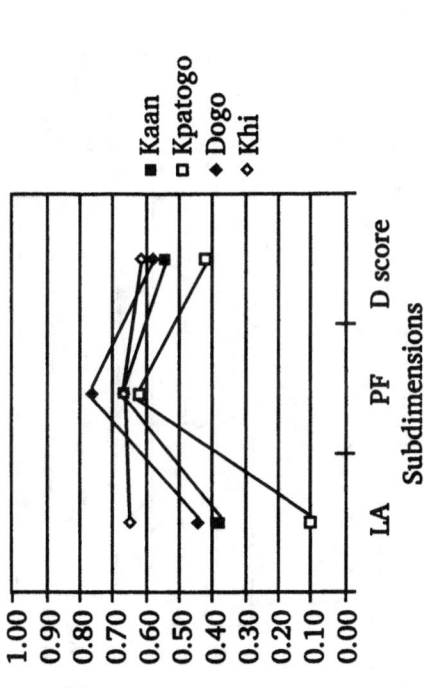

(39) Ethnic Contact judgments of the Jula text

Sample	n	Subdimensions									Age				Sex			
		LA	n	PF	n	D score	E texts	n	Y texts	n	A score	n	E score	n	M score	n	F score	n
Kaan	23	0.46	12	0.73	11	0.59					0.62	13	0.58	6	0.68	14	0.44	9
Kpatogo	15	0.80	10	0.80	5	0.80					0.75	8	0.75	4	—		—	
Dogo	18	0.42	13	1.00	5	0.58					—		—		0.60	10	0.56	8
Khi	14	0.65	10	1.00	4	0.75					0.69	8	0.75	4	0.78	9	0.70	5

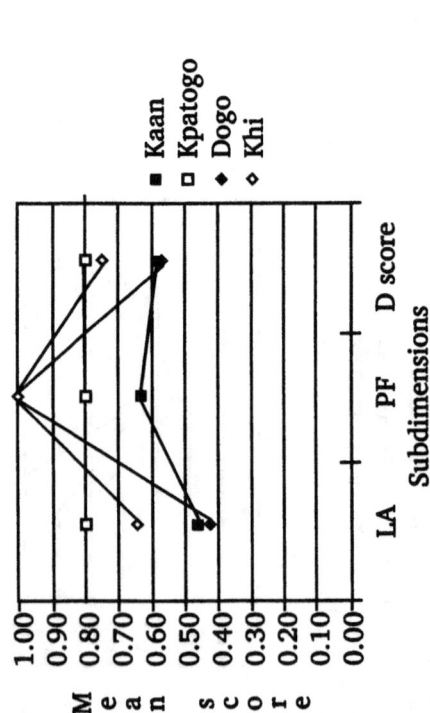

Attitudes toward language awareness

Awareness toward the other language varieties in the region was measured through responses to questions about difficulty of understanding the texts (UN) and the speaking ability (SA) of the text speaker.

Dialect texts.

Kaansa. The graph in (40) shows the identical attitudes held by the Kaan and Kpatogo in this dimension. The Kpatogo feel they have no trouble understanding Kaansa and that the text speakers they heard spoke well and clearly. The Khi and Dogo, while also rating speaking ability very high, were a little weaker on understanding Kaansa. This difference is important in that the D scores of the Dogo and Khi are significantly lower than those of the Kaan and Kpatogo. All of their scores, however, are moderately to strongly positive.

Kpatogoso. In their attitudes about comprehending the Kpatogoso texts, the Dogo and Khi samples were only slightly positive. The Kaan were moderately positive, but that difference disappeared in the D scores when their attitudes toward speaking ability were factored in. In the end, the Kaan, Dogo, and Khi all showed moderate awareness of the Kpatogoso dialect.

Dogose. Dogose was the highest-rated dialect in these subdimensions (cf. (43)). All four groups claimed that they understood Dogose well and that the text speakers spoke clearly. Their responses do not differ much from each other except that the Kaan were a little less positive than all the others. Two comments collected from the Kaan sample give us hints as to why this is the case. A young man from Kérié said that everyone there understood the Dogose spoken in Koro which is located north of Yérifoula and probably where most Dogo come from who have regular contact with the Kaan. The school headmaster in Loropéni is a Dogo from Koro, so is a carpenter who does a lot of work in Loropéni and Yérifoula. In contrast, an adult woman from Yérifoula said that you cannnot understand Dogose unless you live next to the Dogo. The texts they were responding to had been gathered in Béguélé, not Koro, so may have been slightly different than what they were used to.

Within the Kpatogo sample, the elders rated these texts significantly lower than the adults. The elders were moderately positive (.85) while the adults were strongly positive (1.00).

(40) Language Awareness judgments of Kaansa texts

Sample	n	Subdimensions					Age				Sex			
		UN	SA	D score	E texts	Y texts n	A score	n	E score	n	M score	n	F score	n
Kaan	35	1.00	0.95	0.98	0.97	0.97	0.99	22	0.94	9	0.97	20	0.99	15
Kpatogo	25	0.99	0.96	0.98	0.95	0.99	1.00	12	0.94	9	—	—	—	11
Dogo	28	0.83	0.94	0.88	0.84	0.91	—	11	1.00	8	0.86	17	0.92	11
Khi	21	0.71	0.95	0.83	0.82	0.82	0.74	11	1.00	8	0.88	13	0.74	8

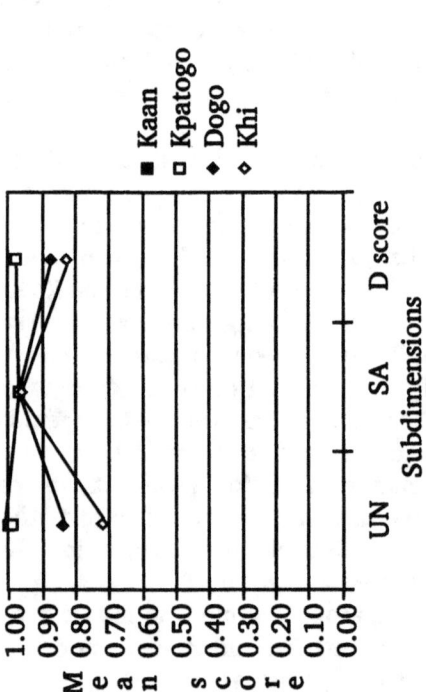

The results

(41) Language Awareness judgments of Kpatogoso texts

Sample	n	Subdimensions						Age						Sex			
		UN	SA	D score	E texts	n	Y texts	n	A score	n	E score	n	M score	n	F score	n
Kaan	35	0.76	0.79	0.77	0.90	17	0.68	18	0.81	22	0.72	9	0.69	20	0.88	15
Kpatogo	25	0.98	1.00	0.99	0.98	10	1.00	15	0.98	12	1.00	9	—	—	—	—
Dogo	28	0.62	0.83	0.72	0.85	13	0.61	15	—	—	—	—	0.74	17	0.69	8
Khi	21	0.62	0.88	0.75	0.81	10	0.72	11	0.72	11	0.94	8	0.69	13	0.84	8

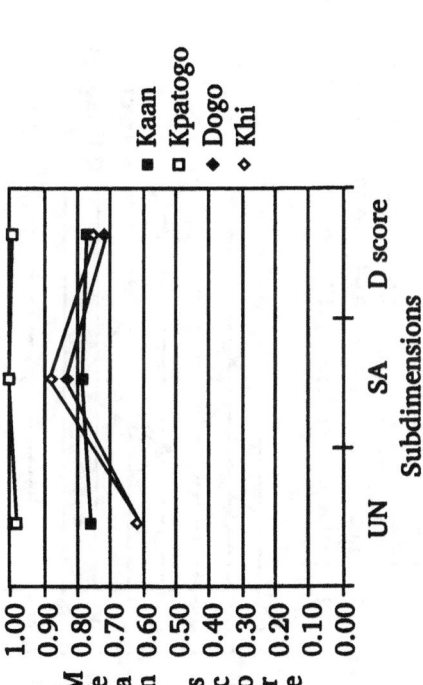

(42) Language Awareness judgments of Dogose texts

Sample	n	Subdimensions							Age				Sex			
		UN	n	SA	n	D score	E texts	n	Y texts	n	A score	n	E score	n	M score	n	F score	n
Kaan	35	0.89		0.99		0.94	0.93	18	0.96	17	0.93	22	1.00	9	0.96	20	0.90	15
Kpatogo	25	0.98		0.91		0.95	0.91	15	0.98	10	1.00	12	0.85	9	—		—	
Dogo	28	1.00		0.89		0.95	0.93	15	0.94	13	—		—		0.97	17	0.91	11
Khi	21	1.00		1.00		1.00	1.00	11	1.00	10	1.00	11	1.00	8	1.00	13	1.00	8

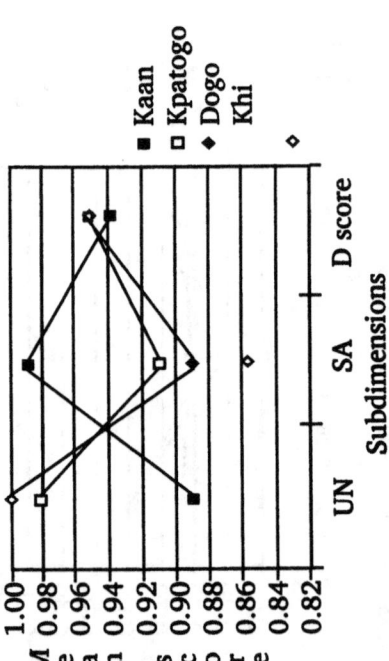

The results

(43) Language Awareness judgments of Khisa texts

| Sample | n | Subdimensions | | | | | | | | | Age | | | | | | Sex | | | |
		UN	n	SA	n	D score	E texts	n	Y texts	n	A score	n	E score	n	M score	n	F score	n
Kaan	35	0.89		0.84		0.86	0.89	17	0.78	18	0.89	22	0.89	9	0.83	20	0.90	15
Kpatogo	25	0.86		0.84		0.85	0.88	10	0.82	15	0.92	12	0.75	9	—		—	
Dogo	28	0.88		0.79		0.83	0.85	13	0.79	15	—		—		0.82	17	0.86	11
Khi	21	0.98		0.95		0.96	0.93	10	0.98	11	1.00	11	0.91	8	0.96	13	0.97	8

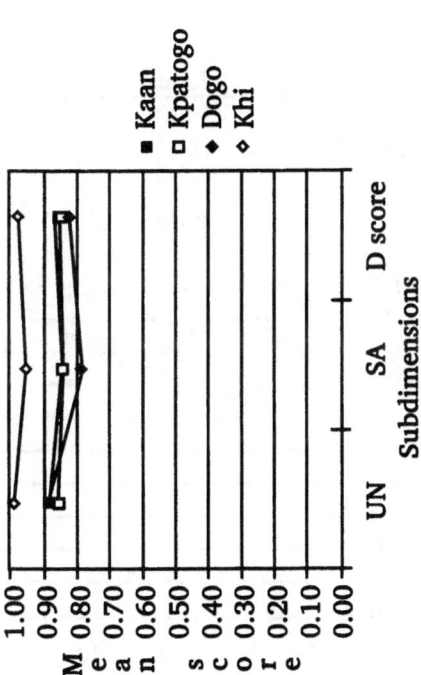

Why is Dogose perceived so positively by all four groups? Two factors that may have influenced their attitudes are the central geographic location of the Dogo community (the three other groups are contiguous to Dogo territory) and their larger population (approx. 12,000). The Dogo travel throughout the region and so have regular contact with the other three groups.

Khisa. The judgments of the Khisa texts are similar to those of the Kpatogoso in that those groups that do not speak the dialect rated the text significantly lower than those who do (cf. (43)). This is what is to be expected, and the fact that this doesn't occur for the Dogose texts, and to some extent the Kaansa texts, is rather startling.

Patterns. In terms of awareness of the language, shown in (44), which includes a perceived ability to comprehend, Dogose emerges as the central dialect. Kaansa, though not as well known among the Dogo and Khi, was highly regarded among the Kpatogo.

(44) Language Awareness judgments of dialect texts: Comparison of D scores

Sample	N	Kaansa	Kpatogoso	Dogose	Khisa
Kaan	35	0.98	0.77	0.94	0.86
Kpatogo	25	0.98	0.99	0.95	0.85
Dogo	28	0.88	0.72	0.95	0.83
Khi	21	0.83	0.75	1.00	0.96

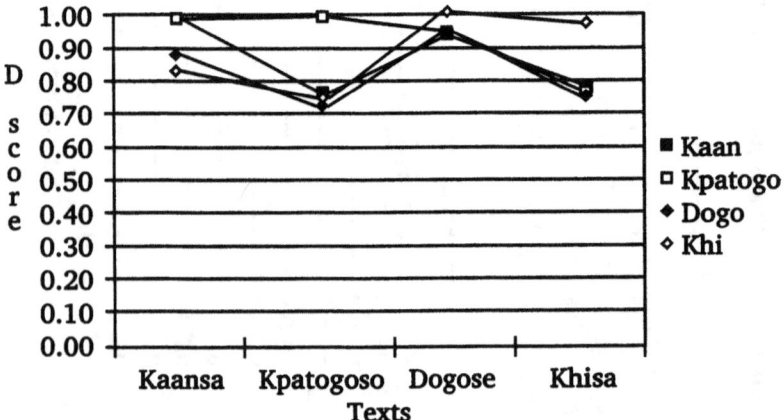

It is interesting to note that, as we saw earlier in the dialect texts of "Attitudes toward ethnic identity", the Kaan and Kpatogo identified the Khisa texts as Dogose. Yet, we have seen above that their judgments of the Khisa texts in this attitude dimension seem to differ noticeably from their judgments of Dogose. This underscores their oral comments to me that they perceived a difference in the two dialects but were unable to name it correctly. It also demonstrates the subtle differences in attitudes that a matched-guise, subjective-reaction approach can elicit.

Lobiri and Jula texts. The Kaan sample rated the Lobiri texts significantly higher[39] than the other samples, which may be an indication of greater bilingualism in Lobiri among the Kaan than the others. In fact, one young Kaan man from Kérié commented, "Everyone here speaks Lobiri." I have no figures for the other groups, but in the next chapter we will see that approximately one third of the Kaan people speak Lobiri at or above FSI skill level three. In spite of the lack of bilingualism data for the other groups, it is obvious from the chart in (45) that the Kpatogo, Dogo, and Khi samples overwhelmingly claim to have little understanding of Lobiri, while most of the Kaan, on the other hand, claim to understand Lobiri.

We also see that these three groups, in spite of their lack of understanding, judged the speaker moderately positively on his speaking ability. These scores are not very different from ratings given other texts that the samples had trouble understanding, and show an unwillingness to attach negative judgments when comprehension is low.

The reactions to the Jula text are markedly different from those of the Lobiri text. The data in (46) reveal very positive attitudes toward comprehension of Jula among all four groups. The only difference between the groups is the Dogo judgment of speaking ability, which is significantly lower than the ratings of the other three groups when their responses are collapsed.[40] While still moderately positive, the others were so positive as to make the Dogo rating seem low. What caused this lower reading were responses to question B-4, "Does he tell his story well?". While most people answered this question positively or with the neutral response (I don't know), a few of the Dogo subjects felt the speaker did not relate his personal account well. Interestingly, no one commented on this question, so I have no individual remarks which might illuminate why some of the Dogo answered this way.

---

[39]Analysis of variance: F obs = 13.37, df = 3, 104, $p < .05$. Post-hoc analysis performed with Tukey's HSD.
[40]X^2 obs = 4.201, df = 1, $p < .05$.

(45) Language Awareness judgments of the Lobiri text

	Subdimensions							Age				Sex			
Sample	n	UN	n	SA	n	D score	E texts n	Y texts n	A score	n	E score	n	M score	n	F score	n
Kaan	35	0.82		0.95		0.95			0.89	22	0.83	9	0.86	20	0.87	15
Kpatogo	25	0.32		0.74		0.53			0.56	12	0.61	9	—		—	
Dogo	28	0.21		0.71		0.46			—		—		0.47	17	0.45	11
Khi	21	0.19		0.86		0.52			0.57	11	0.53	8	0.42	13	0.69	8

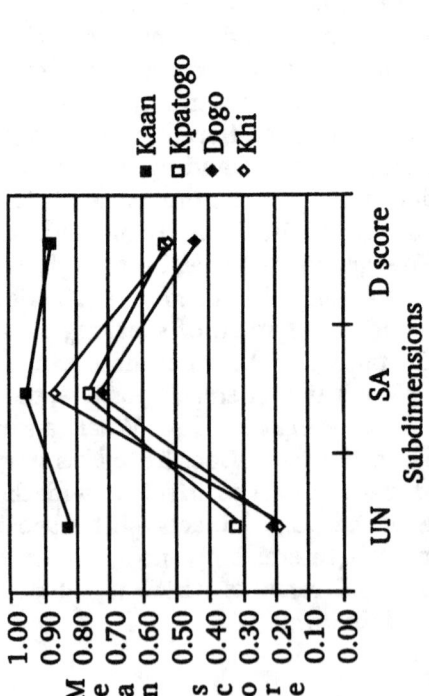

The results

(46) Language Awareness judgments of the Jula text

Sample	n	Subdimensions									Age				Sex			
		UN	n	SA	n	D score	E texts	n	Y texts	n	A score	n	E score	n	M score	n	F score	n
Kaan	35	1.00		0.97		0.99					0.98	22	1.00	9	1.00	20	0.97	15
Kpatogo	25	1.00		0.96		0.98					0.98	12	0.97	9	—		—	
Dogo	28	1.00		0.82		0.91					—		—		0.91	17	0.91	11
Khi	21	1.00		0.95		0.98					0.95	11	1.00	8	1.00	13	0.94	8

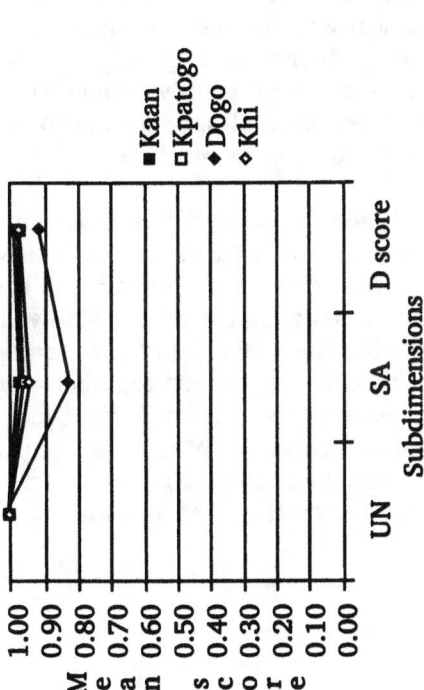

Attitudes toward personal character

Attitudes toward the personal character of the text speakers were elicited through questions probing the subjects' impressions of the general character or personality of the ethnic groups as a whole (GP), of the character of individuals in the speaker's ethnic group (IC), and the character or tenor of the contact the subjects had with each group (CC). Because of the unevenness of the rotation system for these questions, only a few subjects of each group answered the character of contact questions. Consequently, their responses do not weigh heavily on the overall scores for this attitude dimension.

Dialect texts.

Kaansa. The four groups did not differ significantly in their composite scores for these texts in (47). The only differences appear in their GP and CC subdimension scores. The CC scores here are somewhat more informative than for the other texts, since at least ten subjects responded to these questions. The Khi were the most hesitant and neutral, while the Kaan, Dogo, and Kpatogo did not differ greatly from each other. In fact, the four groups did not score significantly differently from each other for any subdimension. They were all moderately to strongly positive about the personal character of Kaansa speakers.

Kpatogoso. We see a similar pattern of response to the Kpatogoso texts, except that the scores in (48) are spread a little wider. The wide difference in CC scores cannot be considered significant because of the low numbers of respondents. Here again, the four groups were moderately to strongly positive in judging the character of the Kpatogoso speakers. When the Kaan and Khi results are grouped together and tested against the Dogo and Kpatogo results (also grouped together), a significant difference emerges, based on a chisquare of their raw scores.[41] The Kaan and the Khi are the most distant and have the least contact with the Kpatogo, and this may be the basis for their shared attitude.

---

[41] X^2 obs = 4.732, df = 1, p < .05.

The results

(47) Personal Character judgments of Kaansa texts

Sample	n	Subdimensions											Age				Sex			
		GP	n	IC	n	CC	n	D score	E texts	n	Y texts	n	A score	n	E score	n	M score	n	F score	n
Kaan	33	0.87	27	0.91	25	0.76	17	0.86	0.86	33	0.85	33	0.90	20	0.75	9	0.86	19	0.85	14
Kpatogo	25	0.76	25	0.88	15	0.87	15	0.82	0.86	25	0.77	25	0.80	12	0.88	9	—		—	
Dogo	28	0.75	28	0.92	18	0.77	15	0.80	0.80	28	0.79	28	—		—		0.82	17	0.77	11
Khi	21	0.71	21	0.91	14	0.60	10	0.75	0.80	21	0.70	21	0.70	11	0.79	8	0.79	13	0.68	8

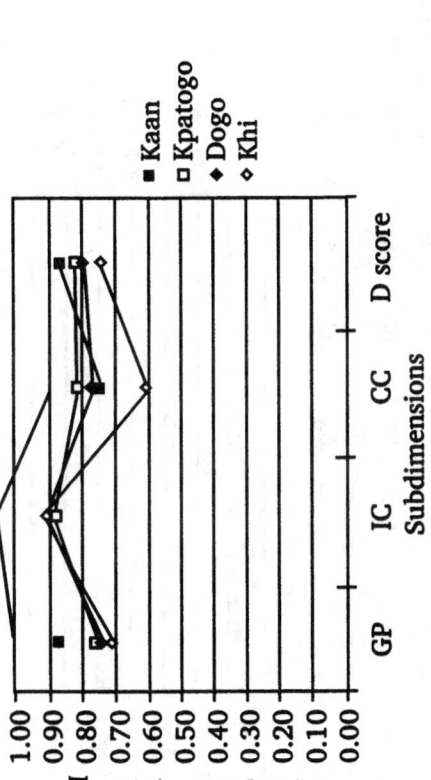

(48) Personal Character judgments of Kpatogoso texts

Sample	n	Subdimensions							E texts	n	Y texts	n	Age A score	n	E score	n	Sex M score	n	F score	n
		GP	n	IC	n	CC	n	D score												
Kaan	33	0.75	16	0.89	18	0.48	10	0.73	0.71	14	0.75	18	0.83	19	0.56	9	0.68	18	0.80	14
Kpatogo	24	0.86	14	0.87	15	0.80	5	0.85	0.89	9	0.83	15	0.83	12	0.92	9	—		—	
Dogo	28	0.83	18	0.80	15	0.80	5	0.79	0.69	13	0.87	15	—		—		0.85	17	0.68	11
Khi	21	0.64	14	0.85	10	0.63	4	0.65	0.50	10	0.80	11	0.61	11	0.75	8	0.62	13	0.72	8

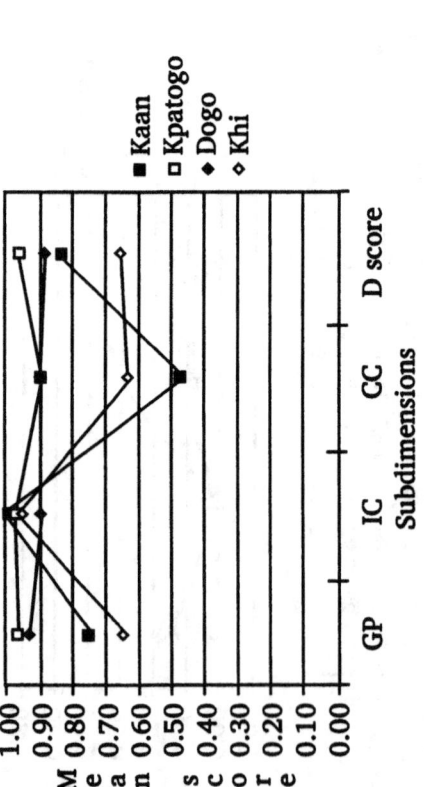

There is one other significant difference which may be seen in the table in (48). The D scores of the elder Kaan subjects were significantly lower than those of the Kaan adults.[42] As a subgroup, the elders of the sample were neutral (.56) while the adults were moderately positive (.83) in their overall rating. It is difficult to explain this without further research. The answer may lie in the increased mobility of the younger generation, or it may be that the elders are more aware of the historical reasons for the split between the two groups and, thus, are less favorably disposed toward the Kpatogo. At this point in my knowledge, I really cannot offer an explanation.

Dogose. There is no readily apparent difference in the four groups' D scores, shown in (49), yet when the Kaan and Kpatogo scores are tested together against Dogo and Khi scores, a significant difference is revealed.[43] The Kaan/Kpatogo group rated the Dogose texts significantly lower than the Dogo/Khi group, though the graph in (49) tells us that these differences occur in the narrow range of moderately positive ratings.

Khisa. The D scores for the Khisa texts are again fairly close to each other, and again a significant difference can be found when some samples are collapsed. In this case, the scores of the Kaan sample are significantly different when tested against those of the Kpatogo, Dogo, and Khi when these last three are treated as a group.[44]

Another significant difference appears in the Kpatogo sample, where the elders gave the Khisa texts a very high overall rating (1.00), while the adults were only moderately positive at .77.[45] Again, the explanation of this difference requires further research.

---

[42]Mann-Whitney test: ASCORE: n = 19, median = 1.0000; ESCORE: n = 9, median = 0.5000; W = 319.0, p < .05.

[43]X^2 obs = 4.940, df = 1, p < .05.

[44]X^2 obs = 7.420, df = 1, p < .05.

[45]Mann-Whitney test: ASCORE: n = 12, median = 0.7500; ESCORE: n = 9, median = 1.0000; W = 103.0, p < .05.

(49) Personal Character judgments of Dogose texts

Sample	n	Subdimensions										Age				Sex			
		GP	n	IC	n	CC	n	D score	E texts	n	Y texts	n	A score	n	E score	n	M score	n	F score	n
Kaan	33	0.85	17	0.84	24	0.47	9	0.76	0.72	18	0.80	15	0.78	20	0.78	9	0.70	19	0.84	14
Kpatogo	25	0.70	15	0.80	15	0.80	5	0.72	0.63	15	0.85	10	0.69	12	0.69	9	—		—	
Dogo	28	0.86	18	0.86	18	0.80	5	0.85	0.79	15	0.90	13	—		—		0.81	17	0.91	11
Khi	21	0.75	14	0.96	14	0.63	4	0.81	0.68	10	0.93	11	0.80	11	0.81	8	0.75	13	0.91	8

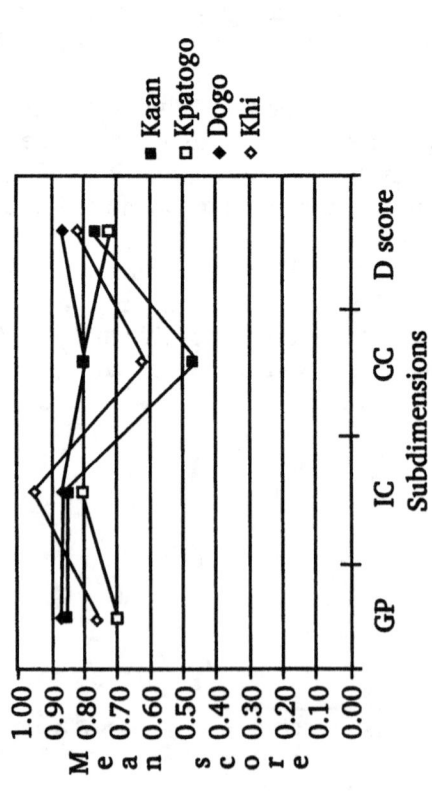

The results

(50) Personal Character judgments of Khisa texts

Sample	n	Subdimensions										Age				Sex			
		GP	n	IC	n	CC	n	D score	n	E texts	n	Y texts	n	A score	n	E score	n	M score	n	F score	n
Kaan	33	0.70	10	0.83	28	0.50	12	0.78	15	0.73	18	0.81	20	0.83	9	0.75	19	0.75	14	0.82
Kpatogo	25	0.80	10	0.85	20	0.90	10	0.86	10	0.78	15	0.92	12	0.77	9	1.00	—	—		
Dogo	28	0.95	10	0.85	23	0.75	10	0.88	13	0.90	15	0.86	—	—			17	0.93	11	0.82
Khi	21	0.93	7	0.91	16	0.86	7	0.93	10	0.95	11	0.91	11	0.86	8	1.00	13	0.94	8	0.91

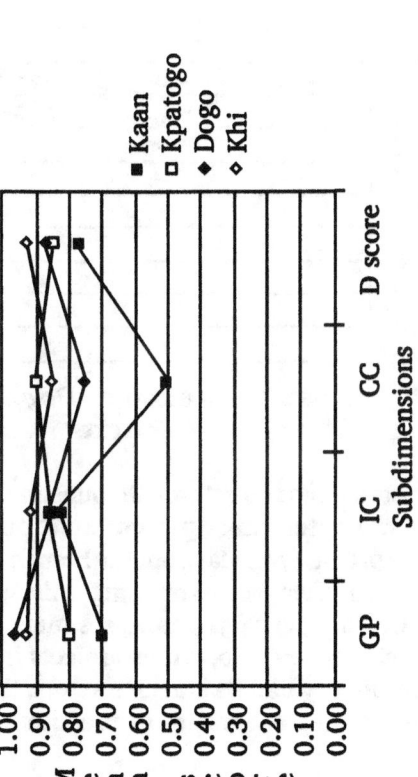

Patterns. The table in (51) demonstrates that in spite of the differences noted above, all four groups think well of each other in terms of personal character. The D scores were very similar and usually fell into the moderately positive range.

(51) Personal Character judgments of dialect texts: Comparison of D scores

Sample	N	Kaansa	Kpatogoso	Dogose	Khisa
Kaan	33	0.86	0.73	0.76	0.78
Kpatogo	25	0.82	0.85	0.72	0.86
Dogo	28	0.80	0.79	0.85	0.88
Khi	21	0.75	0.65	0.81	0.93

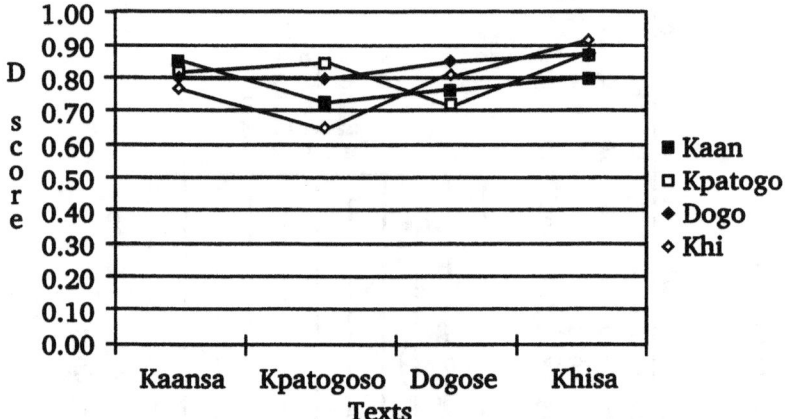

The most frequent comments for GP questions were that "there are both good and bad characters among them" and "here and there [you find bad characters]" expressed in local popular French as "un à un" [one by one]. Another interesting way of expressing this sentiment in local popular French was "Chacun peut pas perdre ses mauvais types" (no one is without their bad characters). So, while subjects in all groups acknowledged that every community had its bad characters, they did not choose to characterize any of the dialect groups as predominantly disagreeable.

The results

Lobiri and Jula texts. For the Lobiri text, the judgments of the Khi and the Kpatogo were significantly lower, in the neutral range, than were those of the Kaan and Dogo, which were moderately positive.[46] The GP judgments of the Kpatogo even dipped into the slightly negative range (.40). The Khi made the most negative comments about the Lobi. Three of the Khi men interviewed affirmed vigorously that there were many bad characters among the Lobi.

While the overall evaluations of the Jula were higher than those of the Lobiri text, a split in attitudes is clearly evident between the Kaan/Kpatogo and the Dogo/Khi in the graph of (53).[47] The Dogo and Khi were strongly positive while the Kaan and Kpatogo were just slightly positive. The primary source of this difference is in their responses to questions about the individual character of the Jula.[48] An adult male Kaan commented, "The Kaan and the Jula can sometimes get into big arguments." The Kpatogo were even less positive and more neutral about the individual character of the Jula, though I recorded no negative comments.

Do we see here the effect of years of Jula domination of the Dogo and Khi? The split in their attitudes corresponds to other important differences such as the use of traditional versus Jula clan names and the maintenance of traditional animism versus the spread of Islam. While the use of Jula as a second language is widespread in all four groups, it may be affective as well as instrumental for the Dogo and Khi. Certainly the Khi evidence attitudes compatible with an eventual shift to Jula as the primary language of the community.

Attitudes toward social status

Attitudes toward the social status of the text speakers and their representative ethnic groups were elicited through questions about the personal importance of the text speaker (PI), perceived educational achievement (ED), and the economic status of the community in question (ES). The D scores gathered in this attitude dimension are presented as a whole in (54) and (55). I will not discuss them in detail because this attitude dimension was not adequately defined or explored by this questionnaire, due primarily to a severe imbalance in the rotation of the questions

---

[46]X^2 obs = 6.944, df = 2, p < .05.
[47]X^2 obs = 5.581, df = 1, p < .05.
[48]X^2 obs = 8.925, df = 1, p < .05.

(52) Personal Character judgments of the Lobiri text

Sample	n	Subdimensions								E texts	n	Y texts	n	Age				Sex			
		GP	n	IC	n	CC	n	D score						A score	n	E score	n	M score	n	F score	n
Kaan	32	0.62	13	0.82	11	0.56	13	0.66						0.72	19	0.56	9	0.58	18	0.75	14
Kpatogo	24	0.40	15	0.60	5	0.80	5	0.52						0.63	12	0.33	9	—		—	
Dogo	28	0.73	15	1.00	5	0.66	8	0.76						—		—		0.74	17	0.80	11
Khi	21	0.45	10	0.50	4	0.71	7	0.55						0.55	11	0.56	8	0.42	13	0.75	8

■ Kaan
□ Kpatogo
♦ Dogo
◊ Khi

The results

(53) Personal Character judgments of the Jula text

Sample	n	Subdimensions											Age						Sex			
		GP	n	IC	n	CC	n	D score	E texts	n	Y texts	n	A score	n	E score	n	M score	n	F score	n
Kaan	33	0.78	16	0.73	15	0.41	8	0.70					0.76	20	0.64	9	0.71	19	0.66	14
Kpatogo	25	0.80	10	0.60	10	0.60	5	0.68					0.58	12	0.78	9	—		—	
Dogo	28	0.81	13	1.00	10	0.80	5	0.88					—		—		0.88	17	0.86	11
Khi	21	0.82	11	1.00	7	0.67	3	0.86					0.86	11	0.88	8	0.85	13	0.88	8

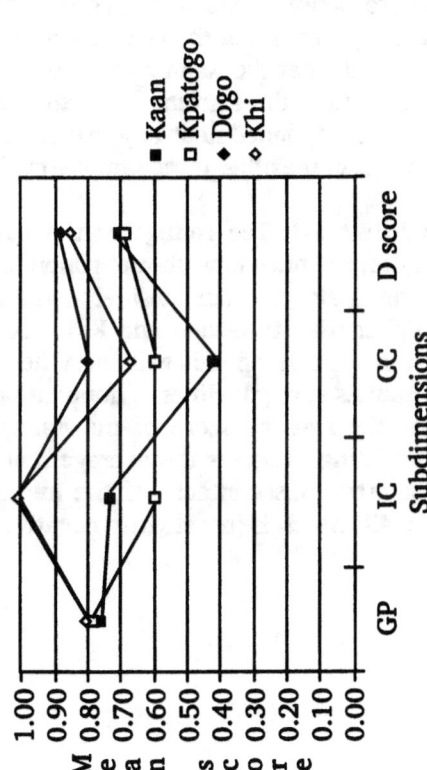

and their distribution across the four questionnaires. In 11 out of 24 ratings of this attitude dimension, tests showed that there were significant differences in the scores elicited by the four questionnaires. Thus, for nearly half of the evaluations, the survey instrument was not reliable for ratings of this attitude dimension. While it is very important to elicit evaluations of perceived social status in any survey of language attitudes, the evaluations gathered here are very limited in their usefulness and capacity to be generalized.

Dialect texts. Despite this limitation, we can observe that for the dialect texts, the stronger subdimension of the two tested was the evaluation of the personal importance of the text speaker. The questions here were an attempt to elicit judgments of a person's status on a village level based on the dialect used. In scanning the scores in this subdimension in the table in (54), we see that most fall into the range of neutral to slightly positive. The only significant variation in responses seems to be in the four groups' evaluations of the Kpatogoso texts. A chisquare of the raw responses to the questions in the PI subdimension reveals that the Kaan rated the Kpatogoso texts significantly differently than the other three groups when the results are collapsed.[49] Most of the Kaan subjects responded neutrally to these questions, whereas the majority of the subjects in the other three samples evaluated this text positively.

Lobiri and Jula texts. The ratings of the Lobiri and Jula texts were based primarily on the questions about economic status. It appears in (55) that the Kaan and Kpatogo, when considered as a group, rated the Jula texts significantly higher than the Dogo and Khi, also when considered as one group.[50] This seems to correspond again with the historical division between the four communities along the lines of domination by the Jula of Kong. It is interesting that the average score of the Kaan/Kpatogo group is .68, a slightly positive rating, whereas the average score of the Dogo/Khi group, the ones who have the most contact with the Jula and the most historical and religious ties is .43, which is just slightly negative.

---

[49] X^2 obs = 13.407, df = 2, p < .05.
[50] X^2 obs = 13.020, df = 2, p < .05.

(54) **Social Status judgments of dialect texts**

Kaansa texts

Sample	n	Subdimensions										Age				Sex			
		PI	n	ED	n	D score	E texts	n	Y texts	n	A score	n	E score	n	M score	n	F score	n
Kaan	35	0.60	34	0.34	19	0.56	0.68	34	0.48	32	0.54	22	0.50	9	0.62	20	0.47	15
Kpatogo	25	0.58	25	0.73	15	0.65	0.63	25	0.70	25	0.76	12	0.51	9	—		—	
Dogo	28	0.57	28	0.23	15	0.52	0.54	28	0.62	28	—		—		0.57	17	0.44	11
Khi	21	0.68	21	0.65	10	0.70	0.74	21	0.74	21	0.51	11	0.91	8	0.82	13	0.50	8

Kpatogoso texts

Sample	n	Subdimensions										Age				Sex			
		PI	n	ED	n	D score	E texts	n	Y texts	n	A score	n	E score	n	M score	n	F score	n
Kaan	33	0.56	33	0.13	12	0.52	0.62	15	0.43	18	0.59	22	0.42	9	0.45	20	0.64	15
Kpatogo	23	0.59	23	0.70	5	0.66	0.75	8	0.62	15	0.63	12	0.67	9	—		—	
Dogo	28	0.70	28	0.40	5	0.70	0.81	13	0.60	15	—		—		0.65	17	0.77	11
Khi	21	0.86	21	0.38	4	0.82	0.85	10	0.80	11	0.77	11	0.94	8	0.83	13	0.81	8

Dogose texts

Sample	n	Subdimensions										Age				Sex			
		PI	n	ED	n	D score	E texts	n	Y texts	n	A score	n	E score	n	M score	n	F score	n
Kaan	34	0.43	34	0.33	12	0.41	0.31	18	0.53	16	0.44	22	0.42	9	0.37	20	0.47	15
Kpatogo	25	0.56	25	0.90	5	0.57	0.45	15	0.75	10	0.67	12	0.47	9	—		—	
Dogo	28	0.63	28	0.00	5	0.55	0.40	15	0.73	13	—		—		0.47	17	0.68	11
Khi	21	0.62	21	0.50	4	0.60	0.32	11	0.90	10	0.68	11	0.44	8	0.50	13	0.75	8

Khisa texts

Sample	n	Subdimensions										Age				Sex			
		PI	n	ED	n	D score	E texts	n	Y texts	n		A score	n	E score	n	M score	n	F score	n
Kaan	35	0.56	34	0.33	15	0.49	0.44	17	0.54	18		0.50	22	0.33	9	0.55	20	0.45	15
Kpatogo	25	0.60	25	0.75	10	0.60	0.40	10	0.73	15		0.60	12	0.67	9	—		—	
Dogo	29	0.59	28	0.10	10	0.49	0.46	13	0.52	15		—		—		0.47	17	0.52	11
Khi	20	0.73	20	0.42	6	0.66	0.65	10	0.68	10		0.61	11	0.71	8	0.56	13	0.81	8

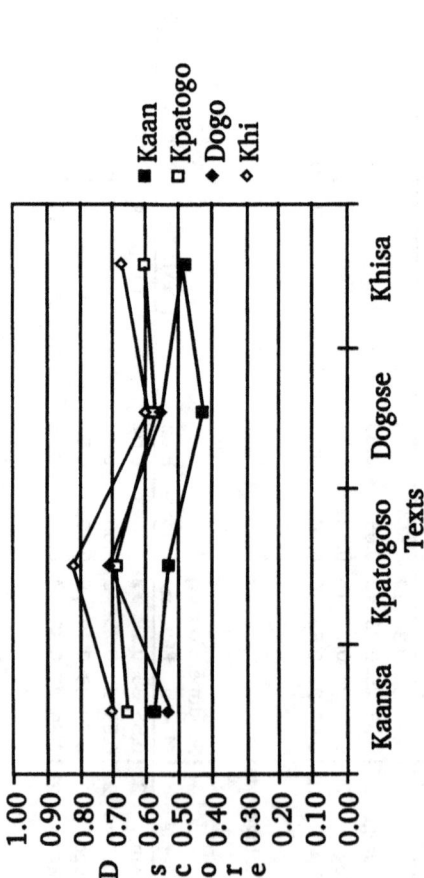

(55a) Social Status judgments of contact language texts

Lobiri text

Sample	n	Subdimensions									Age						Sex				
		ED	n	ES	n	D score	E texts	n	Y texts	n	A score	n	E score	n	M score	n	F score	n
Kaan	34	0.72	16	0.42	33	0.50					0.45	22	0.58	9	0.60	20	0.37	15
Kpatogo	25	1.00	5	0.58	25	0.59					0.60	12	0.58	9	—		—	
Dogo	28	0.25	8	0.52	28	0.48					—		—		0.50	17	0.45	11
Khi	21	0.71	7	0.33	21	0.43					0.41	11	0.44	8	0.42	13	0.44	8

Jula text

Sample	n	Subdimensions									Age						Sex				
		ED	n	ES	n	D score	E texts	n	Y texts	n	A score	n	E score	n	M score	n	F score	n
Kaan	34	0.36	11	0.60	34	0.58					0.54	22	0.65	9	0.62	20	0.54	15
Kpatogo	25	0.90	5	0.80	25	0.81					0.86	12	0.72	9	—		—	
Dogo	28	0.30	5	0.42	28	0.41					—		—		0.46	17	0.33	11
Khi	21	0.00	3	0.45	21	0.42					0.39	11	0.44	8	0.38	13	0.47	8

(55b) Social Status judgments of contact language texts

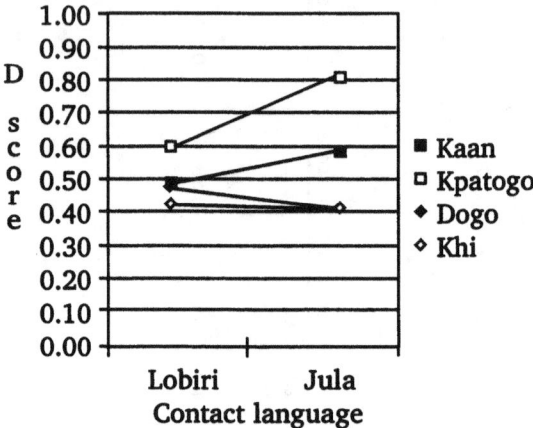

At this point, wherever possible, the evaluations of the Kaansa, Jula, and Lobiri texts will be briefly extracted and compared. This is important because these three sets of texts, recorded by the same young Kaan man, comprised the true matched guise embedded in the survey instrument.

The most readily comparable results for these three texts were in the dimensions of Ethnic Contact and Personal Character. Because of variations in the number and kind of subdimension questions asked of dialect texts versus the Lobiri and Jula texts, I have up till now avoided comparing the evaluations of these two sets of texts. However, these two attitude dimensions used nearly identical subdimension evaluations for both sets of texts and are, therefore, comparable. The scores of the other attitude dimensions can be made comparable after considerable adjustment and weighting of the D scores to compensate for the differences between them, but it is beyond the scope of this book. The tables in (56) display the comparative D scores for these two attitude dimensions.

The wide variation in scores demonstrates the effectiveness of this matched guise. We see that even the Kaan judged this native Kaan man very differently depending on which language he was speaking. Since this was a true matched guise, the only variable which could have caused these diverse scores is that of the language spoken, a clear demonstration that the basic technique of isolating the language variable in an attitude survey developed thirty years ago by Lambert et al. (1960) in Quebec is just as applicable and effective now in a radically different cultural setting when the appropriate adaptations are made for that setting.

(56) Ethnic Contact and Personal Character judgments of the Kaansa, Lobiri, and Jula texts

Ethnic Contact D scores

Subjects	Kaansa	Lobiri	Jula
Kaan	.92	.55	.59
Kpatogo	.72	.41	.80
Dogo	.87	.58	.58
Khi	.85	.61	.75

Personal Character D scores

Subjects	Kaansa	Lobiri	Jula
Kaan	.86	.66	.70
Kpatogo	.82	.52	.68
Dogo	.80	.76	.88
Khi	.75	.55	.86

Since this was an experimental design, there were certain problems that must be considered in order to establish the validity of the scores reviewed above.

Dialect texts versus contact language texts. There was an important difference in the way some of the questions were formulated and grouped depending on whether they were asked of the dialect texts or the contact language texts, Lobiri and Jula. This difference was, in some cases, one of different wording whereas, in other cases, entirely different questions were asked of the contact language texts that were never asked of the dialect texts. This was done because some questions made better sense with different wording for these two texts, and because other questions applied only to the Lobi or Jula communities and not to the four dialect groups. This was the motivation behind creating a whole category of questions just for the Lobiri and Jula texts (the LJ questions in "Survey deisgn" in chapter 5). Often this meant that the Lobiri and Jula texts received fewer questions, with the result that some of the attitudes elicited by them were less well defined. Another result was that in some cases the rotation of the questions was more uneven for these two texts than for the dialect texts.

Basic assumptions. Under "Validity" in chapter 5 I stated three important assumptions undergirding the design of this survey. These assumptions were tested statistically whenever possible. The results of these tests are presented in (98) in appendix 2.

Elder/youth text speakers. The first assumption was that subjects would make the same judgments of a language or dialect regardless of whether they heard an elder or a younger speaker in the test text. Out of eighty opportunities to judge the elder or youth texts, the subjects gave them significantly different overall judgments only three times, that is, less than 4% of the time. These three occasions probably were the direct result of more drastic variation introduced by the question rotation, discussed in detail below. Each case of E-Y text variation coincides with greater questionnaire variation. This assumption therefore holds.

Text sequence variation. The second assumption was that the judgments rendered would not differ according to how the texts were arranged in the two seven-text sequences. In other words, whether a subject heard the Dogose text first or fifth would not affect the way he or she judged that text. Out of 120 opportunities to judge texts embedded in the two sequences, the subjects gave them significantly different overall judgments only eleven times, that is, 9% of the time. In ten out of eleven of these cases the text-sequence variation coincided with greater variation introduced by the question-rotation, which is discussed below. That leaves only one case of independent variation, which clearly demonstrates the validity of this assumption.

Questionnaire variation. At a few points in the preceding presentation of results, I commented on the unevenness of the question rotation system. This unevenness showed up in some attitude dimensions more than in others. Those attitude dimensions which are the best defined showed the least unevenness and the most reliability. Such were the dimensions of Language Awareness and Personal Character. The Ethnic Identity dimension for dialect texts was also well defined. For these dimensions, the use of the rotation system in the four questionnaires produced no significantly different results eighty-six percent of the time. The least reliable results were obtained in the Social Status dimension and for the Ethnic Identity ratings of the Lobiri and Jula texts. In these dimensions, the questionnaires produced even results only forty-seven percent of the time. The other dimension, Ethnic Contact, was consistent sixty-seven percent of the time.

What went wrong here? Remember that the goal was to distribute the questions defining each attitude dimension evenly across the four questionnaires not only in number but also in the way the questions complemented and checked on each other, so that a group of subjects would respond essentially the same way to whichever questionnaire they received. Clearly, I was more successful in accomplishing this for the questions of some attitude dimensions and not for others. Unfortunately, for some attitude dimensions, a group of subjects who responded to, say, questionnaire 1A gave significantly different answers than did those who responded to questionnaire 2B, etc., due to the fact that they had answered different, though similar, questions. A certain amount of this variation must have been due to the small sample sizes and, thus, the even smaller subsamples which responded to each different questionnaire. Larger samples of forty to fifty subjects would probably even out the responses and do a better job of representing the main currents of opinion present in the communities on each questionnaire. There is, however, a disturbing significant relationship between the sample size and the number of instances of questionnaire unreliability,[51] that is, the larger sample sizes (Kaan, 35 and Dogo, 28, average 32) evidence more frequent unevenness of responses than the smaller sample sizes do (Kpatogo, 25 and Khi, 21, average 23). This might suggest that the larger the sample size the more variation will be introduced by the different questionnaires, indicating either a fundamental flaw in the design or a deleterious effect from the lack of random assignment of subjects to questionnaires. I believe, however, that this result can be attributed mainly to the fact that even the larger sample sizes were minimal and may show a wider range of variation than actually exists in the communities.

In view of the preceding discussion, why is it that the results presented in this chapter seem to be so illuminating and seem to make so much sense? Why are they not wildly askew and contradictory? The answer lies in the fact that the problem is with questionnaire reliability, not validity of questions or general approach to measuring attitudes. Except for the unevenness of question rotation, which rendered the four questionnaires unreliable in some applications, the matched guise/subjective reaction approach seemed to work well and elicit interesting, comprehensible, and informative results. The questions that formed the basis for these attitude evaluations were relevant, and they accurately probed real differences in attitude that exist in the communities studied. We will see in chapter 8 how the attitude survey results fit into the sociolinguistic framework constructed by historical background research, the intelligibility tests, and

---

[51] X^2 obs = 6.984, df = 1, p < .05.

ethnographic research. So, while the methodological approach and the questions themselves were valid and very informative, the survey instrument, particularly the system of rotating questions, was uneven in its reliability and needs revision. In addition, larger samples should be taken from each community studied for better representation.

7
Language Proficiency and Use in the Kaan Community

During the first year of my stay in Loropéni, I was puzzled by the easy bilingualism of the inhabitants. Most of the Kaan living in or near Loropéni seemed to speak Lobiri and Jula very well. I had observed some Lobi speaking Jula, some Jula speaking Lobiri, and some Lobi speaking Kaansa. All three languages were used on market days. The pattern of multilingualism I expected to find did not always fit observations of actual use. While I expected Jula, as the regional lingua franca, to dominate in most settings, Lobiri to be secondary, and Kaansa to be limited only to the Kaan community, it became obvious that there were significant deviations from this pattern. For example, I observed a Jula farmer accommodating a Lobi pastor by conversing freely in Lobiri, and on several occasions saw Lobi acquaintances speak Kaansa to some of the Kaan who lived in Loropéni, and even to me, at times, to communicate or just to help me practice my Kaansa. I heard people insist that many Lobi knew how to speak Kaansa, yet observed that most of the time the Kaan interlocutor would accommodate to the Lobi's mother tongue. I saw a young monolingual Kaan woman learn basic conversational Lobiri in a period of about nine months, just by living in Loropéni and having daily contact with the Lobi. During the language attitude survey, I heard many Kaan men and women assert that they could understand Dogose, and that the Dogo could understand them, yet I observed that my language helpers would almost always switch to Jula when interviewing the Dogo.

Added to the mystery of this dynamic situation was the fact that the three languages of the Kaan community repertoire were structurally very different from each other. Kaansa and Lobiri are Gur languages (Naden 1989), while Jula is a Mandé language. Kaansa and Lobiri also differ considerably in their structures and are not mutually intelligible. This trilingualism was not just a matter of people making slight adaptions to learn a related variety, but a full-fledged proficiency in structurally different languages.

To reach an understanding of this dynamic multilingual situation, I planned a secondary survey of the Kaan people which would explore in some depth their own proficiency in Lobiri and Jula as well as record when, where, and with whom they used the languages in their repertoire. Originally, I intended to survey the Dogo community as well, but lacked the time before my stay in Loropéni was finished.

Background and approach

The historical background of the Kaan community in Loropéni was sketched briefly in chapter 3. Their history is presented in much greater detail in the works of Labouret (1931, 1958), Parenko and Hébert (1962), and Père (1982, to appear). In broad strokes, the Kaan were the first to arrive in the Gaoua region in the early part of the seventeenth century, finding the abandoned ruins of prior residents. They settled outside Gaoua until they were uprooted and pushed west by the Lobi, who attacked them from the south and east. The Kaan settled in and around Loropéni for a time, until they were once again pushed out by the Lobi in the mid-eighteenth century. After the Kaan settled outside of Loropéni with their cultural center at Obiré, they began to live in peace with the Lobi and with the Jula, who have built up a small Muslim community in the center of Loropéni. While the general tenor of interethnic relations in and around Loropéni is harmonious, underlying tensions do surface occasionally as conflicts between Lobi and Kaan families or as disputes over the history of settlement of the region.

The method I used to investigate the language use and second-language proficiency of the Kaan people consisted of a direct questionnaire asking subjects to report their habitual language use in particular situations and of a "can-do" scale of language-related tasks which assessed the subject's proficiency in Jula.

Profile of the sample

The table in (16) in chapter 5 presented the distribution of subjects in this sample by age and sex. There were a total of thirty-five subjects in the sample, all of whom were different people than those who participated in the language attitude survey. There were six subjects each from Bopta, Kassita, Soronkina, and Sandi, seven from Obiré, three from Loropéni, and one from Kérié. These villages represent nearly all of the Kaan community that regularly trade at the Loropéni market, excluding those around Djigoué who seldom trade there, and as such provide an adequate sample for investigating community bilingualism.

Only three subjects claimed any amount of formal French education, and a total of eight claimed any external education at all (that is, other than traditional oral education within the ethnic community). Those who had not been to school had received some training during military service, in a rural FJA school, or at the Lobiri-language Bible school run by the Protestant Mission in Bouroum Bouroum twenty-five kilometers north of Gaoua.

The questionnaire asked people if they spoke Lobiri, Jula, and French. No doubt some spoke other languages such as Birifor, Moore, or ethnic languages of Côte d'Ivoire, but proficiency in these languages was not in focus because they are used very little, if at all, in the Loropéni region.

Of the Kaan sample of thirty-five, 29% (10) claimed to speak any amount of French, and all of these were men; no women claimed any proficiency in French. Sixty-six percent (23) claimed any amount of Lobiri, and 100% (35) claimed to know Jula at various levels.

There seems to be a greater number of women who do not speak Lobiri than those who do. In fact, a chisquare analysis[52] of the results shows a significant relationship between sex and proficiency in Lobiri; Kaan women are far less likely to speak Lobiri than Kaan men.

Language proficiency

Due to limited time and other practical constraints, I focused this part of the survey on proficiency in Jula. Lobiri proficiency was measured roughly by asking each subject to compare his or her Lobiri ability with the self-reports of Jula.

Jula proficiency was measured first by an initial four-level self estimate, then by a more lengthy interview using a locally adapted can-do scale of normal speech activities requiring various levels of proficiency.

---

[52] $X^2\text{obs} = 6.311.\ df = 1,\ p < .05$.

Initial estimate

Before talking about specific language tasks, I asked the subjects to give me a quick estimate of their Jula proficiency on the scale listed in (57).

(57) Parle bien   mι nú si tákιrsa   speak well
     Se débrouille   mι nú si   get along
     Ne parle pas bien mι nú si kɛrι kɛrι don't speak well
     Connais pas   mι nú si wa?   don't know

The results of this initial estimate will be compared later in this chapter with the more detailed results from the can-do scales. Many surveys of language use and proficiency in West Africa rely on simple self-ratings such as these to estimate proficiency in an entire community, and I wanted to test the accuracy of this simple measure against one which tries to define proficiency on a more detailed scale and which has some correspondence to the widely used FSI scale of language proficiency.

Can-do scales

The quick estimate was followed by a longer interview where I asked the subjects if they could perform a series of language tasks of increasing difficulty and complexity. The questions required simple yes or no answers, though some offered a third choice, "yes, but with difficulty". Responses were scored by assigning the last level at which the subject could perform all of the tasks, and "plus" levels were given to those who could confidently perform at least two tasks at the next level. For example, a young man from Soronkina gave me an initial estimate of "Je ne parle pas bien", so I started asking him if he could perform the level one tasks. He reported no difficulty with any of those, nor with any of the level two or level three tasks. For level four, he could perform three of the four tasks, and so this was clearly the level at which he started to break down. He could not perform any of the level five tasks. I assigned him at level three-plus because he could perform well at level three yet showed difficulty at the next level. Since he was able to do most of the level four tasks confidently, I assigned him the plus level.

Following this method, I obtained the ratings displayed in (58) for Jula proficiency in the Kaan community. It is apparent that eighty percent of the sample tested at level three or above, and more than a third (thirty-seven percent) of the sample is at level four or above.

Language proficiency

(58)

Level	YF	AF	EF	YM	AM	EM	N	%
0							0	
0+			1				1	
1	1		1				2	
1+							0	
2		1					1	
2+		1		1		1	3	21
3	2		2	1	2	1	8	
3+	2			3	1	1	7	43
4		3		3		2	8	
4+	1		1	1	2		5	37
5							0	

There are no significant relationships between level of proficiency in Jula and either variables of sex or age in this sample. There are, however, some interesting trends that can be seen in (59) and (60).

(59) Jula proficiency by sex

Levels	M	F
Low/Mid (0–3)	6	9
High (3+–5)	13	7

(60) Jula proficiency by age

Levels	Y	A	E
Low/Mid (0–3)	5	4	6
High (3+–5)	10	6	4

First, twice as many males were rated at high levels of proficiency (three-plus to five) as were at low or mid levels (zero to three), while the females were distributed more evenly. Second, twice as many youths were rated at high levels as were at low or mid levels, while adults and elders were also distributed more evenly. Consequently, most of the young males interviewed (seven of nine) tested at high levels of Jula proficiency. Another trend which shows in (58) is that no man tested below level two-plus, while four women did.

Since the chisquare of results did not reach appropriate levels of significance, our conclusions about proficiency distribution by age and sex must be limited to the sample and cannot be generalized to the population on the basis of this research alone. Yet, the differences I have just mentioned may serve as guidelines for further research.

Does the large proportion of youths at high proficiency levels indicate that proficiency in Jula will increase in the community over time? Or does it simply mean that the youth of the Kaan community are at the peak of their Jula proficiency and over time will have less need for the language and thus lose some proficiency? One comment from an older woman of Kassita indicates the latter. She said that when she was young, she spoke Jula well, but that now she has lost her knowledge of the language.

There seem to be two forces at work in the community which affect proficiency in Jula. The first is modernization, that is, improvement of roads, bus services, travel, job opportunities in Côte d'Ivoire, the availability of formal and nonformal education, and literacy. These favor an overall increase in Jula proficiency in the community because they promote contacts with peoples from outside the area, which require a shared language of wider communication.

Second, as youths mature, they marry and need to settle in a particular spot. Those who settle in the Kaan community also settle into what is presently a domain-restricted use of Jula in and around Loropéni, as we will see in the following sections. Their proficiency in Jula will probably stabilize or fall off after ten years or so. Those who settle in other parts of Burkina Faso or in Côte d'Ivoire and only visit the Kaan community would probably use Jula in most domains of life, including some inside the home. Their proficiency would probably increase or be maintained at a very high level.

How these two forces work on particular individuals determines to a large degree what their lifetime proficiency in Jula will be. Probably most of the youths interviewed for this study will find an equilibrium between these two forces. They will settle in the Kaan community, start a family, and maintain several plots of land for subsistence agriculture, yet travel outside the region for part of each year to find extra work for cash.

Results compared

Let us now compare the results of the initial four-point estimate with the results of the can-do scale in (58). Recall that the initial estimate was ordered in descending degree of proficiency, whereas the can-do scale was ordered in ascending degree of proficiency. We should expect, therefore, a negative correlation coefficient if there is a genuine correspondence in scores. The

Spearman rank-order correlation of the two sets of scores is $r_s = -.630$, a moderate and significant correlation showing a substantial relationship between the two measures. This is not too surprising, since they attempt to measure the same faculty in the individual. That the correlation of the two measures was not higher, however, suggests that each measure may elicit reports of different levels of proficiency from the same individual. The general, quick-and-dirty nature of the first measure must be enlightened and defined by a more specific measure if detailed knowledge of language proficiency in the community is desired.

Self-comparison of Lobiri and Jula proficiency

Of those who claimed any amount of proficiency in Lobiri, 46% (16) said they were less proficient in Lobiri than in Jula, while six said they were more proficient in Lobiri, and four said they were equally proficient in Lobiri and Jula.

I arrived at a rough estimate of Lobiri proficiency levels in the community by assigning proficiency at a half-level below the Jula level for those who spoke Lobiri worse than Jula, and by matching the Jula proficiency level for those who reported equal ability in both languages. For those who spoke Lobiri better than Jula, I assigned them a full level higher than their Jula level, except for those who spoke Jula at level four. I assigned these two subjects to level four-plus in Lobiri. This gave me an estimate of the maximum proficiency level in Lobiri in the sample, which is presented in (61).

(61) Estimated Lobiri proficiency in Kaan sample

Proficiency level	Total subjects
2+	5
3	6
3+	6
4	2
4+	4

NB: Lobiri proficiency is not higher than the level marked but may possibly be lower.

To summarize (61), we see that 49% of the sample (17 of 35) speaks Lobiri at level three-plus or below, while six subjects speak at or about level four. So we see that while the majority of both those who speak Jula and those who speak Lobiri are at level three, twice as many people speak Jula at level four (13) as speak Lobiri at the same level (6).

Sixty-five percent (15) of those who speak both Lobiri and Jula learned Jula first and then Lobiri. Three learned Lobiri first, and five couldn't remember which one they learned first. An interesting comment concerning this came from an older man from Obiré, who said, "One does not 'learn' Jula," implying that it is a language one acquires without special effort while growing up.

Seventy-two percent (26) of the full sample expressed a desire to learn Jula better than they already knew it. Fifty-five percent (20) said they would like to learn Lobiri better, including some who said they didn't speak Lobiri at all. I find it interesting that there is such a widespread desire to learn more Jula, even though everyone in the sample speaks some Jula already. This indicates that people see Jula as a desirable asset in their repertoire of linguistic codes. Lobiri is somewhat less desirable, though still seen as useful to many.

Validity of can-do scales

By tracking the number of subjects who claimed they could perform all the tasks for each skill level, we can evaluate to what extent the tasks were aligned in a scale of increasing difficulty and complexity. Do we see a steady decline in the number of people who can perform all the tasks at each level? Were there cases where a task may have been placed at the wrong level, or perhaps was not clearly enough defined and thus elicited responses inconsistent with later responses? The graph shown in (62) demonstrates that there was a gradual decline in numbers of subjects for each level.

(62) Subjects performing all tasks at each skill level

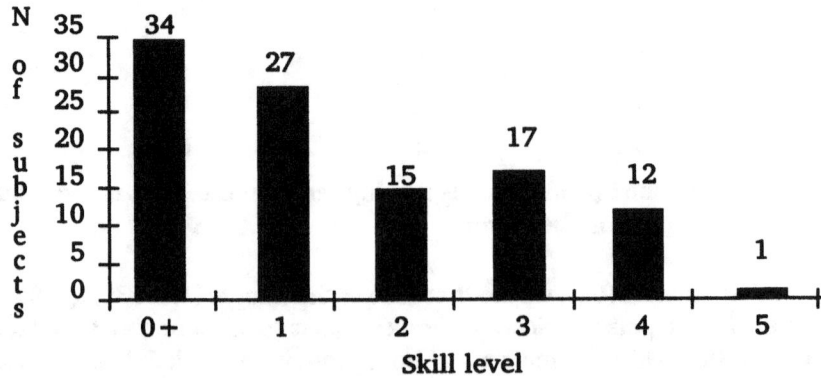

Language proficiency   171

We see, however, that a few more people could perform all of the level three tasks than could do all of the level two tasks. This indicates that at least one of the tasks in level two was either misplaced or poorly worded, which led those whose real proficiency was actually higher to report they had difficulty at this level (but not at the next highest level). The question which seemed to trigger this result was *"Est-ce que quelques fois tu dois pauser pour chercher des mots avant de finir ce que tu veux dire?"*

Some people who tested at level three or level four replied affirmatively that sometimes they had to search for words in order to finish what they wanted to say. Yet, it is not uncommon for native speakers to do this at times, so I took this into account when assigning skill levels based on this scale. Essentially, if a subject consistently reported confidence at performing higher level tasks, an affirmative response to this question was ignored. This question should have been worded more precisely to fit the level two performance criteria (see SIL 1987).

Language use in six domains

There are many occasions in and around Loropéni when Kaan people switch from Kaansa to Jula, Lobiri, or French. Having observed for more than a year many instances of code-switching between these four languages by Kaan multilinguals, I endeavored to systematically investigate self-reports of language use by the Kaan in the situations I had observed. This was done through a direct questionnaire which suggested a whole range of specific, locally common speech situations and asked interviewees which language they habitually use in each. This questionnaire was administered right after assessing the Jula proficiency of each subject using the can-do scale.

The survey questions focused on six domains[53] of language use:

1. *Official:* Interaction with various representatives of the national government: at the police station, at the health clinic, with a school teacher, a rural development worker (l'encadreur), and the veterinarian;
2. *Market:* Interaction when buying or selling selected products, interaction at certain stands, when soliciting certain services, or when counting money;

---

[53]In chapter 5, I mentioned eight domains, including the domains of "topic" and "schooling" not presented here. The responses to questions about topic were not adequate for analysis, indeed, the whole domain as such seems to have been poorly defined for this survey. The school domain questions did not yield many results because so few of the Kaan I interviewed had ever attended school.

3. *Friendship:* Interaction when greeting friends and strangers;
4. *Funerals:* Interaction at local funerals;
5. *Travel:* Interaction when traveling locally or in Côte d'Ivoire; and
6. *Interethnic contact:* Interaction when talking with people from different ethnic backgrounds.

Official. Fifty-seven percent (20) of the sample had used Jula when they had obtained their ID cards. Four subjects had used French, and others had used either Lobiri, or both Lobiri and Jula, depending on the ethnic origin of the agents they dealt with at the time. Nine people, which was about a quarter of the sample, had never obtained a national ID card, so that of the twenty-six who had, more than two-thirds had used Jula for the interaction.

Sixty-nine percent of the sample (24) said they used Jula with the staff of the health clinics in Loropéni or Lorhosso. Four people said they used French, and another four said they used either Jula, French, or Lobiri, depending on whom they were talking to. A young man from Kérié said he spoke Jula with one of the nurses and Lobiri with the Lobi nurse. He added, however, that sometimes he also spoke Jula with the Lobi nurse. An adult woman from Kassita said that, because she could only speak Kaansa, she needed a translator to discuss anything with the clinic workers.

Only about half of the sample (19) said they had opportunities to talk with a school master, and of those, five used French, ten used Jula, and three used either Jula or French, or both. One young man said he used Lobiri, but that was because the school master he had contact with was a Lobi. An elder man from Obiré said he would speak in French, but if there were others nearby whom he wanted to include in the conversation, he would switch to Jula.

Language use with the local development agent was markedly different. This man was a Kaan who had grown up outside his ethnic territory and had returned to Loropéni in the last ten years after the death of his father. Thirty-seven percent (13) of the sample said they would speak in Kaansa with him. Two more people said they would use both Kaansa and French with him, and three others said they would speak in Jula as well as Kaansa. Adding these last five gives us fifty-one percent (18) of the sample using at least some Kaansa with the development agent. Six subjects said they would use Jula, and three said they would interact in French with him. A young man from Kassita commented that he would speak to the agent in Kaansa if they are alone, but if people of other ethnic origin were with them, they would speak in Jula so that the others could understand. One young man from Kérié said the agent's Kaansa was not that good, since he had spent most of his life away from the area. This may explain why some people reported that they code-switched with him, and others said they preferred to speak Jula or French.

The local veterinarian is a Lobi from the Gaoua area. Most of the sample (54%, 19), however, said they used Jula when they spoke with him, and this in spite of the reported Lobiri proficiency among the Kaan. Only a few subjects said they would use Lobiri or French with this development agent. A young man from Obiré said he would speak to these government officials in French when he was at their place of work (school, police station, clinic), but that if he met them elsewhere he would speak to them in Jula.

It is interesting that even though roughly sixty-four percent of the survey sample claimed some knowledge of Lobiri, few people ever use it when carrying out official business with government officials, even when those officials are ethnic Lobis themselves. The preferred language for regular interaction in the official domain is Jula for two-thirds of the sample. The only exception to this pattern is when the official is an ethnic Kaan who speaks Kaansa, and yet even then, 36% (10) preferred to communicate with him in other languages (French, Jula, Lobiri). I propose, then, that in the Official domain, use of Jula is the norm. However, Lobiri may be used when the officer is an ethnic Lobi, and Kaansa is preferred when the agent knows that language.

Market. Concerning habitual language use in the Loropéni market, about half of the Kaan subjects (54%, 19) said they speak their own language most frequently. Most of the others, (40%, 14) said they spoke Jula most often, and two said they spoke either Jula or Lobiri as much as Kaansa in the market.

Shay nut butter (beurre de karité) is a major product of the Kaan community, and the Kaan are known in the area as the ones who produce and sell it, even though some Lobi and Jula also produce it. When asked which language they use when buying shay nut butter in the market, about half of the interviewees (43%, 15) said they use only Kaansa. Most of the others (34%, 12) said they use Jula, Lobiri, or both, as well as Kaansa when buying the butter.

There were some interesting comments to explain this language behavior. One young man said he sometimes speaks in Jula, even to a Kaan seller "because between the Kaan, the prices are higher". He went on to explain that if the seller didn't know him, he might be able to obtain a lower price by speaking in Jula to hide the fact that he was a Kaan. To explain why they sometimes use Jula, others pointed out that they sell it to the Jula, or that they sometimes need to buy it from a Lobi or a Jula. An older man from Kassita mentioned that the Jula do not produce it, but buy it from the Kaan and then resell it at a higher price to others.

Colorful bolts of cloth are sold by Jula merchants, and so it is not surprising that of the twenty-nine interviewees who regularly bought cloth at the market, twenty-seven (or 83% of the sample) used only Jula for the transaction. One adult man from Obiré said he used all three languages at different times, and an older woman from Kassita said she needed a translator to buy cloth.

The Jula have a monopoly on selling freshly slaughtered and inspected beef in the Loropéni market, and so it is natural that all of those interviewees who bought beef said they spoke in Jula for the transaction.[54] More interesting is how the Kaan use their language repertoire to buy pork, which the Jula cannot sell because of religious restrictions. Thirty-three interviewees said they regularly buy pork at the market, and of these, thirteen (37% of the sample) used Lobiri and fourteen (40%) used Jula. Others used Kaansa, or both Kaansa and Lobiri or Jula. Two women from Sandi (Lorhosso) explained their use of Jula saying, "The Lobi understand Jula."

Thirty interviewees (86%) regularly bought *kónyo* 'sugar peas', or pois surcé, another product of the region associated with the Kaan community. Most of these (83%, 29 of the sample) used Kaansa to buy this product.

Why is there such linguistic unanimity for this product and not for shay nut butter? Could it be that the market for shay nut products is wider and thus more interethnic? Could it be, as one young man commented, that the price for this commodity is stable and thus there is no need to hide one's ethnic origin through using Jula to buy at a lower price, nor to buy and resell? Could it be that there is less demand, that for some other reason the Jula or Lobi aren't interested in it, or that only the Kaan sell it, or that the Kaan only buy it from each other?

Lining the Loropéni-Kampti road, along the eastern edge of the market are several stalls or "boutiques" where people buy manufactured goods such as soap, school supplies, batteries, canned or powdered milk, coffee, sugar, sardines, pasta, small tools, and a whole host of other knickknacks. These stands are usually, but not necessarily, tended by Jula merchants. Of the eighteen people (51% of the sample) who replied that they bought things at these boutiques, fifteen (43%) said they used Jula, and the rest said they used either Jula or French.

---

[54] I once heard a meat seller, wearing a Muslim cap, speak fluent Lobiri to someone behind him, then turn and speak fluent Jula to a customer. It is not unlikely that this man was a Lobi Muslim living in the Jula community. Since the Kaan all reported using Jula to buy meat, this indicates that the ethnic origin of the seller has very little bearing on language choice in this particular setting.

Several women prepare large pots of rice or yams accompanied by pieces of chicken floating in spicy peanut sauce. They sell individual portions of this traditional dish to people shopping in the market. Most of the women who sell this food in Loropéni are Jula, and so it comes as no surprise that twenty-three of the twenty-four interviewees who buy prepared food in the market use Jula for the transaction (66% of the sample).

Lining the northern edge of the market, along the Loropéni-Banfora road there are several places to have one's bicycle or mo-ped repaired, two run by Kaan mechanics, others run by Mossi, Lobi, and Jula mechanics. Since there is no ethnic monopoly on this enterprise, we would expect the Kaan to use the full range of their linguistic repertoire when dealing with these repairmen, and that is, in fact, what the interviewees reported. Of the nineteen (54%) who said they frequented the repair shops, six said they usually spoke Jula for this interaction, five said they used Kaansa most often, and the rest (8) reported using different combinations of Kaansa, Jula, Lobiri, and/or French. One young man from Kérié remarked, "It all depends on who you are talking to: Kaan, Lobi, Jula, or French." He added that he would use French when talking to the Mossi.

The currency used in Burkina Faso is the West African CFA franc, which at the time of the research was tied to the value of the French franc at fifty CFA to one French franc. Counting money from a base ten system in one's native language, using the traditional base five system, can get a little complicated. For lower sums, however, it is simplified a bit by the fact that the smallest coin in use in rural areas is the five franc coin, which is conveniently counted as "one". Thus, saying a product costs "five" means it costs twenty-five francs. Though it gets complicated as the numbers get higher, people I observed counting at the market never seemed to have much trouble with the two systems, except when trying to express fairly large (greater than ten thousand francs) and complex sums in Kaansa. When asked which language they preferred to count money in, 86% (30) of all Kaan subjects said Kaansa. Two preferred Jula, and another two used either Kaansa or Jula. This did not really change when I asked what language they preferred when the amount was greater than ten thousand francs. Still 83% (29) preferred using Kaansa, while three preferred Jula. Two others preferred French and either Kaansa or Jula. So we see very little change in preference, even when using the Kaansa base-five system for large and complex amounts of CFA francs.

The table in (63) summarizes the language choice people make in the market when buying particular goods. When the merchants are Jula, or ethnic immigrants such as the Mossi, the obvious language choice is Jula. However, even when the merchants are Lobi or Kaan selling pork or shay nut butter, Jula is still used by more than just a few people. Kaansa is dominant only when buying and selling traditional Kaan products.

(63) Language use for selected market transactions

Product	Merchants	Language used
Shay nut butter	Kaan, some Jula, Lobi	43% Kaansa 34% Jula, Lobiri 17% Jula only
Cloth	Jula	Jula
Meat: Beef	Jula	Jula
Pork	Lobi, Kaan	40% Jula 37% Lobiri
Sugar peas	Kaan	Kaansa
Manufactured goods (boutiques)	Jula, Mossi	Jula
Prepared food	Jula	Jula
Bike repair	Kaan, Jula, Mossi, Lobi	17% Jula 14% Kaansa 23% mixed usage

While we see clearly the dominance of Jula in this market based on a sampling of products, the majority of interviewees still reported using Kaansa most often in the market. No doubt this is due to the fact that people do a lot of socializing in the mother tongue on market day with friends and acquaintances. Yet, it is also noteworthy that 40% of the Kaan subjects reported using Jula most often.

Friendship and greetings. One of the popular settings for interacting with friends is in a small "cabaret" where people often stop after market day to drink millet beer and talk. These cabarets are simply open courtyards of someone's house or cleared areas where women sell millet beer they have made themselves. This is a major source of income for both Kaan and Lobi women. I asked the Kaan subjects which language they speak when they stop at these cabarets after going to the market. Of the twenty-nine (83%) who regularly stop, drink, and talk, seventeen (49%) speak Kaansa, six speak Kaansa and Jula, and only one person (3%) reported speaking Jula alone. The rest speak a mixture of Kaansa, Lobiri, and Jula. Two people commented that the language they chose depended on who they were speaking to, though by the results above we may conclude that the majority talk with other Kaan rather than with Lobi or Jula acquaintances.

For the question of greeting someone you know I emphasized that these were people the subject knew or had previous contact with. This contrasts with the next question which focuses on strangers of certain or uncertain ethnic origin.

When greeting a Lobi, who is an acquaintance, the language of choice is Lobiri for 61% (19) of the interviewees who responded to this question. This closely matches the percentage of the total subjects who claimed any knowledge of Lobiri (64%). Seven subjects said they greeted the Lobi in Jula, and two said they greeted in Kaansa.

There were some interesting explanatory comments for this question. A young man from Bopta said he greeted in Lobiri, but would speak at length in Jula. This is similar to two other comments, one by an older woman from Soronkina who said that she could only greet in Lobiri, but couldn't say anything else. The other comment was from a young man from Sandi, who said, "If you know the Lobi well, you speak in Jula; if you don't know him well, you speak in Lobiri." Apparently, while most greet in Lobiri, some feel more at ease conversing in Jula.

When greeting a Jula, the natural choice was to speak Jula (51%, 18) for the twenty subjects (57%) who answered the question. One woman, however, said she would greet in Kaansa (even though she was evaluated at level two-plus in Jula).

To greet a Dogo whom they know, the majority of Kaan subjects (66%, 23) said they would use Kaansa. Five would use Jula, and another five would greet in Dogose, commenting that they spoke or understood some of that dialect.

The fact that there are so many ethnic groups living in the area and that there is the possibility of meeting people regularly whose ethnic origin one is unsure of led me to ask how the Kaan subjects used their linguistic repertoire to cope with greeting strangers. Seventy-seven percent (27) of the interviewees said they used Jula in this situation, while three said they would greet in Kaansa, and three others would use French.

Several women commented that they would simply say *anίsε*, which is the common Jula greeting to people walking by or arriving from elsewhere. In fact, the Kaan have adopted it into their language and use it among themselves for the same purpose. A young man from Obiré said he would greet an elder in Jula, but a youth in French.

Another common situation where language choice constraints are revealed is when the Kaan are talking in ethnically mixed groups.

When a Lobi is with a group of Kaan, 51% (18) of the interviewees said they would all switch and speak in Lobiri together, while seven said they would speak in Jula. Three subjects said they would continue to speak in Kaansa.

There is an interesting correlation between the estimate I made earlier in this chapter of Lobiri proficiency in the Kaan community and conversational practice reported above. From that estimate it appears that about fifty percent of all the subjects interviewed speak Lobiri at levels three and four. This corresponds nicely to the fifty-one percent mentioned above who said they would switch to Lobiri when a Lobi was with them in a conversational group. What makes this interesting is that FSI level three proficiency is the minimum level where a person feels comfortable in the language and makes few errors in everyday conversational tasks. So, it is tempting to conclude that those who speak Lobiri below level three would prefer to speak either in Jula or in Kaansa when a Lobi is present. A careful scrutiny of individual results, however, shows that there is not a significant relationship between high Lobiri proficiency (as estimated) and reported accommodation to Lobiri in this circumstance; there are apparently other factors as well which determine this language choice.

If a Jula joined the conversation, sixty-nine percent of the sample (24) said they would switch to Jula. Three subjects said they would speak both Kaansa and Jula. An adult man and woman from Sandi, who said they would use both languages, explained that they would greet the Jula in his/her language, then continue the conversation in Kaansa. A young man from Kérié said that whether he switched to Jula depended on whether he wanted the Jula to understand what he was saying.

Potential language behavior in a mixed group of Dogo and Kaan was an enigma for me, because both groups speak Jula well and reported intelligibility between them (average adjusted score of 79/100, as reported by Solomiac (1983) was 'borderline' (Casad 1974:46, Grimes 1987:50). Predicting solely from the intelligibility results, I might guess they would speak Jula together. Yet, the added dimension of perceived intelligibility and perceived ethnic ties, as well as attitudes toward character and contact makes this situation less predictable for the outsider. As it is, 74% (24) of the subjects said they would speak in Kaansa in a group where a Dogo was present. Only four said they would switch to Jula, and, interestingly, four said they would speak in Dogose since they were familiar with that dialect. It is also interesting that the four people who said they would use Dogose are women, and three of them are elders. In contrast to their responses, a young man from Bopta who said he would switch to Jula when Dogo are present, explained his response saying, "because we young people don't understand Dogose." This indicates there may be a difference between generations of Kaan in contact and familiarity with the other groups of their ethnic family.

Of the thirty-three subjects (94%) who responded to this part of the question, thirty-one (89%) said they did not or never have felt ashamed to speak in Kaansa while people of other ethnic origin were listening. Several people were quite adamant, making comments like "No, it's the language of your people!" Two individuals, however, said that sometimes they had felt ashamed, one explaining that it happens when one is traveling in another country.

While about one-half of the sample would accommodate to a Lobi in mixed group conversation, two-thirds would accommodate to a Jula in the same situation, and very few would accommodate to a Dogo. Certainly, there must be a link between community proficiency and accommodation, yet the ethnic and linguistic ties between the Kaan and Dogo seem to mediate to favor Kaansa rather than Jula for mixed groups of Kaan and Dogo.

A young man from Sandi explained to me how he felt most people reacted to the situations I mentioned. Here is a summary of his comments:

> If a Lobi arrives, they greet him in Lobiri but they continue to speak in Kaansa for the conversation. The Lobi takes his leave, and the Kaan reply, in Lobiri. If a Jula arrives, they would all switch to Jula for the entire conversation. If a Dogo arrives, they would both greet and talk in Kaansa, because "he, at least, should understand Kaansa."

Funerals. Though the use of language in religious practice is a wide field of inquiry, I limited this survey to one question about attendance at the funerals of the ethnic neighbors, which is a major social event for the peoples of Loropéni. Fifty-seven percent (20) of the sample said they attend Lobi funerals, and most of those (47%, 16 of the sample) use Lobiri during the event. Let us note once more that the 47% who said they use Lobiri at Lobi funerals closely matched to 50% figure obtained above for those in the community who speak Lobiri at FSI levels three and four, though here again an exact correspondence cannot be established.

Forty-nine percent (17) of the sample said they attend Jula funerals, and all of these used Jula during the event.

Fifty-four percent (19) of the interviewees said they attended Dogo funerals. Among these, most speak Kaansa (34%, 12 of the sample), while some speak Dogose and others use both Dogose and Kaansa. Here again, we do not see people resorting to their common trade language, Jula, to communicate within the ethnic family. Rather, they have found that they can communicate sufficiently with each other using their own dialects.

While it is easy to find individuals in the Kaan community who have travelled to many different towns and cities in the larger region, there are a few places where almost all of the Kaan have travelled: Gaoua, the provincial capital 60 kilometers away via Kampti, and south to Côte d'Ivoire. In the Kaan sample, 49% (17) use Jula exclusively when in Gaoua, whereas six use Jula and either French or Lobiri.

When travelling in Côte d'Ivoire, the Kaan rely on Jula (49%, 17), though many have learned Ivorian or coastal languages as well, such as Kulango (9),[55] Abron, Agni, and Ashanti (two for each). Those Kaan with Ivorian languages in their repertoire learned them during extended stays in Côte d'Ivoire, either as children with their parents, or as young adults working on plantations or doing other forms of manual labor.

Interethnic contact. Thirty-seven percent (13) of the sample said they sometimes work with Lobi acquaintances, but only eight of these spoke in Lobiri when working together. Five people said they used Jula to communicate. Only four people said they worked with Jula acquaintances, and, of course, they used Jula to communicate.

When I asked about working with the Lobi and the Jula, I sometimes suggested appropriate group tasks, such as working together to prepare a field for planting for the men and preparing shay nut butter for the women. Concerning the Jula, one older man from Soronkina commented that the Jula are not farmers like the Kaan, and in another village, my survey assistant and translator commented on this question saying, "The Jula are lazy!", which in this context implied that because some of the Jula do not farm for a living, he felt this meant they were too lazy to do so. During the two years I spent in Burkina Faso and Loropéni, I heard other people comment that the Jula, being merchants, were not good at manual labor and were, therefore, thought of as lazy. This sentiment may also be fueled by a certain jealousy, because the Jula often control important economic links between rural peoples and the towns and cities.

---

[55]The Kulango people live near Bondoukou and Bouna in the northern Côte d'Ivoire, and there are historical and perhaps distant ethnic ties between them and the Kaan. Labouret (1931, 1958), Parenko and Hébert (1962), and Père (1982, to appear) elaborate on these ties.

Sixty-nine percent (24) of the sample said it was permissible for their young men to marry women who only speak Lobiri. It is interesting that of the nine people who disapproved, seven were women. This may be an important difference in opinion between men and women, and is worth exploring in further research. Four men and one woman commented that once a Kaan married a Lobi woman, the wife would learn Kaansa. However, a young woman from Obiré, who did not approve, said, "We would have problems [with that]."

Fewer people, about half the sample (54%, 19), approved of marrying Jula women. Many who did not approve were adamant, saying, "It's not good" or "The Jula do not accept that." One older man from Obiré said, "The Lobi and the Kaan, that's OK. But a Kaan man with a Jula woman, that I've never come across." People were much more positive regarding intermarriage with Dogo women. Eighty-nine percent (31) of the subjects approved of this, most without any comment. An adult woman from Kassita even said, "It's OK if they don't understand each other."

While one can safely assume that, barring special domain or proficiency constraints, the Kaan will speak Lobiri to a Lobi and Jula to a Jula, it was not clear to me if there were situations where the Kaan might use Lobiri with a Jula, for example, or with a Dogo, or use Jula with another Kaan. To probe the logical possibilities of which second language could be used with each ethnic neighbor, I asked the interviewees if they ever had an occasion to speak Lobiri or Jula to people other than the Lobi or the Jula. The results of these questions are presented in the matrix in (64).

(64) Crossethnic language use

Speak:	With someone who is a:			
	Lobi	Jula	Dogo	Kaan
Jula	26 (74%)	—	21 (60%)	16 (46%)
Lobiri	—	8	4	7

This shows dramatically how little Lobiri is used as a language of wider communication, and how much more often Jula is used to speak with other ethnic groups and even with other Kaan in the appropriate situation (such as in mixed groups). One-half to two-thirds of the sample could think of times when they had used Jula with non-Julas, whereas less than one-quarter could think of times they had used Lobiri with non-Lobis.

Some observations and comments which illuminate some of the responses tabulated in (64) follow.

While the survey group was interviewing an adult woman from Kassita, a Lobi man walked by and greeted us in Lobiri. Several in our group replied to his greeting, including the woman I was speaking with. This woman, however, responded in Jula, to which the Lobi replied in Lobiri again. What made this exchange interesting is that soon afterwards, this woman said she never spoke Jula to a Lobi! This is a vivid illustration that people aren't always aware of their language use, especially with highly formulaic utterances such as greetings.

A young man from Kérié said, "There are many Jula who understand Lobiri." Another young man from Kassita said he had spoken Lobiri to a Jula when working together with him in a group to prepare a field. Apparently, there are several Jula who have grown up in Loropéni and, therefore, have learned Lobiri through frequent contact. I observed a few occasions where Jula residents made the effort to speak in Lobiri to Lobi residents. One explanation may be that since the Lobi are in the majority in this region, and they tend to be individualistic and dominant, many Jula learn Lobiri, even though most of the Lobi speak Jula.

A young man from Kassita said he would speak Jula "with a Dogo who lives far from here; he's not going to understand Kaansa." This same man as well as an adult woman from Sandi said they would speak in Jula to the few Kaan who had become Muslim and who lived with the Jula in the center of Loropéni. An older man from Obiré said he would use Jula or Lobiri with Dogo or Kaan interlocutors only if he was in a group with Jula or Lobi participants.

We have seen that only a minority in the sample have had opportunities to work with the Lobi, and not all of those speak Lobiri with them; some choose to speak Jula. Very few ever work with the Jula. While two-thirds of the sample approve of Kaan men marrying Lobi women, several expressed the expectation that the Lobi woman would learn Kaansa. Fewer individuals, about half of the sample, approved of marrying Jula women. There were several negative comments about this possibility. By contrast almost everyone approved of intermarriage with Dogo women and seemed to think there would be no language barrier. The way the sample used Jula and Lobiri across ethnic lines demonstrates clearly how Jula is a language of wider communication, whereas Lobiri is seldom used in the same way.

A summary of language use in the selected domains of this study shows that Jula and French are by far the preferred languages in *official* settings. The only exceptions to this occur when the official is a Lobi or a Kaan, but even with these individuals, many Kaan use Jula or French. Some commented that they would use Kaansa or Lobiri in a personal conversation, but that if they were dealing with official business, especially in the presence of people of other ethnic origin, they would switch to Jula or French.

In the *market*, language use is largely determined by the ethnic origin of the merchants, but Jula is also used with the Lobi at times. Kaansa is limited to transactions with other Kaan. Most of the time, the Jula and Lobi merchants do not accommodate to Kaansa, rather, the Kaan use the different codes in their repertoire to establish communication and transact business. The Kaan do most of the accommodating. However, most find it easiest to count money in their own language.

In casual conversations, such as at cabarets near the market, about half the sample normally conversed with other Kaan in Kaansa, and about one-quarter would also converse in Jula or Lobiri. When *greeting friends* in passing, most (61%) accommodate to Lobiri for Lobi friends, and just about all of them will greet Jula acquaintances in Jula. However, there is little accommodation for Dogo friends. For *greeting strangers* of unknown ethnic origin, the Kaan rely on Jula. When talking in mixed groups, half of the sample would accommodate to the Lobi, but two-thirds would accommodate to the Jula, and again we see that few (about one-quarter) would switch languages to accommodate Dogo participants.

Similar patterns emerge in language use at *funerals*. Most of those who attend Lobi or Jula funerals speak those languages well, so it is normal that they would accommodate in those settings.

About one-half of the sample rely exclusively on Jula when they *travel* to Gaoua or Côte d'Ivoire. Others use French, Lobiri, or Ivorian languages to supplement their use of Jula where appropriate.

With regard to *interethnic contact*, only about a third of the sample had opportunities to work with Lobi acquaintances, and not all of them (just one-quarter of the sample) use Lobiri when they do so. Even fewer work with Jula friends, but Jula is the language of interaction for all of them. The issue of intermarriage revealed that there is a much greater permissiveness for Kaan men to marry Lobi women than Jula women, and while several people expressed the expectation that a Lobi wife would learn and accommodate to her husband's language, few expressed that sentiment for Jula wives. In fact, even though half the sample approved of the idea of taking a Jula wife, several people made strong negative remarks about the idea. For intermarriage with the Dogo, a large majority approved and felt there would be no trouble with communication. A short study of crossethnic use of Lobiri and Jula confirmed that Jula is used much more often as a language of wider communication than Lobiri whose use seems to be limited to direct contact with the Lobi.

There seems to be a striking absence of any well-defined diglossia in the data presented in this chapter. Even though we might say that French functions as the "high" language, yet so few of the Kaan speak French, and really it is little used outside of the school and the government offices in Loropéni, that it functions primarily as a "dummy high" (Platt 1977, Fasold 1984). There are some similarities to Mkilifi's triglossia (1978), or "double overlapping diglossia" (Fasold 1984:45) in Tanzania, but there are very important differences as well. Jula as the trade language does not share the same status as Swahili, for it does not yet have a widely recognized standard written form nor any place in the school curriculum.

Instead of well-defined diglossia, we see a pattern of habitual, though not always strict, accommodation toward Lobiri and Jula. This accommodation pattern can be symbolized by the diagram in (65).

(65) Pattern of linguistic accommodation among the Kaan in Loropéni

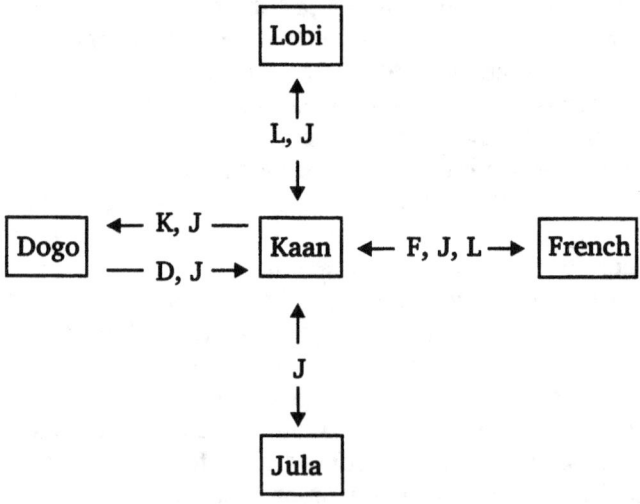

Since their community was the focus of this study, the Kaan are represented in the center of the diagram. The arrows show communication links and are labelled with the language(s) used by most of the sample according to their survey responses. When more than one language is used, they are listed in order of dominance from left to right. By dominance, I mean the language which is most appropriate according to the repertoire of each individual. So, in speaking to the Lobi, for example, it is best to use Lobiri if the individual has enough proficiency and if the domain allows it. The next best choice is Jula.

The box labelled "French" represents not just any French nationals with whom the Kaan may have contact, but anyone, black or white, whose primary mode of communication is in French. People such as government officials, school officials, development workers, anthropologists, missionaries, and tourists are included in this category.

Note that communication between the Dogo and the Kaan is the only case of nonreciprocal language use. Also note that I have not represented individual cases of bilingualism on the part of the Lobi or Jula, that is, when Lobi or Jula residents converse in Kaansa to the Kaan. While such situations do occur, they are rare enough to be exceptions rather than the rule.

From the survey results, it seems safe to say that Jula is the dominant language in Loropéni. While it is true that the Lobi are more numerous and enjoy ethnic dominance, and that some life-long Jula residents speak Lobiri, it is also true that official events in Loropéni always have a simultaneous Jula translation but not always a Lobiri translation. It is also true that one-third to one-half of the Kaan I surveyed use Jula to speak with the Lobi depending on the situation and the complexity of the discourse, while few have ever used Lobiri with Jula speakers. It is also true that in a mixed group many Kaan said they would switch to Jula to include Jula participants, but said they would only greet Lobi participants in Lobiri then continue to talk in Kaansa. It is also true that, in spite of community-wide proficiency in Jula, many Kaan said they desired to learn more, whereas proficiency in Lobiri is less widespread, and people are less interested in learning more. All this leads me to conclude that Jula is dominant in social and economic arenas, whereas Lobiri is an important ethnic language due to the numerical advantage of the Lobi in the region.

I found it interesting how widespread was the report that Kaan people normally speak in Kaansa to the Dogo. When I visited several Dogo villages for the language attitude survey, I observed that the two Kaan language assistants who accompanied me at different times used more Jula than Kaansa. When gathering texts with Philippe Farma in Béguélé, it was obvious that the Dogo elder I interviewed felt much more comfortable talking with Philippe in Jula than in Dogose. Since I was trying to record Dogose texts, Philippe kept gently reminding the elder to speak in Dogose when he lapsed frequently into Jula to get his point across. Philippe himself ended up asking all of the interview questions in Jula.

Similarly, Jean-Baptiste Suwa accompanied me on the survey trips to Dogo villages, and he seemed to prefer talking in Jula, especially when it was important to communicate carefully and effectively. He would often explain my questions (asked originally in Kaansa) in Jula to make sure they were understood well.

The headmaster of the school in Loropéni is a Dogo from Koro. He explained how the Kaan and Dogo communicate by saying that even though they understand each other sometimes, they find it easier to speak in Jula.

It seems then that many Kaan hold the ideal that they and the Dogo should understand each other, but the observed reality is that they understand each other better in Jula. Perhaps the best interpretation of the majority reports of speaking Kaansa with the Dogo is that those with frequent contact have gained a passive understanding of Dogose, and likewise for the Dogo who live near the Kaan. Incidences of successful communication in the two dialects, along with positive attitudes toward shared ethnic identity and contact, have given many Kaan the impression that the two dialects should be completely intelligible.

8
Integration of the Research

This chapter attempts to integrate the findings from the language attitude (chapter 6) and language proficiency and use (chapter 7) surveys with the historical and linguistic background data presented in chapters 2–4. The relationship between measures of linguistic similarity and social attitudes will be explored. Models developed by Mackey, Batiana, Cooper, and Lewis will be employed to gain a broader perspective and deeper understanding of the dynamic multilingualism of the Kaan people. Finally, an attempt will be made to integrate the language attitude and proficiency and use data into the framework of Gumperz' notion of communicative economy.

Dialect and attitude issues

What relation does dialectal variation have with intelligibility between dialects and attitudes toward those dialects? If related, what dimensions of attitude correspond best with intelligibility and lexical similarity? What does this interplay of variation, intelligibility, and attitudes tell us about dialect boundaries, language classification, and the language/dialect distinction? By integrating the research presented in the preceding chapters we will attempt to answer these questions.

Let us now compare the research into the lexical similarity and intelligibility of the four dialects done by Solomiac (1983), presented in chapter 3, with the results of the language attitude survey reported in chapter 6. In the tables and charts to follow, LEXSIM is Solomiac's lexical similarity figure, which is actually a shared cognate percentage between the different dialects. INTELL is the adjusted intelligibility score from Solomiac's survey. The other statistics in the tables are the results of the attitude study presented by dimension.[56] All the scores have been transformed to the same scale with the low point at 0.00 and the high point at 1.00. Solomiac's intelligibility scores were incomplete, so the lack of a score is marked in the table by a line and on the chart by a large empty circle.

Kaansa. Example (66) displays the integration of lexical similarity, intelligibility, and attitude scores for Kaansa. Note from the table and chart that the Kpatogo[57] had the highest shared cognate and intelligibility scores of the three dialects related to Kaansa, as well as the highest evaluation of language awareness and personal character of the Kaan. Yet, they had the lowest evaluation of shared identity and contact. Note also that the Dogo and the Khi are remarkably similar in all of their scores.

(66) Integration of scores for Kaansa

Lg/Group	LEXSIM	INTELL	Attitudes			
			EI	EC	LA	PC
Kaan	1.00	1.00	0.98	0.92	0.98	0.86
Kpatogo	0.81	0.90	0.51	0.72	0.98	0.82
Dogo	0.68	0.79	0.67	0.87	0.88	0.80
Khi	0.71	0.76	0.69	0.85	0.83	0.75

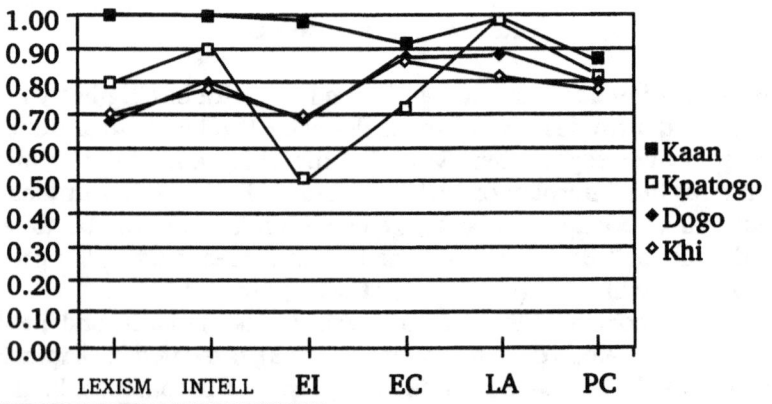

---

[56]EI = Ethnic Identity, EC = Ethnic Contact, LA = Language Awareness, and PC = Personal Character.

[57]In the discussion that follows, whenever I refer to the attitudes of the Kpatogo, Dogo, Kaan, or Khi, I refer to those expressed by the samples of those communities in this study. An accurate representation of group attitudes requires larger, more representative samples.

Dialect and attitude issues

Kpatogoso. Example (67) displays the integration of lexical similarity, intelligibility, and attitude scores for Kpatogoso. Solomiac did not test the intelligibility of Kpatogoso among the other dialects.

(67) Integration of scores for Kpatogoso

			Attitudes			
Lg/Group	LEXSIM	INTELL	EI	EC	LA	PC
Kaan	0.81	—	0.77	0.72	0.77	0.73
Kpatogo	1.00	1.00	0.95	0.90	0.99	0.85
Dogo	0.69	—	0.53	0.88	0.72	0.79
Khi	0.72	—	0.56	0.68	0.75	0.65

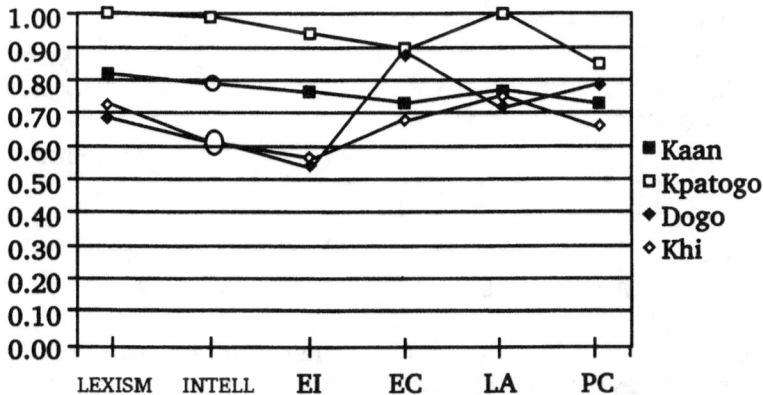

In spite of a strongly positive attitude about frequent contact with the Kpatogo, the Dogo are only moderately aware of Kpatogoso and just slightly positive about shared ethnic identity. Their low ethnic identity score is matched by the Khi, who also share with the Dogo an equal percentage of cognates with Kpatogoso.

The Kaan, who share more cognates with Kpatogoso than the other dialects, are similar to the Khi in their attitudes about contact and language awareness, yet show a more positive attitude toward shared ethnic identity than the Khi or the Dogo.

Dogose. Example (68) displays the integration of lexical similarity, intelligibility, and attitude scores for Dogose. Solomiac did not gather data on the intelligibility of Dogose to the Kaan.

(68) Integration of scores for Dogose

Lg/Group	LEXSIM	INTELL	Attitudes			
			EI	EC	LA	PC
Kaan	0.68	—	0.68	0.73	0.94	0.76
Kpatogo	0.69	0.95	0.40	0.78	0.95	0.72
Dogo	1.00	1.00	0.97	0.90	0.95	0.85
Khi	0.82	0.99	0.83	0.79	1.00	0.81

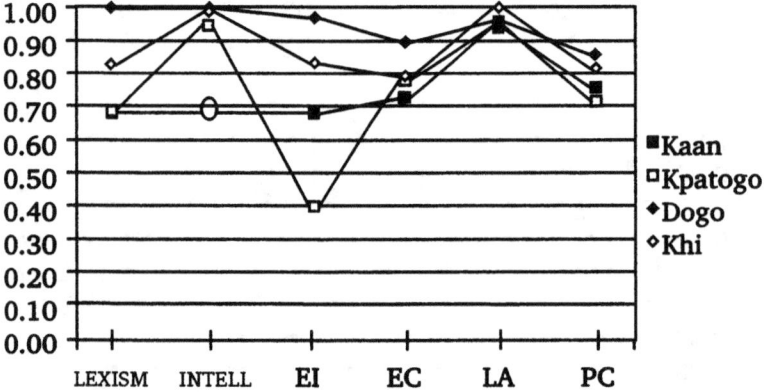

What is striking here is the high intelligibility scores and language awareness assessments of the Khi and Kpatogo, yet the low, slightly negative attitudes toward shared ethnic identity that the Kpatogo hold toward the Dogo. The Khi, however, show much more positive attitudes toward shared identity with the Dogo. The Kaan also show high language awareness yet hold a moderate view of shared identity with the Dogo. This seems to indicate on the surface that high intelligibility, similarity, or general language awareness does not entail positive attitudes of shared identity.

The Khi, with eighty percent shared cognates, and the Kpatogo, with seventy percent shared cognates, show near complete understanding of Dogose.

Khisa. Example (69) displays the integration of lexical similarity, intelligibility, and attitude scores for Khisa. Here again, Solomiac did not test the intelligibility of the Khisa among the Kaan nor the Kpatogo.

Dialect and attitude issues

(69) Integration of scores for Khisa

Lg/Group	LEXSIM	INTELL	Attitudes			
			EI	EC	LA	PC
Kaan	0.71	—	0.72	0.70	0.86	0.78
Kpatogo	0.72	—	0.44	0.75	0.85	0.86
Dogo	0.82	0.77	0.89	0.78	0.83	0.88
Khi	1.00	1.00	0.98	0.88	0.96	0.93

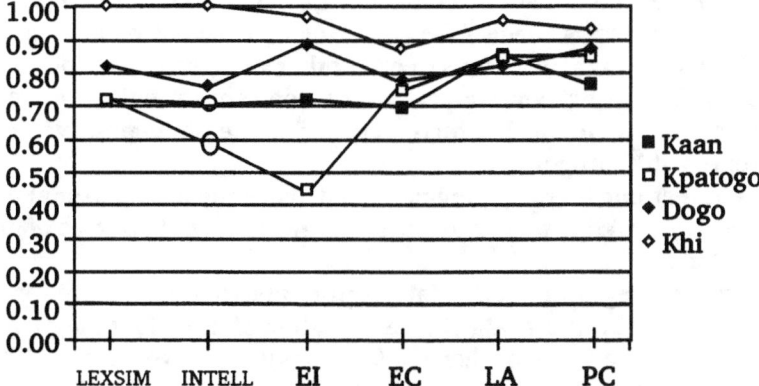

The Dogo, who share about eighty percent cognates with Khisa show much less comprehension of Khisa than the Khi did of Dogose. This is clear evidence of non-reciprocal intelligibility between these two groups. In fact, when we compare the integrated scores of the Dogo and Khi for Dogose and Khisa, we see that the only areas where they really seem to differ are in intelligibility and language awareness.

It is also interesting to note the low ethnic identity rating the Kpatogo gave the Khi, in spite of rating ethnic contact, language awareness, and personal character pretty much the same as the Dogo and the Kaan did.

Patterns. The pattern that becomes evident immediately in these integrated scores is the close relationship between intelligibility scores and judgments of language awareness. When converted to ranks,[58] these scores show a high correlation coefficient[59] and, thus, a marked relationship. This is not really surprising since the language awareness judgments are responses to

---

[58]The attitude survey scores are consistently treated as ranks in this research.
[59]*rho* = .742, significant at $p < .05$.

questions about perceived intelligibility (the subdimension Understanding) as well as speaking ability and familiarity with the dialect.

Another pattern that is immediately evident is that judgments of shared ethnicity (EI) seem to be unrelated to the other language attitude dimensions or to lexical similarity or intelligibility. For example, the Kpatogo show consistently low ethnic identity scores, regardless of similarity of dialects or other measures. We may conclude, then, that if there is any attitude of distinctness or separation between these four groups, it is most evident in their attitudes toward shared ethnic identity.

In most cases, attitudes toward language awareness are more positive than attitudes toward ethnic contact. This indicates that these groups do not need to perceive themselves as having extensive, frequent contact in order to gain a high awareness of each other's language varieties. A notable exception to this, however, is that the Dogo are strongly positive about their contact with the Kpatogo, but are moderately positive in their awareness of Kpatogoso.

Like the ethnic identity judgments, attitudes towards personal character seem unrelated to other attitudes assessed here, or to degree of linguistic similarity.

From the integration of the data as presented above, can we formulate an hypothesis about the relative classification of these four language varieties? Should we think of them as four languages, two, or one? The fact that each group has a distinct name which sets off its variety from the others would favor a classification of four languages. But the close similarity of form and comprehension between Khisa and Dogose, as well as between Kaansa and Kpatogoso would favor a classification of two languages with two dialects each. The lack of a single language name which encompasses all four varieties would lead us away from classifying these as one language, yet the responses and comments to question D1-2 about judging the dialects as the same language show a real sense of shared linguistic ties among the four groups, even though there was no consensus about speaking the same language. The comments people made about this question reveal two themes: some said "X dialect is the same language, but there are differences"; others said "X dialect is not the same language, but we can understand each other." What do we make of this ambivalence?

We can conclude from these data that the Dogo and the Khi are very close to each other and that Dogose dominates Khisa in several ways. First, their high lexical similarity (82%) does not correspond to reciprocal intelligibility. Dogose is highly intelligible to the Khi (99%), but Khisa is much less intelligible to the Dogo (77%). Correspondingly, the Dogo are moderately positive about their awareness of Khisa, while the Khi are strongly positive about their awareness of Dogose. Dogose then dominates Khisa in intelligibility and in attitudes toward language awareness. Another interesting manifestation of this dominance is found in their attitudes toward shared ethnic identity. The Dogo are more positive about sharing identity with the Khi than the Khi are about sharing identity with the Dogo. One might characterize the Dogo attitude as: "We sort of understand them, and we sort of know about their dialect, but they really are the same as us," whereas the attitude of the Khi toward the Dogo might be: "We understand them well, we know all about their dialect, but we're a little different from them." Perhaps the area where the similarities between the Dogo and the Khi shine through is in their judgments of the Kpatogo and Kaan. Their judgments of the Kaan are almost identical, as are their measurements of lexical similarity and intelligibility in relation to Kaansa. For Kpatogoso, they are virtually identical in measurements of lexical similarity and in judgments of ethnic identity and language awareness. However, the Dogo differ from the Khi in their judgments of ethnic contact and personal character of the Kpatogo.

Describing the relationship between Kaansa and Kpatogoso is more difficult. Since we lack complete intelligibility data for Kpatogoso, we must rely on the judgments of language awareness, which, as we have seen for the comparative data available, correlated closely with intelligibility scores. Thus, we see that both the Kaan and Kpatogo hold identical, strongly positive attitudes about language awareness toward Kaansa, but are distinctly different toward Kpatogoso, where the Kaan are moderately positive instead. The greatest difference between these two groups is how they view shared ethnic identity. The Kaan are moderately positive in this regard, but the Kpatogo are neutral, which is much lower than the Kaan rating. And while the Kaan also judge the Dogo and Khi moderately positively for shared identity, the Kpatogo are neutral to slightly negative towards them. The Kpatogo seem to have a deep attitude of separation and distinctness from the other three communities, at least with regard to shared ethnicity.

However, the Kaan and Kpatogo do share similar dialect features and attitudes which allow us to class them together, and as with the Dogo and Khi, the larger of the two groups may be seen as dominant in some sense (language awareness, sense of shared identity). Yet, the Kaan and Kpatogo do not share similar attitudes toward the other two groups; there is a greater attitudinal gulf between them than between the Dogo and Khi.

We have seen very little evidence of any categorical relationship between different dimensions of social attitudes and level of intelligibility. When groups are at the intelligibility threshold,[60] their social attitudes toward each other vary greatly, for example, from slightly negative to strongly positive concerning shared ethnic identity. This demonstrates how important it is to investigate language attitudes when dialects co-exist at this threshold level. One cannot properly group threshold dialects based on intelligibility data alone; their attitudes toward each other must be taken into account.

There is sufficient evidence in the data to conclude that Dogose and Kaansa are the prestige dialects. They were the most widely recognized and understood dialects, people had the most consistent frequent contact with them, and they seemed to be psychological/attitudinal reference points. However, there is a marked lack of any particular, specific indicators of prestige such as the will to identify ethnically with these two dialects (indeed, the will seems to be in the opposite direction, to separate one's group as ethnically distinct from these two), or higher attributed social status or personal character evaluations to speakers of Kaansa and Dogose. So at best we may say that Dogose and Kaansa hold prestige through wider language awareness and, perhaps, by virtue of their larger communities.

Bilingualism and language use issues

Mackey's bilingualism model

Bilingualism in the Kaan community can be described using Mackey's (1968) model. Though this model is intended for the description of bilingualism in an individual, it is also useful for describing bilingualism as a property of a community.

There is a high DEGREE of bilingual proficiency in Jula in the community (all of the sample knew some Jula; 80% spoke it at level two-plus or above), and a lesser degree of proficiency in Lobiri (66% of the sample knew some Lobiri; most spoke it no better than at levels two-plus to three-plus). This was established by the can-do rating of Jula proficiency and the estimate-by-comparison rating of Lobiri proficiency.

All of the domains surveyed and presented in chapter 7 fall into this category of external FUNCTION, which Mackey describes as one which is "determined by the number of areas of contact, and by the variation of each in duration, frequency, and pressure" (1968:557). We saw in chapter 7 that Jula dominated these domains, but was not exclusive except when a particular domain was controlled exclusively by ethnic Jula (such as the sale of beef in the market). Generally, the Kaan would accommodate to the language of

---

[60]At the intelligibility threshold, adjusted scores fall between 75 and 85 (Casad 1974:46).

the interlocutor and would not insist on speaking Kaansa unless they had no other means of communication or when on home turf, such as in conversation with other Kaan or in the case of interethnic marriage, where a Kaan man would insist that a Lobi wife learn and use Kaansa at home.

Mackey mentions "pressure" as a factor in determining the type of bilingualism one finds in a community. By this he meant external forces which encourage the use of one language over another. In the Kaan community, there is a great deal of economic pressure to know Jula, by virtue of its role as the regional trade language, and proficiency in Jula allows the speaker not only to trade locally with other ethnic groups, but it also provides a lingua franca for extensive travel outside the immediate region.

In addition, there is a certain political and administrative pressure to learn at least elementary French because this is the official language of the country and also a world language. It holds some prestige, yet is not really practical for local usage. Only approximately twenty-nine percent of the Kaan know any amount of French, and most of the things they can do in French locally, they can accomplish more efficiently in Jula or Lobiri.

Historical pressure intersects with economic and demographic pressure, and these together largely account for the bilingualism in Lobiri and Jula in the Kaan community. The early influx of the Lobi into Kaan territory, and their subsequent dominance by aggression and later by sheer force of numbers, has made it necessary for many Kaan to learn Lobiri. The economic pressure brought about by Jula control of trade was combined with the expansion of the Wattara Jula of Kong, and later, the raids of the army of Samori at the end of the last century. Though the Kaan were never subdued by the Jula in the same way as the Dogo and Khi, they felt the effects of the Jula control of the region surrounding them.

Finally, for the Kaan Christians, there is religious pressure to learn Lobiri, because the church in Loropéni is dominated by the Lobi. Sermons are habitually in Lobiri, and the Scriptures used are a Lobiri translation of the New Testament. In addition, the Kaan pastoral trainees are trained at a mission-run Bible school taught primarily in Lobiri.

The language proficiency and use survey did not systematically explore any of what Mackey calls internal functions, that is, internal speech and thought, various forms of mental and spiritual activity such as dreaming, counting, praying, reckoning, cursing, and some forms of magic or traditional religion. The only internal function dealt with in chapter 7 is counting money, and for that activity, the Kaan overwhelmingly preferred to use Kaansa, even with large and complex sums.

ALTERNATION of two codes was explored in this survey in relation to the interlocutors in an encounter. While most of the Kaan interviewed said they would speak to a Jula in Jula without alternation, there was a variety of interesting responses and comments for when people spoke with Lobi or Dogo acquaintances. Some would greet a Lobi in Lobiri and then converse in Jula. Others would choose Lobiri or Jula depending on how well they knew the Lobi interlocutor. For conversation with the Dogo, most Kaan said they could speak in Kaansa. Observations of such encounters, however, revealed that people use both Kaansa and Jula.

Another interesting situation of alternation occurred when a small group of Kaan switched to Lobiri or Jula for the whole conversation when they were joined by a Lobi or Jula acquaintance. A few people said they would only switch languages to greet, but continue the conversation in Kaansa.

Finally, note here the observation that in the Official domain, one hears frequent code-mixing and borrowing of French into Jula or Lobiri.

The use of features of one language while speaking another, while not a focus of this research, would no doubt provide some fascinating data for future work. How do the Kaan trilinguals keep their language repertoire sorted out? How does the mother tongue, Kaansa, interfere with the form of the Lobiri or Jula one is speaking? In situations like those described at the end of chapter 7, where the Kaan participants may switch between four languages in a matter of minutes, one wonders how the structures of the languages might interfere with each other when used in rapid succession. These and other issues of interference in this multilingual setting are worth further study.

Urban and rural models of language use in Burkina Faso

Batiana's (1985:16) model of language use in urban settings in Burkina Faso was presented in chapter 3. It is reproduced in (70) for ease of reference.

(70) Urban multilingualism in Burkina Faso

	Language		
Place	Local vehicular language (Moore/Jula)	Official vehicular language (French)	Mother tongue (Lyele)
Market	+	+	−
Work	−	+	−
Home	−	−	+

Though simplified, this model fits the broad patterns of language use in the urban areas of Burkina Faso, such as Ouagadougou, Koudougou, and Bobo Dioulasso. Outside of the cities, however, language use may become more complex, as it does in Loropéni. Using the same style of table, the broad patterns of language choice found among the Kaan in Loropéni is displayed in (71) as they were presented in chapter 7.

One difference between the model presented in (71) and Batiana's in (70) is that French plays less of a role in everyday life in the rural setting than in urban life, and the role that it does play is less exclusive: in official domains one is just as likely to hear Jula used as French. French is not used much in the marketplace, whereas the mother tongue is often used as much as or more than the regional trade language. Another difference is the addition of a dominant ethnic language (DEL = Lobiri) into the model. This would be necessary for any community with minority and majority ethnic communities living in close contact who both must use a lingua franca different from either of their own languages. A final difference is the more frequent use of the mother tongue, not just in the market and at home, but in casual friendships with residents, even occasionally with long-time residents of the dominant groups.

(71) Rural multilingualism in Loropéni

Domain	Official language (French)	Local vehicular language (Jula)	Dominant ethnic language (Lobiri)	Mother tongue (Kaansa)
Official	+	+	−	−
Travel	+	+	+	−
Interethnic contact	−	+	+	−
Market	−	+	+	+
Friendship	−	+	+	+
Home	−	−	−	+

Pervasiveness, dominance, and the lingua franca

Perhaps by reflecting on the criteria for evaluating lingua francas presented in chapter 2, we may enlighten our discussion of the proposed dominance of Jula in Loropéni. Cooper's (1982b) scaled criterion variables for evaluating the pervasiveness of language behavior were (1) awareness (knowledge of the innovation, i.e., Jula or Lobiri as a second language), (2) evaluation (attitude toward the personal usefulness of the innovation), (3) proficiency (appropriate use of the innovation), and (4) usage (frequency and purpose of use).

We have already discussed at length the proficiency and usage aspects of this issue. Proficiency for Jula is clearly higher and more pervasive in the community than proficiency in Lobiri. For the variable of usage, we saw in the study of selected domains that Jula is used in most domains in one way or another, as well as in crossethnic situations, while Lobiri was limited to direct contact with the Lobi.

The awareness and evaluation of Lobiri and Jula in the Kaan community was assessed by the attitude survey presented in chapter 6. Awareness was assessed by the Language Awareness (LA) attitude dimension questions, and the evaluation of the two languages was assessed by the Ethnic Identity (EI), Ethnic Contact (EC), and Personal Character (PC) attitude dimensions. The results of the these judgments of Jula and Lobiri from the Kaan community are reproduced in (72).

(72) Kaan awareness and evaluation judgments of Lobiri and Jula

	EI	EC	LA	PC
Jula	0.46	0.59	0.99	0.70
Lobiri	0.44	0.55	0.89	0.66

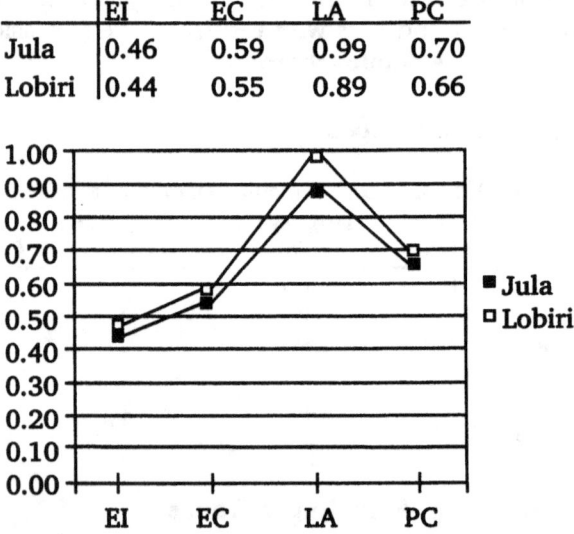

The table and chart show that the Kaan are highly aware of both languages, yet differ in this attitude dimension.[61] This Language Awareness dimension, however, seems to be the only real difference in the way the Kaan view the two languages. Their evaluations of Jula and Lobiri in terms of ethnic identity, ethnic contact, and personal character hardly differ at all. They are quite neutral about sharing ethnic identity and the

[61]This difference, however, does not attain the appropriate level of significance as measured by the Wilcoxon t test for dependent samples.

nature and frequency of contact together. Also, they are just slightly positive about the personal character of the Lobi and the Jula.

What does this tell us about the pervasiveness of Lobiri and Jula in the Kaan community? Simply that high awareness, frequent usage, relatively high proficiency are not accompanied here by evaluations that would indicate any kind of shift to either language at present. Use of these two languages seems to be driven by the practical demands of living side-by-side in Loropéni, and in the case of Jula, by the communication needs of traveling outside the region.

Since the issue of pervasiveness did not distinguish Lobiri from Jula as a lingua franca for the Kaan community, let us now consider Scotton's (1982) values for lingua francas and see how they apply to this situation. She distinguishes between secondary official languages or non-official lingua francas and minor, locally-based lingua francas, the main distinction between them being that locally-based lingua francas are tied to a specific ethnic group, and their use often indicates a relation of dominance or authority (i.e., dominated or subordinate groups use this language when speaking with the dominant or superordinate group). In contrast to this, non-official lingua francas are not necessarily ethnically-based and do not automatically indicate an authority relationship. In addition, this type of lingua franca allows for wide spatial mobility and does not identify the user as the member of a socioeconomic class, nor is it attached to educational achievement or formal speech events.

These distinctions are very helpful in illuminating the differences between Jula and Lobiri for the Kaan. Lobiri certainly holds an element of ethnicity that Jula does not: witness the finding that the Kaan reported using Lobiri primarily and nearly exclusively with the Lobi, whereas they used Jula not just with Jula, but also with the Lobi, the Dogo, and with government officials in official domains. In addition, Lobiri does carry a certain value of dominance or authority. Though this was not mentioned in chapter 7, my observations show that most often the Lobi of Loropéni will address a Kaan in Lobiri, rather than Jula. We did see in chapter 7 that the Kaan will accommodate to the Lobi by greeting and conversing in Lobiri when the individual has the necessary proficiency to do so. Even the fact that some Kaan reported speaking Jula to the Lobi shows that they do not expect the Lobi to know or speak Kaansa, and must, therefore, switch languages to accommodate to them. In addition, the cases of Jula residents speaking Lobiri mentioned in chapter 7 are best explained by Scotton's distinction between lingua francas. The local, ethnic dominance of the Lobi impels those of any ethnic origin who speak Lobiri to use it in some situations.

Types of bilingual communities

Lewis (1985) set out to establish a typology of bilingual communities in order to facilitate comparison and thus generate hypotheses about the interaction of a community's social structure and setting with its linguistic repertoire. Unfortunately, Lewis does not consider sub-Saharan African communities in this proposed typology, but draws examples from Europe, North America, and the Soviet Union, with an occasional reference to South Africa. In spite of the fact that a vast, populous area where multilingual communities are quite common is left out of the typology, some of the analysis of variables affecting community bilingualism may be helpful for understanding the research presented in the previous chapters.

The four groups studied here fit best into Lewis' category of stable communities, which can be identified in terms of geographic/demographic stability and linguistic stability. The Kaan and Dogo are geographically and demographically stable; the Kpatogo have geographic but not demographic stability (i.e., the population seems to be diminishing, primarily through emigration), and the same is probably true of the Khi. In addition, the Khi probably don't have linguistic stability, as they seem to be in the throes of a language shift.

Isolation, as one aspect of stability, is shared by all four groups. They also have a kind of social boundedness (i.e., the Kaan vis-à-vis the Lobi, and the Kpatogo vis-à-vis everyone else), and yet significant numbers of people from all four groups travel regularly and do not shun the concomitant interethnic contact. Even in their geographical isolation they regularly encounter other local ethnic groups at regional markets.

Lewis states that in stable communities, bilingualism is found mostly along the periphery, among those with external contact (1985:55). Among the Kaan, we see a stable, isolated community with historical ties to the land ("indigenousness" Lewis calls it) and for whom language is closely tied to ethnic identity. According to Lewis' model, these factors should produce limited, peripheral bilingualism, and yet, in this research we see a community saturated with bilingualism.

Part of the problem of applying Lewis' typology to these communities is the lack of any definition which takes into account West African types of isolation and stability. While it is true that the Kaan, Dogo, Kpatogo, and Khi lack easy access to major population centers, they do not lack access to the dominant ethnic groups of the region. In addition, their stable communities are marked by the seasonal migration of a good portion of the young adult male population seeking work for cash in other countries or contiguous regions. Yet, they habitually return to the community to work their ancestral fields and perform the traditional rites which keep the community cohesive.

Other variables from Lewis that explain this apparent weakness in the model are differences in economic development between contact groups, the history of the settlement of a region, and the status relationships between groups in contact. The small Jula communities in West Africa, such as the one in Loropéni, influence and control important economic resources, including the trade of most goods that are not produced locally, as well as some that are (such as fresh beef). Their connections with other Jula communities throughout the region have made their language the lingua franca, and thus, made it essential for the survival of the indigenous groups in the region to learn Jula as a the language of trade and travel.

The mass immigration of the Lobi into traditional Kaan territory, and the conflict it engendered at the time, has also made proficiency in Lobiri important for the Kaan.

While the social status of the Kaan, Lobi, and Jula is much the same (peasant farmers), the Jula have a higher economic status by virtue of their greater involvement in trade. By weight of their numbers, the Lobi enjoy a greater influence on local affairs than the Kaan. Thus, control of important economic activity and demographic superiority form the socioeconomic underpinnings of the language dominance and patterns of accommodation found in Loropéni. These are also the key variables which have created the environment which has given birth to a type of bilingual community that does not fit easily into Lewis' model.

As Lafage (1979, 1986) points out, social stratification and the concomitant patterns of language use vary as much according to relevant cultural structures as socioeconomic realities. Thus, the models of bilingual communities developed for Europe, the Americas, and parts of Asia will not automatically fit the communities of sub-Saharan Africa, just as models and frameworks developed for East Africa will not always transfer to West Africa. It is hoped that the research presented in this book will serve as raw material for the eventual construction of adequate models of multilingual communities for rural West Africa.

The communicative economy

Using Gumperz' (1976) concept of communicative economy as it relates to language maintenance and shift, let us discuss two situations presented in this work: first, indications of a shift toward Jula among the Khi (and perhaps the Dogo), and second, the language repertoire of the Kaan and the Kpatogo.

The Khi and the Dogo

There are written historical records of two significant changes in the communicative economy of the Khi in the past 250 years. The first, in 1714, was the invasion of the Wattara from Kong, which submitted the Khi and the Dogo to this Jula dynasty. The slaves of the Wattara invaders may have become a separate subculture called the Bambadion, as discussed at the end of chapter 3. What this did to the communicative economy of the era was to strengthen and cement the role of Jula as an important regional lingua franca, making it essential to the Khi and Dogo for survival. It also may have weakened the economic position of the two communities because they were pillaged and made vassals to Kong. Certainly Samori's overthrow of the Wattara and subsequent plunder of Dogo and Khi territory at the close of the next century further impoverished them, hinging their survival more securely on the adoption of Jula for trade and contact. Yet, the event which seems to have set the Khi on the direct path toward language shift, and which distinguishes them in that respect from the Dogo, was their mass conversion to Islam in 1935 through the preaching of Yaya, a Guinean itinerant preacher. Thus, they were linked to the Jula not just through political and economic domination, but also through a common religion. Comments gathered while surveying the Khi indicate that not only do they use Jula in all domains,[62] but also that at least one village (Dabokiri) has switched entirely to Jula for intramural communication Coulibaly (1984:41).

In the light of these historical changes, let us examine the attitudes toward Jula held by the Khi and Dogo, as well as those held by the Kpatogo and Kaan. Example (73) displays a table and chart of the results of the attitude survey of these four groups as they were gathered in reference to Jula.

---

[62]Solomiac (1983) recorded comments that sometimes in Mangodara Khi children speak to their parents in Jula. During my survey visit, I collected similar comments from the people I interviewed. During the interviews themselves (which were almost all conducted in Jula), I noticed several participants and observers talking to each other in Jula or code-switching from Khisa to Jula.

The communicative economy 203

(73) Kaan, Kpatogo, Dogo, and Khi attitudes toward Jula

Group	EI	EC	LA	PC
Kaan	0.46	0.59	0.99	0.70
Kpatogo	0.29	0.80	0.98	0.68
Dogo	0.57	0.58	0.91	0.88
Khi	0.64	0.75	0.98	0.86

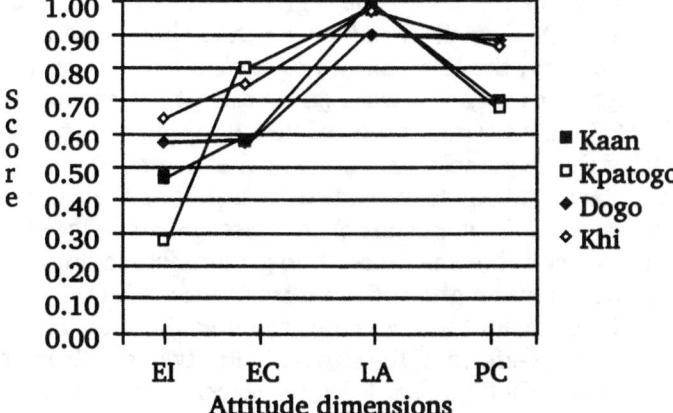

The data in (73) show that in many ways the Khi and the Dogo held more positive attitudes toward the Jula than the Kpatogo and Kaan. In the crucial area of ethnic identity, the Khi and Dogo were the most positive of the four about sharing ethnicity with the Jula, though granted their score fell only in the slightly positive range. This is contrasted, however, with neutral and moderately negative attitudes held in this dimension by the Kaan and Kpatogo. When collapsed together as one group, the Dogo and Khi have a combined ethnic identity score that is significantly higher than the combined score of the Kaan/Kpatogo group.[63]

The Khi and Dogo were also the most positive about the personal character of the Jula, scoring in the strongly positive range, while the Kaan and Kpatogo were just slightly positive in their evaluations. This is a significant difference between these two subgroups.[64] While all groups had extremely high awareness of the Jula language, the Khi (along with the Kpatogo) were among the groups with the highest regular contact with the Jula.

---

[63] Analysis of variance: $F = 16.61$, df = 1, 106, $p < .05$.
[64] Analysis of variance: $F = 7.82$, df = 1, 105, $p < .05$.

These attitudes are compatible with the observations and reports described above, and show that in both language use and language attitudes, the Dogo and especially the Khi are showing traits that accompany a language shift. The Dogo community is not as far along the path toward such a shift because it is a large, diffuse community where the religious ties to the Jula are not as complete as is the case with the Khi.

The Kaan and the Kpatogo

From their migration into the Gaoua region around 1650 (Parenko and Hébert 1962, Père 1982) until the advent of the Lobi toward the end of the eighteenth century, the Kaan and the Kpatogo lived in contact with each other,[65] fighting off (not always successfully) the attempts of the Wattara Jula of Kong to extend their influence to that corner of the region. Because of this regional dominance of the Jula of Kong, it is very likely that the Kaan and Kpatogo made Jula a part of their community speech repertoire from the very start of their settlement in the Gaoua region. However, the split between these two groups, which must have occurred in the early to mid-eighteenth century, seems to have isolated the Kpatogo from the constant harassment of the invading Lobi and Birifor, which had devastating effects on the size and vitality of the Kaan community. As the Lobi and the Kaan settled into peaceful (though not always friendly) coexistence at the beginning of the nineteenth century, the Lobi language became an important and necessary addition to the speech repertoire of the Kaan community. By contrast, however, it seems to have had little importance for the Kpatogo farther north, who by their own reports speak very little Lobiri and have little regular contact with the Lobi, in spite of their close proximity. Thus, the communicative economies of the Kaan and Kpatogo diverged with the immigration of the Lobi. In view of this history, let us examine the Kaan and Kpatogo attitudes toward Lobiri and Jula.

The tables and charts in (74) and (75) show vividly the differences between the attitudes of the Kaan and the Kpatogo toward these two languages of contact.

---

[65]Though not always peacefully. Parenko and Hébert (1962:428) mention a conflict between them which ended in the pillaging of Kpatogo villages by Bongo, a leader of the Khi allied with the Kaan.

The communicative economy 205

(74) Evaluations of Jula and Lobiri by the Kaan

	EI	EC	LA	PC
Jula	0.46	0.59	0.99	0.70
Lobiri	0.44	0.55	0.89	0.66

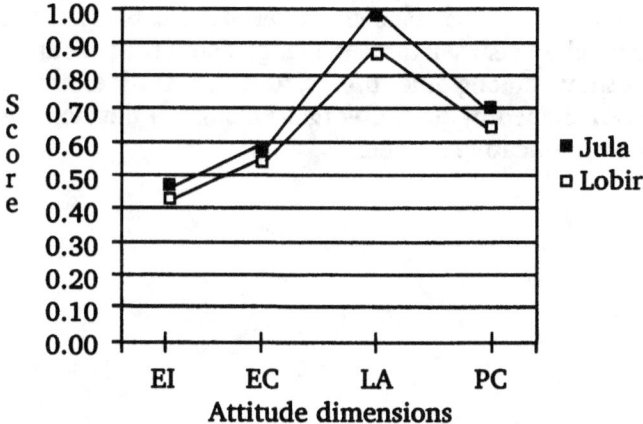

(75) Evaluations of Jula and Lobiri by the Kpatogo

	EI	EC	LA	PC
Jula	0.29	0.80	0.98	0.68
Lobiri	0.32	0.41	0.53	0.52

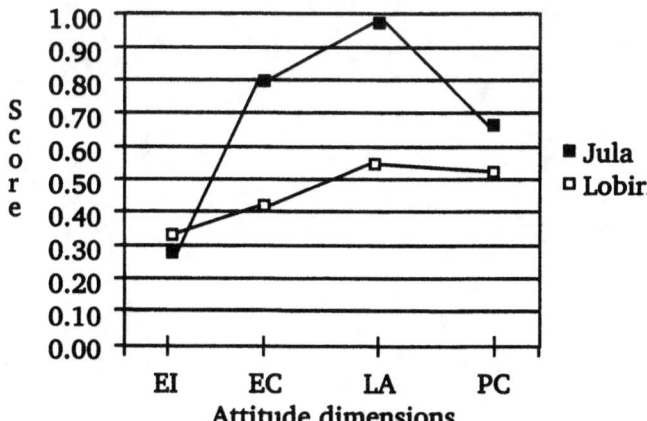

As we saw above, the Kaan hold very similar attitudes toward Jula and Lobiri; the Kpatogo, on the other hand, view the two languages very differently. While they hold moderately to strongly positive attitudes toward contact with the Jula and awareness of their language, they are slightly negative to neutral in these same dimensions for the Lobi. And, whereas the Kaan were neutral to slightly negative about shared ethnic identity with these two groups, the Kpatogo are slightly to moderately negative. The Kpatogo even rated the personal character of the Lobi lower than that of the Jula and much lower than the Kaan judged both the Lobi and Jula.

These results show, among other things, how the attitudes of these two groups have been shaped by their divergent historical development and their distinct communicative economies.

9

Summary and Conclusion

Summary of research results

Chapter 6: The language attitude survey

Attitudes toward shared ethnic identity. The Kaan, Kpatogo, Dogo, and Khi sample groups perceived little difference between Dogose and Khisa and tended to judge the one as they had the other in this attitude dimension. Many identified Khisa as Dogose when asked to name the dialect, but in their comments showed that they heard some differences between the dialects though they were unfamiliar with the Khi community.

The Khi sample showed a split along generational lines: the older subjects judged shared ethnicity with the Dogo, Kpatogo, and Kaan significantly more positively than the younger subjects did. This seemed to back other historical and anecdotal evidence that the Khi are in the process of a language shift toward Jula. Other evidence for this shift is found in the moderately positive attitude among the Khi about sharing traditions with the Jula, in contrast to the moderate to strongly negative attitude of the other three groups.

It was noteworthy, too, that all four groups were neutral to slightly negative about shared ethnicity with the Lobi. This shows that Labouret's (1931, 1958) classification of the Kaan (and by extension, the other three groups) within the Lobi branch is not a sentiment shared by the groups themselves.

Attitudes toward interethnic contact. There was not wide variation in the attitudes recorded for this dimension. All four samples were moderately to strongly positive about contact with each other. The Kaan and Kpatogo judged the Dogo and Khi very similarly, as if they did not really distinguish between the two groups. This is in line with the previous finding that the Kaan and Kpatogo tended to identify the Khisa text as Dogose.

Attitudes toward language awareness. Dogose is the central dialect in terms of this dimension of attitudes, that is, everyone was familiar with it and claimed to understand it. Kpatogoso was the least recognized dialect.

Only the Kaan sample showed positive attitudes toward the Lobi in this dimension; the rest were decidedly negative. By contrast, all four samples showed very positive attitudes about familiarity with Jula.

Attitudes toward personal character. The four dialect samples think well of each other's character (moderately positive). By contrast, the Khi and Kpatogo judged the Lobi significantly lower (neutral) than the Dogo and Kaan did. An interesting difference in attitudes became evident in evaluations of the Jula texts: the Dogo and Khi judged Jula significantly higher (strongly positive attitudes) than the Kaan and the Kpatogo did (slightly positive). This adds more weight to the indicators that both the Dogo and the Khi are shifting to Jula. The use of Jula in these communities may have an affective component (wanting in some way to share in Jula culture) as well as an instrumental motivation (speaking Jula for practical purposes).

Attitudes toward social status. The measurement of attitudes toward social status was not well defined by the survey instrument and proved to be unreliable. The ratings of the dialect text were based primarily on attitudes concerning the personal importance of the text speakers, while ratings of the Lobiri and Jula texts were based primarily on judgments of the economic status of the text speakers. The Kaan and Kpatogo samples rated the Jula texts significantly higher (slightly to moderately positive) than the Dogo and Khi did (slightly negative). This corresponds to the historical split in the four communities with regards to direct influence of the Jula of Kong, though the direction of their attitudes is unexpected.

Chapter 7: The language proficiency and use survey

Proficiency in Jula. All of the subjects in the sample of the Kaan people spoke some Jula; eighty percent of the sample speaks at level two-plus or above, while thirty-seven percent speaks at level four or above. There were no significant differences in the distribution of Jula proficiency in the sample by age or sex, but there were interesting trends in the data. Twice as many men spoke Jula at high levels of proficiency as did at low levels, whereas women were more evenly distributed among the levels. There were twice as many youths at high levels of proficiency as at low levels, while other age groups (adults, elders) were more evenly distributed among the levels. These trends could indicate that either proficiency in Jula is on the rise in the younger generation, or young people are at the peak of their Jula proficiency and will level off or decline as they grow older.

Lobiri proficiency. Two-thirds of the sample reported speaking some Lobiri, and most of these (forty-eight percent of the total sample) speak it at levels two-plus through three-plus. This amply demonstrates a higher community proficiency in Jula than in Lobiri, yet shows that Lobiri is also widely used.

Dominance patterns. The study of language use in different domains revealed that Jula is the dominant second language of the Kaan community, as it is used in the widest range of domains. Lobiri, on the other hand, is restricted to use with the Lobi, and is generally not used as a language of wider communication. One striking example of this is that one-third to one-half of the Kaan sample reported having used Jula with a Lobi (depending on the domain and the complexity of the discourse) while very few ever use Lobiri with a Jula speaker.

The Kaan and the Dogo. Many subjects reported that the Kaan could converse with the Dogo using their own dialects without difficulty in comprehension. However, observations of this kind of contact during survey visits to Dogo villages with Kaan language assistants showed frequent use of Jula when careful communication was important, or to clarify, explain, or comment on things that had been said in Kaansa. It was concluded that passive understanding of Dogose or Kaansa was gained by those of both groups with frequent contact with each other, but without frequent contact, comprehension was more difficult, and quite often Jula was used to fill in the gaps. Instances of successful interdialectal communication coupled with a sense of shared cultural identity and history contributed to the widespread attitude that the two groups could communicate with each other in their own dialects.

Chapter 8: The analysis of integrated data

Dialect and attitude issues. We saw in the analysis of linguistic similarity measures and attitude results that a close relationship exists between intelligibility scores and language awareness. This contrasted vividly with the lack of any apparent connection between attitudes toward shared ethnicity or personal character and linguistic similarity. Shared ethnicity seems to be the one attitude dimension where these four groups distinguish themselves the most from each other.

In most cases, attitudes toward language awareness were more positive than attitudes about interethnic contact, which suggests that very frequent contact between these groups is not a prerequisite for high awareness of their dialects. A notable exception was found in the Dogo attitudes toward the Kpatogo. The Dogo were strongly positive about frequent contact with the Kpatogo, but only moderately aware of their dialect.

The question of whether to classify these dialects as four, two, or one language was discussed, and it was shown that while it is fairly easy to consider Dogose and Khisa as two dialects of the same language, both structurally and attitudinally, it is difficult to think of Kaansa and Kpatogoso in the same way, primarily due to the attitude of ethnic separation among the Kpatogo. That being said, the Kpatogo still have more linguistic and attitudinal bonds with the Kaan than with the Dogo or Khi, and certainly the Kaan view them as their closest ethnic cousins. What emerged from the discussion was the fact that Dogose and Kaansa have a certain prestige by virtue of their wide recognition and their larger communities.

Bilingualism and language use issues.

Models of bilingualism. Mackey's (1968) model for the description of bilingualism was used to synthesize the data from chapter 7. Under the category of "function", various types of pressure were discussed which promote and support the different languages spoken by the Kaan. Jula was backed by economic pressure, French by administrative pressure, and both Jula and Lobiri by historical and demographic pressure. The small group of Kaan Christians experience religious pressure to learn Lobiri because of the established church among the Lobi, the Lobi-language Bible school run by the Protestant Mission, and the Lobiri translation of the New Testament and other religious literature.

The code-switching data from chapter 7 was examined under the category of "alternation", and it was shown that most code-switching was reported when the Kaan spoke with Lobi acquaintances. In such cases individuals varied as to whether they would switch to Lobiri or Jula, and for how much of the interaction.

The aspect of "interference" between two or more languages was not dealt with in this study, but it was noted that the situation in Loropéni is ripe for research into that area.

Batiana's (1985) model for urban language use in Burkina Faso was compared to a suggested model for rural language use based on the research in Loropéni. It was shown that language use in Loropéni was in some ways more complex than in the urban centers of Burkina Faso, because of the restricted role of French and the wider roles of local ethnic languages.

Frameworks for interpreting language roles. Pervasiveness and dominance with regard to the role of Jula as the lingua franca in Loropéni was then discussed. Cooper's (1982b) criterion variables for evaluating the spread and pervasiveness of a language proved inadequate for distinguishing the roles of Jula and Lobiri, but Scotton's (1982) set of values for lingua francas did provide the framework for a useful analysis. Jula lacked specific ethnic associations and was used in a wider variety of situations than Lobiri. Yet, Lobiri enjoyed a certain amount of local ethnic dominance which explained the regular Kaan accommodation to Lobiri as well as the cases of longtime Jula residents speaking Lobiri.

Bilingual communities. In examining Lewis' (1985) typology of bilingual communities through comparison with the bilingual data from the Kaan community, it was concluded that there are too many characteristics of bilingualism among the Kaan that were not properly accounted for by his work. The Kaan, Dogo, Kpatogo, and Khi seemed to fit his definition of stable communities, but the bilingualism and attitudes found among them differed in important ways from what Lewis' typology indicated should exist. This served to emphasize the point made by Lafage (1986) that new sociolinguistic models are needed to adequately explain the kinds of variation in language form and use found in West Africa.

Chapter 5: Methodology

Since small sample sizes restrict the applicability of the conclusions cited above, perhaps the primary contribution of this book is in its adaptive methodology: the adaptation of the matched guise/subjective reaction test to a rural, nonliterate setting, the use of a can-do scale for estimating second-language proficiency in a community, and the combination of direct methods (questionnaires, self-ratings) and indirect methods (observations, matched guise) in sociolinguistic research.

The matched guise/subjective reaction test. The validity and effectiveness of the matched guise approach was demonstrated by the wide range of judgments given to the Lobiri, Jula, and Kaansa texts, all of which were recorded by the same individual Kaan language helper. It showed that people rated the same speaker in very different ways depending on which language he was speaking.

The experimental design of this survey rested on some basic assumptions: the equality of text speakers, the equality of text sequences, and the equality of questionnaires (that is, the reliability of the rotation system). The first two of these assumptions were shown to be valid and backed by empirical tests of the data. The third assumption was defensible for some applications of the questionnaires (i.e., for measuring the dimensions of Personal Character, Language Awareness, and the dialect evaluations of Ethnic Identity), but not for others (Social Status, Ethnic Contact, Lobiri and Jula ratings of Ethnic Identity). This was traced to the imbalance in the system of distributing the questions and texts among the four different questionnaires. However, while the reliability of this survey design needs improvement, the validity of this approach was established by the correspondence of the attitude results to the historical and cultural background of the four communities studied, as well as complementary relationships within the results themselves. In other words, there are problems with reliability, but there is also evidence to establish the internal and external validity of this design.

Language proficiency assessment. It was also demonstrated that language proficiency in a community can be assessed through the development of a can-do scale drawn from the FSI or SLOPE skill level descriptions and adapted where necessary to the local situation. While oral proficiency interviews are a better alternative when time, personnel, and other factors allow, a carefully constructed scale of self-reports can give a researcher a broad understanding of the distribution of second-language proficiency in a community. The form of this method is practical and manageable enough for small research teams to use and can be combined with larger surveys of language attitudes and use in rural communities.

Direct versus indirect attitude assessment. This research has shown that attitudes are complex and do not always follow other indicators of linguistic or ethnic similarity, so there is a danger in relying on a few informal questions to assess language attitudes in a survey. The responses to Solomiac's (1983) direct questionnaire which asked for opinions about the intelligibility of dialects leave one with the surface impression that there is easy, unhindered comprehension between the dialects. However, not only do Solomiac's intelligibility tests tell a different story, but the indirect language attitude research showed a variety of attitudes among these four groups, some positive, some neutral, some even negative. While the responses Solomiac received probably correspond best to the language awareness attitudes discussed in chapter 6, the addition of the other attitude dimensions in this study helped define, explain, and set in context the responses Solomiac received to his direct questionnaire.

All research methods have their limitations; they fall on a continuum from simple and practical, yet lacking depth or precision, to complex and elaborate, requiring careful training and extra effort, and yet providing detailed, precise data. The research presented here used a variety of methods from several points along this continuum: participant observation, historical research, informal interviews, a direct questionnaire, simple and elaborate self-reports, and a complex indirect elicitation of attitudes. The data they yielded give us a multifaceted image of the interaction of language and social life among the Kaan people, their ethnic family, and their ethnic neighbors.

Conclusion

This research demonstrates that detailed, insightful data can be gathered concerning language attitudes and use among rural, nonliterate peoples of West Africa. Data-gathering techniques are not limited by oral communicative norms to direct questions or simple self-reports of proficiency and use. Instead, researchers can adapt indirect assessment techniques to fit the exigencies of the cultural milieu and still collect valid, informative data, provided these data are crosschecked through complementary investigative methods such as participant observation and direct interviews.

If we are to seriously consider the insights gained into the role of language attitudes in minority communities elsewhere in the world, we may propose that differences in language attitudes will not only reflect historical events, but will contribute to the determination of future events which will continue the evolution of the communicative economy of each of the groups studied in this research.

The maintenance of linguistic and cultural distinctives within a community will hinge upon their interaction with the social and economic changes ahead; their choice of ways to interact with and respond to change is in part influenced by their attitudes toward the languages and people who are the conduits of social change. It is therefore important for linguists, anthropologists, missionaries, development workers, and other agents of social change to pay close attention to the interplay of language attitudes, language use, and social conditions while introducing changes into the communicative economy of a people, not just for the success or failure of the specific program, but also for the preservation of the dignity and adaptive vitality of the culture undergoing change.

Appendix 1

Village Data

(76) Kaan villages

Village	Kaan name[66]	PH[67]	CNRST[68]	S[69]	Meaning or etymological source
Begehon	bèyèhɔ́ŋ		*	*	colline contennant une terre salée
Bingassa	bĩŋgàsà			*	Dioula, lit.: 'tomber mourir'
Bingélé	péŋgěnǐ		*	*	aller une fois voir sans l'accord de quelqu'un (pérí kèrè)
Bobéta	pɔ́bətʰǎ	*	*	*	lieu d'éclatement (pábánthǎ)
Buroyo	burɔ́ʔjò			*	la source
Deeba	dɛɛba			*	Dioula: 'le grand bas-fond'
Djigoué	yɔ̀fɩ́ŋgà			*	l'eau blanche
Dougafissa	dɔ́yɔ́fĩsà		*	*	les sabots du buffle

[66]Koffi Farma of Obiré is the source of the pronunciation and the meaning or etymology.
[67]Mentioned in Parenko and Hébert (1962).
[68]Mentioned in an unpublished survey report by the Centre Nationale de Recherches Scientifiques et Techniques (CNRST), Ouagadougou.
[69]Noted and confirmed during this survey.

Appendix 1

Village	Kaan name	PH	CNRST	S	Meaning or etymological source
Duguro	dúyurò			*	anciennement (?)
	hòpìkòkò			*	
Horkonso	hòrəkɔ́nsɔ̀			*	beaucoup de forêts
Itabuntanga	ìtʰàbùntáŋgà		*	*	puits royal
Kabti	kʰàbətʰì		*	*	à coté de l'haricot blanc (khàbì wá thɛ̀?)
Karankasso	ɲɓyʋtʰã̀			*	boire chez moi (ɲúgí mí thã̀)
Kassitan	kàjítʰã̀		*	*	lieu de refus (kàu mín thã̀)
Kérié	kɛ̀rìjɛ̀		*	*	sur les rochers (kɛ̀ʔrìyɛ̀)
?	kɛ̀ŋgɛ̀		*	*	
Kontan	kʰɔ̃̀ntʰã̀		*	*	
Kungoguro	kṹgoguro			*	Dioula: 'c'est mon problème personnel'
Lérébi	dɛ̀rəbí		*	*	habitude (dɛ̀rìbìrìmà)
Lokosso/ Sandi/ Lorhosso	sắnní	*		*	danser, se perdre (sán téu)
Loropéni	dɔ́yɔ́pɛ́nnnɛ̃̀	*		*	buffle gras comme un melon (dɔ́wɛ́ nɔ́ʔnì mípɛ́nnì)
Mugonsi	mṹyɔ́nsì			*	ronger, détruire, manger (múgíʔkirima)
Namiyari	nāmījarɪ			*	il est temps de te lever
Namuyi	mṹí			*	le bubal
Nyanigbana	ɲānīgbānā			*	'face rouge' (avoir des problèmes)
Nyimiyé	ɲímíɲɛ̀			*	l'oeil demande (yíbí ɲíŋ)
Obiré	òòpírigɛ̀	*	*	*	granite noir
Ouatan	wáátʰã̀		*	*	lieu de tomber (wáa thã̀)
Ouodo	wɔ̀ʔrì			*	être sâle, clôturer (wɔ́ʔmà)
Poéyé	kpɔ̀ì			*	
Sanékogoro	sắnnűkóyərò			*	

Village Data

Village	Kaan name	PH	CNRST	S	Meaning or etymological source
Sarafiguiré	sàyəfṹhɛ̀ʔrì		*	*	traverse ici à l'autre côté
Saramassi	sáŋmásì			*	Dioula: 'le moment n'est pas arrivé'
Segué	sàògè		*	*	mettre là
Sogonhorgo	sɔ̀yɔ̃ŋhɔ̀rəgɔ̀			*	forêt des Dioulas
Soronkina	sɔ̀yɔ̃ŋkʰìnã̀	*	*	*	route des Dioulas
Tawouro	táhùrò			*	autre arbre
Toetan	tṍʷétʰã̀			*	qui n'as pas de problèmes chez lui? (máa dáʔrì tɔ́ ú thã̀)
Togo	tógò		*	*	
Tonhébé	tṹbì	*		*	sucer l'os du poisson (tṹmà)
Wurokun	wúrókʰũŋ			*	regretter, partir
Yérifoula	hɛ̀ʔrìfɪrà	*	*	*	tourterelle blanche
Yinataura	ɲĩnátɔ́ɔ́rà			*	Dioula: 'pour cette année qui reste'
Zono	sɔ́nnɔ̃́	*	*	*	augmenter la quantité (sɔ́nígɔ́rì)

(77) Kpatogo villages

Village	Kpatogo name[70]	PH	SL[71]	S
Bantou	gbàntú			*
Dahinikorosso	dằɲíní		*	*
Diassara	ɟàsàrà	*	*	*
Gbengué	gbɛ̃̀ɲɛ̀	*	*	*
Kamilidaga	kàmìlìdáyá		*	*
Karanga	kàrằngá		*	*
Legbindi		*		
Massamo			*	*
Mounji			*	*
Ouérin	wɛ̀rɛ̃́	*	*	
Tonkoro	túkɔ̀rɔ̀		*	

---

[70]Phonetic transcriptions of local pronunciations.
[71]Mentioned in Solomiac (1983).

(78) Dogo villages

Name	Dogo name	PH	SL	S[72]
Bangbara	gbaŋgbara			*
Balgogo		*	*	
Bazé	bàwɛ̀			*
Béguélé	begele	*	*	*
Boborola		*		
Bogoté/Bokote		*	*	
Bossié		*		
Dahinikorosso		*		
Dapala		*		*
Dérégoué		*		
Dibi	dìwí			*
Doutié		*		
Flélélo	flandé			*
Gangassé		*		
	gbɛ̀r[ɛ]gbɛ́			*
	gbɔ́gá			*
Gouedanga		*		
	gɔ̀wɛ́ɩ			*
Nizélé	ɲ́zédè	*	*	*
	kằgàlié			*
Kien		*	*	
Kokanko	kɔ́gɔ́ríkɔ́rɔ́	*		
Konamissé	kɔ́námìsí	*		
Konkan		*	*	
Koro	kɔ́ɔ́rɔ			*
Kouendi		*		
Kouéré	kpele	*	*	*
Logué		*		*
Mado		*		
Nerekedaga		*		
Ngolofesso		*		
Norokama		*	*	*
Npoun/Kpoun	kpú	*	*	
Ouangoro	wằgɔ́gɔ́			*

---

[72]Includes villages from a word list by Lassina Ouattara.

Village Data 219

Name	Dogo name	PH	SL	S
Ouo	wòò	*	*	*
Pambie Soukoura	pàmíe sókórá	*		
Poikoro		*	*	
Safia		*		
Sanmbola	sǎpʊ̀là			*
Sampobien		*		
Sidéradougou		*		*
Siekoro		*		
Sikongo		*		
Sirakoro		*	*	*
Soucié	sìsié			
	súkúrání			*
Toukoro	gɔ̀yà	*		*
Zangazoli		*	*	

(79) Khi villages

Name	Khi name	PH[73]	SL	S
Bandakélésso	sósígbò	*	*	*
Dabokiri		*	*	*
Farakorosso		*	*	
Mangodara	mǎŋgɔ̀dáyá	*	*	*
Massadéhirikoro	gbɛlɛgbʊ	*	*	*
Sirakoro		*	*	*
Tonbikorosso				*
Yaya/Diaya		*	*	

---

[73]Parenko and Hébert did not distinguish between the Khi and the Bambadion, calling them all "Komono." Thus they list far more villages than Solomiac, who limited his to the Khi alone. Here I present only the "Komono" villages of Parenko and Hébert which are also mentioned by Solomiac.

(80) Village characteristics

	Access[74]	Government presence	Nearest clinic	Nearest market	Ethnic composition
Kaan villages					
Yérifoula	SR	Ec(prim), CDR, Del	In town	In town	K/L/J/A
Loropéni	MR	Pre, Pol, Ec (prim), CDR	In town	In town	K/L/J/A
Obiré	FR	Ec(prim), Del	Loro, Yéri	Loro, Yéri	K
Soronkina	P	Del	Loropéni	Loropéni	K/L
Saramassi	P	Del	Djigoué	Djigoué	K/L/A (Peul)
Lorhosso/ Sandi	SR	Del, Ec (prim)	In town, Loro	In town, Loro	K/L/J
Kerié	P	Del	Loro	Loro	K
Kpatogo villages					
Karanga	P	Del	Diassara	Bandjigui	Kp
Ouérin	P	Del	Diassara	Kursi (Lobi)	Kp
Kamilidaga	P	Del	Diassara	Koro (Dogo)	Kp
Gbéngué	FR	Del	Diassara	Kursi (Lobi)	Kp
Diassara	FR	FJA, Del, (CDR?)	In town, fr9/87	Kursi (Lobi)	Kp
Dogo villages					
Béguélé	P	Del	Ouo, Yérifoula	Yéri	Dg
Koro	FR	Del, Ec (prim)	Dipeo, Yéri	Koro	Dg/L/J
Nizélé	P/FR	Del	Ouo	Ouo	Dg
Ouo	MR	Pre, Ec(prim), CDR, Del	Ouo	Ouo	Dg/L/Pl/J
Sidéradougou	MR	Pre,Pol,Gen,Ec, CDR,Del,Au	Sidéra- dougou	Sidéra- dougou	Dg/L/J/A

---

[74]MR = main road; SR = secondary road; FR = former road; P = path.

Village Data

	Access	Government presence	Nearest clinic	Nearest market	Ethnic composition
Khi villages					
Massadéhirikoro	SR	Del	Mangodara	Mango, Sirakoro	Kh
Mangodara	MR	Pre, Pol, Gen, Dou, Ec, CDR, Au	In town	In town	Kh/L/J/A
Sirakoro	SR	Del	Mangodara	In town, Mango	Kh/J
Bandakélésso	SR	Del	Mangodara	Mango, Sirakoro	Kh

Appendix 2

Language Attitude Survey Data

(81) Total sample for language attitude survey by ethnic group and village

Kaan villages	Elder		Adult		Youth	
	Male	Female	Male	Female	Male	Female
Kérié	1		2	3		
Loropéni		1			1	
Obiré			1		2	
Lorhosso	3	2		1		
Sagamassi			3	3		
Sorokina		1	2	2	1	
Yérifoula	1		3	2		
Totals	5	4	11	11	4	
	9		22		4	
Total sample	35					

Kpatogo villages	Elder		Adult		Youth	
	Male	Female	Male	Female	Male	Female
Diassara	4		1			
Gbengué	2		1	2		
Kamilidaga			2	1	1	1
Karanga	1		4			
Ouérin	1	1	1		2	
Totals	8	1	9	3	3	1
	9		12		4	
Total sample	25					

Dogo villages						
Béguélé		1	1	2	2	
Koro	1		2	2	1	
Nizélé	1		1	3	1	
Ouo			3	1	1	
Sidéradougou		1	2	2		
Totals	2	1	8	10	7	
	3		18		7	
Total sample	28					

Khi villages						
Bandakéléssó	1	1	2	2		
Mangodara	3					
Massadéhirikoro			2	3	1	
Sirakoro	2	1	1	1	1	
Totals	6	2	5	6	2	
	8		11		2	
Total sample	21					

(82) Kaansa (Loropéni) attitude survey texts
Elder speaker (KE), 17 seconds

sèɛrɛ̀ wã́ã̌,
kʰà kʰà? mìnìmà bòsé kɔ́? nű̀nà
ʋ́ bʋ dììgì wɛ̀rà
tʊ̃̀wã́ páã́ná? mìnì wɛ̀rà
kʰàjì wá mɛ́ɛ́ nʊ̃̀ŋɨ̀rɔ̃̀ŋ
hágíjé bà
wósì wá bɛ́ɛ́ nʊ̃̀ŋɨ̀rɔ̃̀ŋ
tɔ́ɔ́rá mì jà? tʰààgìrá nʊ̃m mʋ̃̀
bòsí sɔ̀yɔ̃̀mbìrà jí? sómájárì wɛ̀rà
tʰɔɔ̀rà mí bʋ̀ kʰììbì kpɔɔ̀gɔ̀
ná mì wɔ́nní dé sʋ̀mìnà wã̀?

I was saying, I said that a sickness can get you for a whole year. Yet I've been treated now. Everywhere it hurts, the back, your whole body hurts (...), your head hurts... The sickness the Julas call 'somaya' [jaundice or malaria]. I suffered for ten days without being able to work in the fields.

(83) Kaansa (Loropéni) attitude survey texts
Elder speaker (KY), 17 seconds

sìrá bà tàrà mì jóó bã̀fɔ́rà
ĩ̀ jóó nã́nà mã̀ʃí kɔ́ tágí ba kɔ́r bʋ̀
mã̀ʃí wá dɔ́gírá bʋ̀ mì kɛ̀mmá kʰɨ̀ɨ̀gɛ̀
mì físìjà tákpɛ̀kɛ̀rà
jɛ̀ kʰɛ̀ dékì ĩ̀ jèè bʋ́
dé mì kʰòr múúkìrì kpààgɔ̀ ĩ̀ kɛ̀ŋ
ná kʰɨ̀ɨ̀gìrà búmà kí kù? kpààgìrá
ĩ̀ mákírá ná mã̀ʃíná pɨ́ɨ́ wà? jɛ̀ mí kɛ̀mmá pɨ́ɨ́?ùmà ĩ̀ kʰɛ̀ dékì sɔɔ̀ gì bʋ́
ʋ̀ kʰòr dégémbì ísã́ã̀?nà ĩ̀ námɛ̀
ʋ́ wààtìrá kʰà? pìmà pì khú séjèmà
tí jɛ̀ nʊ̃̀wã̀ mí kű̀ŋ tákìrsì wà?
jɛ̀ pí khà? pì kpégɛ̀ ĩ̀ kɛ̀ŋ ná sì jɛ̀ jóó wà?
tí kpànàà bʋ̀ pí tʋ̀má pí khú séé
pí kpégɛ̀ tírá dééri mí dégémbù wáá páã́ kàlɛ̀ mɛ́ɛ́?nà

After that I went to Banfora to work with a grain mill. Something got stuck inside the machine; I thought it was a piece of metal. I folded back the cloth covering and reached in with my hand to get the flour out so that I could see if it was a piece of metal, and if it could come out. It happened that the machine was not off, though I thought it was off and that I could push my hand in there. It grabbed three fingers and crushed them. At that time, they would cut them off. I was not at all happy about that, so they said they would stitch them up and then see, otherwise, afterward they would cut them off. They stitched them, that's why my fingers happened to heal stuck together like this. I really suffered.

(84) Kpatogoso (Diassara) attitude survey texts
Elder speaker (KpE), 60 seconds

ham bu dı sísáã
mı wɔ́nní di tɔ́ mɪ́ní wã kʰwĩ
mı ba jóó gao
ĩ ná ópéré ná baa
ĩ kɔnjá tı jımi thĩ tṹwã? dɛ́?
mı fɔlɔfɔlɔ thĩ ʋra dɔhũŋboso khuɾı kɔ́r mı
sı ta waatı dɛ́ʋ gɛ́rʋ ná hɛ̃ to mí hũ fa
mı jóó ɟɛbugu ná kpṹ dı gĩkpo ná ferıgbi má?nĩkpo
pí tɔ sɛ́ɛ́ mı
dɔ́ɔ́gɔ tɔ ba kɔ́r mı
nɔyaja duɲɲi wɛra
ná kı wɔ́ɔ́rɔ́ ja sóó mɛ́?na
ná mʋ kɔ́r kʰaatɛ kɛʋ
mʋ kʰʋɾı gbasĩĩ kɔ́ŋgbo kɛmɛ́sáã mı thĩ se ʒɛ́ɛ́ ʋ
ná tı ja tı ba hũ khá dɛ?
ná mʋ jıĩni mɛ ná tı kɔŋ gbıbı
ɛ̃hɛ̃ɛ̃ nɔyɔja dóóni nıpɛ jaa dé ná mũ jóó opere mṹ hu
mı kha? é?
ná mı jóó ópéré ná hu
ná mı hu kı jɛ ba jɛ̃ŋ kɔkɔna wa?
mı nu kı kɔna wɔ̃ thoona?

For three years I was not able to eat. I went to Gaoua to have an operation... [unintelligible] But at the beginning of my life I had sleeping sickness. Back then I would sit like this and sleep like this. Then I went to Diebougou and got shots for a year and six months. After that I had another sickness like stomach aches. If you get that, you grab and push right here. If it makes a noise it calms down, it calms down and then settles on the other side. Then it feels a little better. People came and said, if you go for an operation, you're going to die. I said, "Eh! If I go for an operation and die, if I die, won't my stomach leave me in peace?" I didn't feel anything after that.

(85) Kpatogoso (Diassara) attitude survey text
Younger speaker (KpY), 35 seconds

ná ba mʊ ja khã dé nétʰɩnɩgɩ só bosé tɪ̃ɛ gɔ mʊ̃ɔ̃ do ná bose wɔ́r gɔ mʊ̃ɔ̃ do cogo cogo...bose gɔ sʊrɔ̃ cɔ mɛ kʰááne bʊ fɛ ná heʔna naŋga kĩ pɔ́ɔ́mɔ na sɔ́ɔ́ kɩɾɩga kɩɾɩga kɩ bʊ́ bɔ́ɔ́ tɛ pe bu gí bʊ jɛ pɔ́ɔ́mɩna sʊɛ bɔɔ tɛ foi bʊ́ waʔ...bosé kɔ́ sʊrɔ̃ jɪ̃ã na jé bʊ haarɩ fɔʔ nɩpɛ fʊ̃ʊ̃gɛ̃ ĩ tʰagɔ mɩgɛ tʊm ba ja tʊ̃wã?

If you become somebody, sickness will come upon you. Sickness can come upon you no matter what. [unintelligible] I have been sick, but where we are today, living in poverty, that's what is more difficult. If it's not things like that, if it's not poverty, otherwise there's not much with us. [unintelligible] But I was sick once. There were even people there crying, wailing around my head. I didn't know if I was going to get better.

(86) Dogose (Béguélé) attitude survey text
Elder speaker (DgE), 19 seconds

sʊɛ bósía sʊɛ kha bʊ́wá mɩ gbɔ dɛ béɛ́ kha nomma ná mʊɛ tʰɪ̃ɛ tʊʊ wó na kʰwɛ̃ɛ̃ná pɩ kʰá pēma dá nɪ̃ɪ̃sē kɩ boso biibi pɩ jɛ bʊ́ ná dɔtɔr nʊɛ ɔ nʊɛkʰa tɔ jɛ wáʔ sʊɛ dáhásé pɩ pʰɛɛnɩ na bos o mʊɛ áálí

This sickness, it's my whole body that hurts. At that time I was a child. But back then, if one talks about the old days..., they dug up roots for treating the children. There wasn't any dispensary or other thing. They treated illness with roots, and I was healed.

(87) Dogose (Béguélé) attitude survey text
Younger speaker (DgY), 22 seconds

mɪ bam fárá mɪ borí mɪ warɪ na nõ maʔnɪ ja na kpagĩŋ kpɪbɪ na bose sɪɛ wan sóó nɛtʰɪnɛ gbɔdɔ má do dɔɔnɪ o wágátɪ bʊ? mʊ́ bʊ? mõ tʰũ? ɔ wágátɪ bʊ mʊ bo? na tá na tá mɔgɔ dɔ́ɔ́ le fe bose mɪɛ níɛ ɔɔ kʰɛrɛ fara

When I came here, I was sick. I had fallen from a tree and was hurt. As for illness, you're never done with it. There are times when you are in good health. There are times when you are sick. I went away to be with my family, and I was treated there.

(88) Khisa (Mangodara) attitude survey text
Elder speaker (KhE), 32 seconds

*ɛɛ mí júú hɔrgɪra
kɪ dún plandiʒo
mobili plandiʒo
li…kwɔ́jága
ná ɟina nɔ̃ɔ̃ le mobili ba kóó plandiná
pɪ bʊ́? ĩŋkaní
mobili o wa sʊrɪ wa plandi húúrí
yɛ́?…plandi húúgó kɔ? neena wa?
plandi wá?
mɪ kuʔrima yo?
mɛə dúùnũ mɪ kuʔri
plandi huʊró
pʊká niina húú wá?
ɔ́ʔɔ̃́? na mɪ kúʔro
na tɪra mɪ kuʔri mobili horokira*

He was in Côte d'Ivoire. At that time he wanted to be a chauffeur. He became an apprentice. One day, as they left, his colleague had an accident near a ravine, in which an apprentice died. They said, "We had an accident, but no one died, only the apprentice." Huh? The apprentice is not a person? [laughter] Ah, so that's it. He says, "If the apprentice is not a person…" [laughter] So he got out of there.[75]

---

[75]This is a spontaneous translation given at the time of recording by another elder in the group. He translated the story into French; this is my rendering of his translation into English.

(89) Khisa (Mangodara) attitude survey text
Younger speaker (KhY), 78 seconds

sōmajá gɔ́ʔ mɪ
na mɪ jibiri sáĩŋgá
nɛ mɪ nṍnɛ̃ sáĩŋga
nɛ mɪ mɔ́ga nõõsa
mɪ... pɪ jú kʰʊ mɪ bʊsʊŋgʊ
farfɪ́n bʊsʊŋgʊ
na bʊsʊŋgʊʔʊ
na kɪŋkɪnã wã?
lɛɛ...sɪ ba sɪ́rgɪ́nɪ́
mɪ...mɪ jánɪ́ sɪɪkalamma
mɪ...na pɪ jú mɪ dɔtɔrɔ bʊŋgʊ
na piiʔ hṹnã́ʔnɪ mɪ́nɪ́
bɪm baʔ án dɔ́gana
si jáá si kalamã́ã́ wa?
naa...si ju dɔtɔrɔ wa bʊsʊŋgʊ wa?
ná jʊɪ na omo?
na tɪ́ɪ́gɪ́
na jɪ́bɪ́rɪ́ na horo? na baana
na kpã́ɪ́nɪ́
na si dé mɪ hṹ mũka fṍõnsa
mɪ tʰɪnɛ beɛmɛ lɛɛ ʊm bɛrmɪ bʊsʊŋgʊ mɪ bá sɪkalamá wa?
mɛ jékɪ́nɪ́ ba sɛ́ɛ́ nɪ́tɪnagá wa?
na sɪ nogo jana
na mɪ kuuro
na farafɪrɪ bʊsʊŋgʊ bʊ?
na mɪ lɛ́ɛ́ lɪ́ mɪ kuuro
na si tanɪ sɛnɛgao

I had contracted jaundice. First, I treated it indigenously, then, when it wasn't working, they took me to the dispensary. I was almost unconscious. I wasn't aware anymore of what was happening; I was like, somewhat crazy. They put me on an IV. At one point they say I tore out the IV and threw it aside and went home. The nurse couldn't put up with me anymore and I went home. And everything I did, I... I wasn't conscious anymore. But afterwards I... thanks to God, even so I... they treated me indigenously and...[I got better]. I almost died.

(90) Jula attitude survey text
Young Kaanse speaker (JY), 38 seconds

a tun tara ɛɛ
kuu foro la
ka taa...nɛrɛtigɛ
n ka sandʒi tun nana o wagatila
ka...nɛrɛ jiri
mbon nan jɛlɛla nɛrɛ jiri kan an tɛ bɛn a kɛra kum
a kɛra komu gwan le bara
o watira ne tun jɛlɛla ka to ka nɛrɛtigɛ
ne senw bɔraji
ne bɔraji kana bɛn
nɛrɛ jiri dʒu koro
foo n tun tise ka kuma
n tun jana kumu n bɛna sa
n ka n na na wuli

We had gone off to the yam fields to gather nere pods. It was raining then, and one couldn't climb [a tree] without falling. It was slippery, as if someone had rubbed gumbo on it. So I climbed [the tree] to gather nere pods, and my feet slipped, and I fell off the nere tree. I thought I was going to die, but I didn't.

(91) Lobiri attitude survey text
Young Kaanse speaker (LY), 21 seconds

sɪ-n kɔɔ dʒaal poo jɔ hulẽ paar
dɪ mɪ kɔɔ gbaan unu sanfaan
ĩ tʃa ĩ dʒalna ĩ hʋ jwɔn
dɪ bɔɔ kɛ mɪ-n tʃasɪ ĩ kãsɪ kʋlan hʋɛ
mobiri kɔɔ tʰʋ mɛr a kpɛɛ
dɪ mɪ kɔɔ hale mobiri balɔ
a kpɪɛr ma kʰire
se mɪ kɔɔ tʰer
ma kʰə

We were going to the marsh to bathe. I took the soap from my mother to wash with, but when I ran across the main road, a car hit me. I was under the car. I thought I was going to die, but I didn't, and I got out of there.

(92) Questions relating to Ethnic Identity

B-2: *tʊ́nɪ thĩĩne sɛɛrɛɛ mɛ́ʔ-naa*
What race speaks like that?

Subdimension: Shared Language (SL)
D1-2: *ʊ́ ná mʊ́ sɛɛrɛra ma kpoogo báa*
Are his language and your language the same?

Subdimension: Arbitration (AR)
S3-2: *mʊ kágáʔ dé ʊ wɔ́nní thɪɪ fáa nɪ́pɪ báa*
Do you think he can judge for the people here?

Subdimension: Family Relations (FR)
S4-1: *pí thĩĩna ná í thĩĩna ma kpoogo báa*
Are their families similar to your families?

S1-1: *nɪ́pí pā̃tí ʊ́rɛ wɛra pɪ yeema fáa hapɪ báa*
Do people like him marry women from here?

D2-4: *nɪ́pí sɛɛrɛɛ mɛ́ʔnɪ wɛra pí hũŋgira bʊ́ thĩnáa*
People who talk like that, are there some in your family?

Subdimension: Shared Traditions (ST)
S1-2: *nɪ́pí pā̃tí ʊ́rɛ wɛra pí mambɪra ma kpokpo ná í wá bɪrɪ báa*
Are the traditions of people like him different from yours?

S4-2: *nɪ́pí pā̃tí ʊ́rɛ wɛra pí mambɪra ma kpoogo ná í wá bɪrɪ báa*
Are the traditions of people like him the same as yours?

S1-3: *nɪ́pí pā̃tí ʊ́rɛ wɛra pí busɪ ná í wá sɪra ma kpoogo báa*
Are the funerals of people like him the same as yours?

S2-2: *nɪ́pí pā̃tí ʊ́rɛ wɛra pí busɪ ná í wá sɪra ma kpokpo báa*
Are the funerals of people like him different from yours?

Subdimension: Cultural Maintenance (CM)
S2-1: *nɪ́pí pā̃tí ʊ́rɛ wɛra pɪ thooma khʊ̃ɪʔ nɪ́pɪ wá mambɪra báa*
Do people like him follow the traditions of the elders?

S3-1: *nɪ́pí pā̃tí ʊ́rɛ wɛra sɛ́ɛ-bɪrɪma khʊ̃ɪʔ nɪ́pɪ wá mambɪra báa*
Are people like him abandoning the traditions of the elders?

Subdimension: Shared Religion (SR)
LJ2-1: *nípí pátí ʋrɛ wɛra pí khũna ma kpokpo ná faa wá khũnáa*
Is the religion of people like him different from yours?

LJ1-1: *sɔgɔmbɩra níma pí thãná kɔ́ŋ í tara fará báa*
Are there more Muslims among them than here?

(93) Questions relating to Ethnic Contact

B-3: *nípí pátí ʋrɛ wɛra kɔ́m-bɩruma fará bá pí sɩrgɩ déyéŋ-gɩruma fará báa*
Are there many people like him around here, or is their region far from here?

Subdimension: Linguistic Accommodation (LA)
D2-1: *nípí sɛɛrɛɛ mɛ́ʔnɩ wɛra pɩ wɔ́nnɩ nú fáa sɛɛrɛrɩ báa*
Can people who speak like that understand the language here?

LJ1-4: *nípí sɛɛrɛɛ mɛ́ʔnɩ wɛra pɩ wɔ́nnɩ sɛɛʔ mʋ́ thĩ́sɛɛrɛra báa*
Can people like him speak your language?

Subdimension: Personal Familiarity (PF)
S1-4: *nípí pátí ʋrɛ wɛra mʋ tʋ bɩ tákɩrsa bá mʋ tʋ bɩ tákɩrsɩ waʔ báa*
Do you know people like him well or not well?

S3-5: *nípí pátí ʋrɛ wɛra mʋ másabɛ ní í kɛŋgɩra báa*
Do you have friends among people like him?

S4-4 *nípí pátí ʋrɛ wɛra pɩ báa tɔnnɛɛma fará báa*
Do people like him come through this village?

(94) Questions relating to Social Status

Subdimension: Personal Importance (PI)
D1-4: *ʋ sɛɛrɛɛma mʋ kemmá ʋra pãama ʋ́ nɩɩná báa*
Does he speak like he's someone important in his village?

D2-2: *wáɩ wɛra ʋ sɛɛrɛɛ pátí ʋ dé ɲɩsíbɛ́ɛ waʔ báa*
Does this man speak like he doesn't want to be a "grand type"?

Language Attitude Survey Data 233

D3-2: ʋ sɛɛrɛɛma mʋ́ kemmá ʋra déeri dugutígí báa
Does he speak like a village chief?

Subdimension: Economic Status (ES)
LJ1-3: nɩ́pɩ́ pātɩ́ ʋ́rɛ wɛra kɔ́ŋɔ́ŋ bʋ wá sʋmɩyɛ́ kpokpo bá sʋŋ kpoori báa
Are there many people like him who do a different kind of work for a living, or is their work the same as yours?

LJ2-2: wagɩ́ʔrɩbɛ nɩ́ bá nɩ́kpórbɩ ɩ́ tara fará báa
Are there more traders or officials among them than there are here?

LJ1-2: nɩ́pɩ́ hense nɩ́ báa
Are there rich people among them?

Subdimension: Education (ED)
S3-4: nɩ́pɩ́ pātɩ́ ʋ́rɛ wɛra nɩ́ kɔ́ŋɔ́mbɩ déeri dákorso yɛ sɛɛʔ táfɩrsa ɩ́ tara fáa nɩ́pɩ báa
Among people like him, are there many who have gone to school and speak French, more so than among the people here?

(95) Questions relating to Personal Character

Subdimension: Group Personalities (GP)
S1-5: nɩ́pɩ́ pātɩ́ ʋ́rɛ wɛra nɩ́thɩná pɩ́yāʋ nɩ́ báa
Are there bad characters among people like him?

S2-4: nɩ́pɩ́ pātɩ́ ʋ́rɛ wɛra nɩ́ kɩ́rba nɩ́ báa
Are there good characters among people like him?

Subdimension: Individual Character (IC)
S4-3: nɩ́pɩ́ pātɩ́ ʋ́rɛ wɛra pɩ kpónnóʔma fáa nɩ́pɩra báa
Do people like him respect the people here?

D1-5: tárɩ́ ʋ́ sɛɛrɛɛ mɛ́'nɩ wɛra ʋ wɔ́ɔmɛ yɛ wɔ́nnɩ́ thɩ nɩ́na báa
Is the one who is speaking wise and able to judge people in his village?

Subdimension: Character of Contact (CC)

S3-3: *nípí pātí úrɛ wɛra ĩ na bíra ma kpímma báa*
Do you have disputes with people like him?

S3-5: *nípí pātí úrɛ wɛra mú másabɛ ní ĩ kɛŋgɩra báa*
Do you have friends among people like him?

(96) Questions relating to Language Awareness

Subdimension: Understanding (UN)

B-1: *nú-muni sɛɛrɛ wá bíɛ?*
Did you understand everything?

D1-1: *sí númina nʊʊma báa*
Is it easy to understand?

D3-3: *nípí pātí úrɛ wɛra sí númina kpɩnɩma báa*
Is it difficult to understand people like him?

Subdimension: Speaking Ability (SA)

B-4: *wáɩ wɛra sɛɛ? ú khũɩ? wá múɩna tákɩrsɩ báa*
Does this man tell his story well?

D1-3: *wáɩ wɛra sɛɛrɛra ʋ yésɩ báa*
Are this man's words clear?

D2-3: *ʋ sɛɛrɛɛma dɔgɩnsɔ báa*
Does he "speak in his throat"?

D3-1: *ʋ sɛɛrɛɛma nú phiyɛŋge bá ʋ sɛɛrɛɛma nú yésɛŋge báa*
Does he "speak with his mouth closed" or "his mouth open"?

Subdimension: Familiarity (FM)

S2-3: *mʋ kágá? dé ú thĩsɛɛrɛ kɩrɩ-ʋrɩ báa*
Do you find that his language is nice/pretty/good?

LJ2-3: *sɛɛrɛ dómó ú pɩ sɛɛrɛɛ ní ú ná fa wára ma kpoogo báa*
Is it the same manner of speaking the language that one hears here?

(97) Attitude survey questionnaire 1A: Final form

Nom: Village:

Questions de base

1	2	3	4	5	6	7	B-1-LA:	Est-ce que tu as tout compris?
							B-2-EI:	Quelle race parle comme ça?
							B-3-EC:	Les gens comme lui, est-ce qu'il y en a beaucoup ici, ou bien leur région est loin d'ici?
							B-4-LA:	Est-ce que cet homme raconte bien son histoire?

Questions pour les textes dialectaux
Ensemble D1

	2				6	D1-1-LA:	Est-ce qu'il est facile à comprendre?
1	2	3		5	6	D1-2-EI:	Est-ce que sa langue et ta langue sont les mêmes?
	2				6	D1-3-LA:	Est-ce que cet homme parle clair?
	2				6	D1-4-SS:	Est-ce que tu penses qu'il parle comme un homme important dans son village?
	2				6	D1-5-PC:	Celui qui parle comme ça, est-ce qu'il a la sagesse pour juger les gens?

Ensemble D2

		3		5		D2-1-EC:	Les gens qui parlent comme ça, peuvent-ils comprendre la langue d'ici?
		3		5		D2-2-SS:	Est-ce que cet homme parle comme il ne veut pas être "grand type"?
		3		5		D2-3-LA:	Est-qu'il parle dans la gorge?
		3		5		D2-4-EI:	Les gens qui parlent comme ça, y en a-t-il dans ton clan/famille?

Ensemble D3

1	D3-1-LA:	Est-ce qu'il parle avec la bouche fermée ou la bouche ouverte?
1	D3-2-SS:	Est-ce que tu penses qu'il parle comme un chef de village?
1	D3-3-LA:	Les gens comme lui, est-ce qu'ils sont difficile à comprendre?

Questions pour les textes en Lobiri, Dioula

Ensemble LJ1

7	LJ1-1-EI:	Est-ce qu'il y a des musulmans chez eux? Plus qu'ici?
7	LJ1-2-SS:	Est-ce qu'il y a des gens riches chez eux?
7	LJ1-3-SS:	Les gens comme lui, est-ce qu'il y en a beaucoup avec un travail différent, ou bien est-ce que le travail est le même?
7	LJ1-4-EC:	Les gens comme lui, est-ce qu'ils peuvent parler la langue de ta race?

Ensemble LJ2

4	LJ2-1-EI:	Les gens comme lui, est-ce que leur réligion est différente de la réligion ici?
4	LJ2-2-SS:	Est-ce qu'il y a des commerçants ou bien des fonctionnaires chez eux, plus qu'ici?
4	LJ2-3-LA:	La façon de parler qu'ils parlent là-bas, est-ce que c'est la même façon de parler la langue ici?

Questions partagées
Ensemble S1

1	5	7	S1-1-EI:	Les gens comme lui, est-ce qu'ils se marient avec les filles d'ici?
1	5	7	S1-2-EI:	Les gens comme lui, est-ce que leurs traditions sont différentes des vôtres?
1	5	7	S1-3-EI:	Les gens comme lui, est-ce que leurs funérailles sont les mêmes que les vôtres?
1	5	7	S1-4-EC:	Les gens comme lui, est-ce que tu les connais bien ou pas bien?
1	5	7	S1-5-PC:	Les gens comme lui, est-ce qu'il y a des mauvais types chez eux?

Ensemble S2

2	S2-1-EI:	Les gens comme lui, est-ce qu'ils suivent les traditions des anciens?
2	S2-2-EI:	Les gens comme lui, est-ce que leurs funérailles son différentes des vôtres?
2	S2-3-LA:	Est-ce que tu trouves que sa langue est bon/joli?
2	S2-4-PC:	Les gens comme lui, est-ce qu'il y a des bons types chez eux?

Ensemble S3

3	6	S3-1-EI:	Les gens comme lui, est-ce qu'ils laissent les traditions des anciens?
3	6	S3-2-EI:	Est-ce que tu penses qu'il peut juger les gens d'ici?

3	6	S3-3-PC:	Les gens comme lui, est-ce que vous faites des palabres avec eux?
3	6	S3-4-SS:	Les gens comme lui, est-ce qu'il y a beaucoup chez eux qui ont fait l'école et qui parlent français, plus que les gens d'ici?
3	6	S3-5-ECPC:	Les gens comme lui, est-ce que tu as des amis parmi eux?

Ensemble S4

4	S4-1-EI:	Est-ce que leurs familles sont commes vos familles?
4	S4-2-EI:	Les gens comme lui, est-ce que leurs traditions sont les mêmes que les vôtres?
4	S4-3-PC:	Les gens comme lui, est-ce qu'ils respectent les gens d'ici?
4	S4-4-EC:	Les gens comme lui, est-ce qu'ils se promènent dans ce village?

Information personnelle

1. Nom du village:
2. A. Nom de famille/clan:
   B. Autres noms:
3. Age: (Vieux, Adulte, Jeune, M/F)
4. Religion: (Animist, Catholique, Protestant, Musulman)
5. Travail:
6. Maison: (banco/paille, banco/tôle, ciment/tôle)
7. A. Marié(e):
   B. Combien de femmes:
   C. Combien d'enfants:
8. Bicylette/moto/voiture:
9. Ecole/formation:
10. Relation du réseau:
11. Voyages dans la région: (Loropéni, Obiré, Koro, Diassara, Ouo, Mangodara, Sidéradougou, Côte d'Ivoire.)

Language Attitude Survey Data

(98) Results of statistical tests on language attitude survey scores
(SD = p < .05; Y = yes)

A	B	C	D	E	F	G	H	I	J	K	L	M	N	O	P	Q	R	S
Dim.	Subj.	Texts	Etext	Ytext	SD	Ascore	Escore	SD	Mscore	Fscore	SD	Med TS-A	Med TS-B	SD	Quest.	SD	Dscores	SD
EI	K	K	0.98	0.99		0.98	0.94		1.00	0.95		1.00	1.00				0.98	Y
EI	KP	K	0.51	0.46		0.49	0.61					0.50	0.36				0.51	
EI	D	K	0.67	0.63					0.68	0.64		0.66	0.61				0.67	
EI	KH	K	0.69	0.62		0.56	0.83	Y	0.72	0.63		0.69	0.65				0.69	
EI	K	KP	0.73	0.82		0.77	0.75		0.72	0.80		0.50	0.50				0.77	Y
EI	KP	KP	0.98	0.93		1.00	0.87					1.00	1.00				0.95	Y
EI	D	KP	0.52	0.50					0.59	0.44		1.00	1.00				0.53	
EI	KH	KP	0.47	0.64		0.41	0.77	Y	0.59	0.50		0.67	0.67				0.56	Y
EI	K	D	0.77	0.57		0.70	0.74		0.68	0.68		0.83	0.67				0.68	Y
EI	KP	D	0.42	0.37		0.39	0.51					0.50	0.33				0.40	Y
EI	D	D	0.99	0.95					1.00	0.94							0.97	Y
EI	KH	D	0.78	0.87		0.76	0.96	Y	0.82	0.85		0.83	1.00				0.83	Y
EI	K	KH	0.63	0.79		0.80	0.67		0.65	0.81		0.92	0.58		1A/4B	Y	0.72	Y
EI	KP	KH	0.24	0.55	Y	0.50	0.44					0.50	0.17	Y	1A/2B	Y	0.44	Y
EI	D	KH	0.87	0.91					0.88	0.90		1.00	1.00				0.89	
EI	KH	KH	0.95	1.00		0.95	1.00		0.97	0.98							0.98	
EI	K	L				0.46	0.40		0.42	0.42		0.17	0.65	Y	1A/2B, 2B/3A AB, 3A/4B	Y	0.44	
EI	KP	L				0.36	0.26					0.17	0.50	Y	1A, 3A/2B, 4B	Y	0.32	
EI	D	L							0.39	0.64	Y	0.17	0.67	Y	1A, 3A/2B, 4B	Y	0.49	
EI	KH	L				0.38	0.48		0.38	0.43		0.17	0.38		1A, 2B/3A, 4B	Y	0.40	
EI	K	J				0.43	0.50		0.49	0.43		0.59	0.50		1A/AB	Y	0.46	
EI	KP	J				0.32	0.24					0.00	0.50	Y	4B/1A, 3A	Y	0.29	Y
EI	D	J							0.50	0.66		0.33	0.50				0.57	
EI	KH	J				0.61	0.54		0.64	0.56		0.67	0.50	Y			0.64	

240 Appendix 2

A Dim.	B Subj.	C Texts	D Etext	E Ytext	F SD	G Ascore	H Escore	I SD	J Mscore	K Fscore	L SD	M Med TS-A	N Med TS-B	O SD	P Quest.	Q SD	R Dscores	S SD
26 EC	K	K	0.90	0.94		0.94	0.82		0.96	0.87		1.00	1.00				0.92	
27 EC	KP	K	0.71	0.86		0.79	0.81					0.75	0.63			Y	0.72	Y
28 EC	D	K	0.86	0.93								1.00	1.00		4B/2B, 3A		0.87	
29 EC	KH	K	0.86	0.85		0.78	0.91		0.91	0.80		1.00	1.00		1A/2B	Y	0.85	
30 EC	K	KP	0.77	0.63		0.73	0.71		0.93	0.72		1.00	1.00			Y	0.72	see X2
31 EC	KP	KP	1.00	0.70		0.94	0.88		0.68	0.78		0.50	1.00				0.90	see X2
32 EC	D	KP	0.96	0.65					0.80	0.94		0.70	1.00		3A/2B, 4B	Y	0.88	
33 EC	KH	KP	0.75	0.50		0.50	1.00		0.67	0.70		0.75	1.00		2B/3A	Y	0.68	
34 EC	K	D	0.72	0.75		0.75	0.79		0.67	0.80		0.50	1.00		1A/3A, 4B, AB	Y	0.73	
35 EC	KP	D	0.77	0.80		0.72	0.94										0.78	
36 EC	D	D	0.87	1.00					0.85	1.00					1A/3A	Y	0.90	
37 EC	KH	D	0.73	1.00		0.86	0.80		0.63	1.00							0.79	
38 EC	K	KH	0.82	0.55		0.72	0.57		0.57	0.80							0.70	
39 EC	KP	KH	0.70	0.80		0.75	1.00										0.75	
40 EC	D	KH	1.00	0.50	BDL (.06)				0.75	0.82					1A/2B, 4B	Y	0.78	
41 EC	KH	KH	1.00	0.71		0.80	1.00		0.89	0.88							0.88	
42 EC	K	L				0.62	0.41		0.59	0.48							0.55	
43 EC	KP	L				0.38	0.56										0.41	
44 EC	D	L							0.61	0.50		0.50	0.00	Y	1A/2B	Y (BDL)	0.58	
45 EC	KH	L				0.50	0.71		0.62	0.60							0.61	
46 EC	K	J				0.62	0.58		0.68	0.44							0.59	
47 EC	KP	J				0.75	0.75					1.00	0.50	Y	2B/3A	Y	0.80	see X2
48 EC	D	J							0.60	0.56							0.58	
49 EC	KH	J				0.69	0.75		0.78	0.70							0.75	see X2

Language Attitude Survey Data

A Dim.	B Subj.	C Texts	D Etext	E Ytext	F SD	G Ascore	H Escore	I SD	J Mscore	K Fscore	L SD	M Med TS-A	N Med TS-B	O SD	P Quest.	Q SD	R Dscores	S SD
50 LA	K	K	0.97	0.97		0.99	0.94		0.97	0.99							0.98	Y
51 LA	KP	K	0.95	0.99		1.00	0.94										0.98	Y
52 LA	D	K	0.84	0.91					0.86	0.92							0.88	
53 LA	KH	K	0.82	0.82		0.74	1.00		0.88	0.74							0.83	
54 LA	K	KP	0.90	0.68	Y	0.81	0.72	Y	0.69	0.88	BDL (.057)	0.69	1.00	(No)	2B/AB	Y	0.77	
55 LA	KP	KP	0.98	1.00		0.98	1.00										0.99	Y
56 LA	D	KP	0.85	0.61	Y				0.74	0.69		0.75	1.00	Y	1A/2B	Y	0.72	
57 LA	KH	KP	0.81	0.72		0.72	0.94		0.69	0.84							0.75	
58 LA	K	D	0.93	0.96		0.93	1.00		0.96	0.90							0.94	
59 LA	KP	D	0.91	0.98		1.00	0.85	BDL (.057)									0.95	
60 LA	D	D	0.93	0.94					0.97	0.91							0.95	
61 LA	KH	D	1.00	1.00		1.00	1.00		1.00	1.00							1.00	
62 LA	K	KH	0.89	0.78		0.89	0.89		0.83	0.90							0.86	
63 LA	KP	KH	0.88	0.82		0.92	0.75										0.85	
64 LA	D	KH	0.85	0.79					0.82	0.86							0.83	
65 LA	KH	KH	0.93	0.98		1.00	0.91		0.96	0.97							0.96	Y (BDL)
66 LA	K	L				0.89	0.83		0.86	0.87							0.89	Y
67 LA	KP	L				0.56	0.61										0.53	
68 LA	D	L							0.47	0.45							0.46	
69 LA	KH	L				0.57	0.53		0.42	0.69	Y						0.52	
70 LA	K	J				0.98	1.00		1.00	0.97							0.99	
71 LA	KP	J				0.98	0.97										0.98	
72 LA	D	J							0.91	0.91							0.91	
73 LA	KH	J				0.95	1.00		1.00	0.94							0.98	

A Dim.	B Subj.	C Texts	D Etext	E Ytext SD	F Ascore	G SD	H Escore	I SD	J Mscore	K Fscore	L SD	M Med TS-A	N Med TS-B	O Quest.	P SD	Q SD	R Dscores	S SD
74 PC	K	K	0.86	0.85	0.90		0.75		0.86	0.85							0.86	
75 PC	KP	K	0.86	0.77	0.80		0.88										0.82	
76 PC	D	K	0.80	0.79										1A/3A, 4B	BDL (.059)		0.80	
77 PC	KH	K	0.80	0.70	0.70		0.79		0.79	0.68							0.75	
78 PC	K	KP	0.71	0.75	0.83		0.56	Y	0.68	0.80							0.73	see X2
79 PC	KP	KP	0.89	0.83	0.83		0.92										0.85	
80 PC	D	KP	0.69	0.87													0.79	
81 PC	KH	KP	0.50	0.80	0.61		0.75		0.85	0.68							0.65	see X2
82 PC	K	D	0.72	0.80	0.78		0.78		0.62	0.72				2B/AB	Y		0.76	see X2
83 PC	KP	D	0.63	0.85	0.69		0.69		0.70	0.84							0.72	see X2
84 PC	D	D	0.79	0.90													0.85	
85 PC	KH	D	0.68	0.93	0.80		0.81		0.81	0.91							0.81	
86 PC	K	KH	0.73	0.81	0.83		0.75		0.75	0.91				1A/AB, 2B, 3A/4B, AB	Y		0.78	see X2
87 PC	KP	KH	0.78	0.92	0.77		1.00	Y	0.93	0.82							0.86	
88 PC	D	KH	0.90	0.86					0.94	0.91				4B/2B, 3A	Y		0.88	
89 PC	KH	KH	0.95	0.91	0.86		1.00		0.58	0.75							0.93	
90 PC	K	L			0.72		0.56										0.66	
91 PC	KP	L			0.63		0.33					0.00	1.00	1A/2B, 4B	Y		0.52	
92 PC	D	L							0.74	0.80							0.76	
93 PC	KH	L			0.55		0.56		0.42	0.75							0.55	
94 PC	K	J			0.76		0.64		0.71	0.66							0.70	BDL (.055)
95 PC	KP	J			0.58		0.78		0.88	0.86							0.68	see X2
96 PC	D	J							0.85	0.88							0.88	
97 PC	KH	J			0.86		0.88										0.86	

Language Attitude Survey Data

	A Dim.	B Subj.	C Texts	D Etext	E Ytext	F SD	G Ascore	H Escore	I SD	J Mscore	K Fscore	L SD	M Med TS-A	N Med TS-B	O SD	P Quest.	Q SD	R Dscores	S SD
98	SS	K	K	0.68	0.48		0.54	0.50		0.62	0.47					3A/4B	Y	0.56	see X2
99	SS	KP	K	0.63	0.70		0.76	0.51	Y									0.65	
100	SS	D	K	0.54	0.62					0.57	0.44					1A/2B, 4B/3A	Y	0.52	
101	SS	KH	K	0.74	0.74		0.51	0.91	Y	0.82	0.50	Y						0.70	
102	SS	K	KP	0.62	0.43		0.59	0.42		0.45	0.64					3A/1A, 2B, AB	Y	0.52	Y
103	SS	KP	KP	0.81	0.62		0.67	0.75								3A/AB	Y	0.68	
104	SS	D	KP	0.81	0.60					0.65	0.77							0.70	
105	SS	KH	KP	0.85	0.80		0.77	0.94		0.83	0.81							0.82	Y
106	SS	K	D	0.31	0.53		0.44	0.42		0.37	0.47					1A/4B	Y	0.41	
107	SS	KP	D	0.45	0.75		0.67	0.47								1A/3A, 4B	Y	0.57	
108	SS	D	D	0.40	0.73					0.47	0.68							0.55	
109	SS	KH	D	0.32	0.90	Y	0.68	0.44		0.50	0.75					1A/2B, 3A, 4B	Y	0.60	
110	SS	K	KH	0.44	0.54		0.50	0.33		0.55	0.45					2B/4B (seeK-KO-HSD.TXT)	BDL	0.49	
111	SS	KP	KH	0.40	0.73		0.60	0.67								2B/1A, 3A, 4B	Y	0.60	
112	SS	D	KH	0.46	0.52					0.47	0.52					1A/4B 2B/3A, 4B	Y	0.49	
112	SS	KH	KH	0.65	0.68		0.61	0.71		0.56	0.81		0.50	1.00	Y	2B/1A, 3A	Y	0.66	
114	SS	K	L				0.45	0.58		0.60	0.37							0.50	
115	SS	KP	L				0.60	0.58										0.59	
116	SS	D	L							0.50	0.45							0.48	see X2
117	SS	KH	L				0.41	0.44		0.42	0.44							0.43	see X2
118	SS	K	J				0.54	0.65		0.62	0.54							0.58	see X2
119	SS	KP	J				0.86	0.72										0.81	Y
120	SS	D	J							0.46	0.33							0.41	
121	SS	KH	J				0.39	0.44		0.38	0.47							0.42	

Appendix 3

Language Proficiency and Use Survey Data

(99) Language use questionnaire: Final form

Nom: Village:
Questions d'usage de la langue

Lobiri/Dioula/Français
Domaine 1: Officiel
OF1. Quelle langue as-tu parlé quand tu as obtenu ta carte d'identité? (Où)
OF2. Quelle langue parles-tu quand tu vas au dispensaire? (Où)
OF3. Quelle langue parles-tu en parlant avec
  A. le maître d'école
  B. l'encadreur
  C. le vétérinaire?

Domaine 2: Le marché
MK1. Quelle langue parles-tu le plus souvent au marché de
  A. Loropéni
  B. Yérifoula
  C. Lorhosso
  D. Koro
  E. Ouo?

Quelle langue parles-tu quand tu achètes...
MK2. du beurre de karité
MK3. des pagnes
MK4. de la viande
    A. boeuf
    B. porc
MK5. des pois sucrés
MK6. quelque chose dans une boutique (boîte de sardines, boîte de lait)
MK7. quelque chose à manger (du riz-sauce)?
MK8. Quelle langue parles-tu quand tu fais réparer un vélo ou un vélomoteur?
MK9. A. Quelle langue préfères-tu pour conter de l'argent?
    B. Quand la somme est grosse (plus que 10.000 francs)?

Domaine 3: L'amitié
    Quelle langue parles-tu...
FR1. au cabaret en venant de/en quittant le marché
FR2. quand tu rencontres sur la route un____ que tu connais?
    A. Kaan
    B. Lobi
    C. Dioula
    D. Dogo
FR3. quand tu salues un étranger dont tu ne connais pas l'ethnie
FR4. avec tes amis Kaan quand il y a des ____ avec toi en même temps?
    A. Lobi
    B. Dioula
    C. Dogo
FR5. Est-ce qu'il t'est arrivé d'avoir honte de parler en Kaansa pendant que des gens d'autres ethnies t'écoutent?

Domaine 4: La religion
RL1. Quelle langue parles-tu dans vos prières
    A. en groupe
    B. seul?
RL2. Est-ce que tu assistes aux funérailles des
    A. Lobi
    B. Dioula
    C. Dogo?

Domaine 5: Les voyages
TR1. Quelle langue parles-tu le plus souvent quand tu voyages à
   A. Gaoua
   B. Loropéni
   C. Yérifoula
   D. Lorhosso
   E. Koro
   F. Ouo
   G. Banfora
   H. Bobo-Dioulasso
   I. Sidéradougou
   J. Côte d'Ivoire?

Domaine 6: L'école
   Est-ce que tu as parlé...
SC1. en ___ en classe à l'école
   A. Kaansa
   B. Dogose
   C. Dioula
   D. Lobiri
SC2. à l'extérieur de l'école avec tes camarades
SC3. en jouant au football avec eux?

Domaine 7: Le sujet
SJ1. A. Est-ce que tu parles de la politique en
      Kaansa
      Lobiri
      Dioula
      Français?
   B. (Quand tu parles de la politique) est-ce que tu emploies beaucoup de mots en:
      Français
      Dioula
      Lobiri?
SJ2. Quand tu racontes à tes amis dans le village ce qui est arrivé au marché, est-ce que tu emploies:
   A. beaucoup de mots en
      Français
      Dioula
      Lobiri
   B. quelques mots de...seulement

C. Jamais de mots de...?

Domaine 8: Le contacte inter-ethnique
CT1. A. Est-ce que tu travailles avec des Lobi/Dioula pour
　　　　préparer un champ (hommes)
　　　　préparer le beurre de karité (femmes)?
　　B. Quelle langue parles-tu avec eux?
CT2. Est-ce que tu penses que c'est bon de permettre aux jeunes hommes Kaan de se marier aux femmes qui parlent
　　　　uniquement le...
　　A. Lobiri
　　B. Dioula
　　C. Dogose
　　D. Kaansa?
　　Est-ce qu'il arrive que tu parles...
CT3. Dioula avec un Lobi?
CT4. Lobiri avec un Dioula?
CT5. Dioula avec un
　　A. Dogo
　　B. Kaan?
CT6. Lobiri avec un
　　A. Dogo?
　　B. Kaan?

Questions finales: Compétence
PA1. Est-ce que tu parles le Lobi mieux que le Jula?
　　Le Jula mieux que le Lobi?
　　Les deux au même niveau?
PA2. Quelle langue est-ce que tu as appris d'abord?
　　Les deux en même temps?
PA3. Est-ce que tu désires de parler le ____ mieux que tu le fais maintenant?
　　A. Lobiri
　　B. Dioula
　　(Est-ce que tu penses que tu parles le ____ bien maintenant, et que ça suffit pour parler avec tout le monde et dans toutes les circonstances?)
　　A. Lobiri
　　B. Dioula

Nom:　　Village:　　Age:　　Sexe:　　Ecole:

(100) Jula proficiency self-rating questionnaire: Final form

Nom: Village:
Mesures de compétence en langue Dioula

Estimation initiale de compétence:

1. parle bien
2. se débrouille
3. ne parle pas bien
4. connais pas

0. Niveau 0+ ("zéro plus")

0.1. Est-ce que tu connais seulement quelques phrases et expressions parce que on les entend souvent?	oui- un peu seulement; non- beaucoup
0.2. Tu ne peux pas vraiment causer avec les gens.	oui- peux pas; non- peux

1. Niveau 1

1.1. Est-ce que tu peux saluer les gens avec facilité?	oui/oui- difficile/ non
1.2. Tu peux dire à quelqu'un de quel village tu viens, qui est ton père (ton vieux), quel est ton clan (famille), d'où tu viens, où tu vas, et ce que tu vas faire là-bas.	oui/oui- difficile/ non
1.3. Est-ce que c'est vrai que souvent les Dioulas doivent parler lentement et prononcer bien et répéter pour que tu puisses comprendre ce qu'ils disent?	oui- ils font comme ça; non- je comprends tout
1.4. Quand tu parles, est-ce qu'il arrive que tu ne peux pas finir une phrase parce que tu ne trouves pas les mots que tu cherches?	oui- ça m'arrive; non- ça n'arrive pas

2. Niveau 2

2.1. Tu peux expliquer en détail les relations dans ta famille: qui habite dans ta cour, où habitent tes oncles et tes frères et soeurs, qui est marié avec qui, quels sont leurs enfants, toujours en employant les bons mots Dioula.
oui/oui- difficile/non

2.2. Tu peux causer avec un Dioula au sujet des évenements de la semaine passée: qui est tombé malade, qu'est-ce qui se passe au marché, si on trouve assez à manger, quels sont les grands palabres du village, etc.
oui/oui- difficile/non

2.3. Quand les Dioulas parlent de ces choses tu peux comprendre presque tout.
oui/oui- difficile/non

2.4. Quand tu parles Dioula, tu peux parler assez vite...
oui/oui- difficile/non

...mais pour parler des choses compliquées tu ne peux pas parler aussi vite.
oui- parle pas vite; non- parle vite toujours

2.5. Est-ce que quelques fois tu dois pauser pour chercher les mots avant de finir ce que tu veux dire?
oui- je dois pauser; non- je ne pause pas

3. Niveau 3

3.1. Tu ne fais pas beaucoup de fautes, même quand tu parles rapidement à propos des affaires compliquées.
oui- pas de fautes; non- il y a des fautes

3.2. Quand tu écoutes à deux Dioulas en train de discuter vivement quelque chose d'important, tu comprends tout ce qu'ils disent.
oui/oui- difficile/non

3.3. Tu peux accompagner un malade au dispensaire et expliquer le problème en profondeur au docteur (dire comment à ton avis il est tombé malade, quand la maladie a commencé, qu'est-ce que le malade a mangé, où il fait mal, etc.).
oui/oui- difficile/non

3.4. Tu peux expliquer à un ami Dioula un problème dans ta famille, ou disputer avec quelqu'un quand tu n'es pas d'accord avec lui.
oui/oui- difficile/non

4. Niveau 4

4.1. Tu connais des blagues, devinettes, proverbes, et injures des Dioulas, et quand tu les entends, tu ris avec eux. — oui/oui- difficile/non

4.2. Tu peux vivre et travailler chez les Dioulas avec facilité et confiance. — oui/oui- difficile/non

4.3. Tu peux rendre un témoignage élaboré dans un jugement officiel, et tu peux expliquer en détail les faits d'un événement que tu as expérimenté. — oui/oui- difficile/non

4.4. Tu ne fais presque jamais de fautes en parlant. Tu trouves toujours facilement les mots pour dire exactement ce que tu veux dans toutes les circonstances. — oui/non

5. Niveau 5

5.1. Quelques fois les Dioulas ne savent pas que je ne suis pas un Dioula aussi. — oui/non

5.2. Quelques fois, tu trouves que c'est plus facile de t'exprimer en Dioula qu'en ta langue maternelle. — oui/non

5.3. Tu peux conter et faire des calculs très vite en Dioula. — oui/non

5.4. Tu comprends les paroles des chansons Dioula à la radio. — oui/non

5.5. Tu connais la vie et les habitudes des Dioulas aussi bien que tu les connais pour ta propre ethnie. — oui/non

References

Agheyisi, Rebecca and Joshua Fishman. 1970. Language attitude studies: A brief survey of methodological approaches. Anthropological Linguistics 12(5):137–157.

Akere, Funso. 1981. Sociolinguistic consequences of language contact: English versus Nigerian languages. Language Sciences 3(2):283–304.

Akere, Funso. 1982. Language use and language attitudes in a Yoruba suburban town: A sociolinguistic response to the factors of traditionalism and modernity. Anthropological Linguistics 24(3):344–362.

Alexandre, Pierre. 1971. Multilingualism. In Thomas A. Sebeok (ed.), Current trends in linguistics, 7: Linguistics in sub-Saharan Africa, 654–663. The Hague: Mouton.

Alexandre, Pierre. 1972. Languages and language in black Africa. Evanston, Ill.: Northwestern University Press. Translated by F.A. Leary from the French edition, Langues et langage en Afrique noire. Paris: Payot. 1967.

Batiana, André. 1985. Variation linguistique et comportements langagiers dans la communauté lyèlLoropéni. Thèse de doctorat de 3ème cycle. Université de Nice (Faculté des Lettres et Sciences Humaines).

Battestini, Simon P. X. To appear. Reading signs of identity and alterity: History, semiotics and a Nigerian case. African Studies Review.

Battestini, Simon P. X. n.d. The interface between writing and speech in West Africa. ms.

Bender, M. L., R. L. Cooper, and C. A. Ferguson. 1972. Language in Ethiopia: Implications of a survey for sociolinguistic theory and method. Language in Society 1:215–233.

Bendor-Samuel, John T. 1980. Is a sociolinguistic profile necessary? Paper presented at the 14th Congress of the West African Linguistic Society, Cotonou, Benin, April 14–18, 1980.

Bendor-Samuel, John T. and Rhonda L. Hartell. 1989. The Niger-Congo languages: A classification and description of Africa's largest language family. Lanham, Md.: University Press of America.

Binger, Louis Gustave. 1892. Du Niger au Golfe de Guinée par le pays de Kong et de Mosi, 2 vols. Paris: Hachette.

Bourhis, Richard. 1982. Language policies and language attitudes: Le monde de la francophonie. In Ellen Ryan and Howard Giles (eds.), Attitudes toward language variation, 34–61. London: Edward Arnold.

Bourhis, Richard and Howard Giles. 1976. The language of cooperation in Wales: A field study. Language Sciences 42:13–16.

Brewster, E. Thomas and Elizabeth S. Brewster. 1976. Language acquisition made practical. Oakland, Cal.: Lingua House.

Bruhn, Thea C. 1984. Country status report: Senegal. Language/Area Reference Center. Washington, D.C.: Center for Applied Linguistics.

Calvet, Louis-Jean. 1981. Les langues véhiculaires. Collection "Que sais-je", Number 1916. Paris: Presses Universitaires de France.

Calvet, Louis-Jean. 1982. The spread of Mandingo: Military, commercial, and colonial influence on a linguistic datum. In Cooper, 184–197.

Casad, Eugene H. 1974. Dialect intelligibility testing. Norman, Okla.: Summer Institute of Linguistics.

Chambers, J. K. and Peter Trudgill. 1980. Dialectology. New York: Cambridge University Press.

Claessens, Jan. 1981. Regards sur la Haute Volta. Poitiers: Collectif Tiers-Monde.

Conover, W. J. and Ronald L. Iman. 1981. Rank transformations as a bridge between parametric and nonparametric statistics. The American Statistician 35:124–133.

Cooper, Robert L. 1980. Sociolinguistic surveys: The state of the art. Applied Linguistics 1(2):113–128.

Cooper, Robert L., ed. 1982a. Language spread: Studies in diffusion and social change. Bloomington: Indiana University Press.

Cooper, Robert L. 1982b. A framework for the study of language spread. In Cooper, 5–36.

Cooper, Robert L. and Joshua A. Fishman. 1974. The study of language attitudes. International Journal of the Sociology of Language 3:5–19.

Coulibaly, Bakary. 1984. Le jula véhiculaire de Haute Volta: Phonologie, morphologie, syntaxe, et règles de transcription orthographique. Thèse de doctorat d'état en linguistique. Université Descartes, Paris.

Delafosse, Maurice. 1912. Haut-Sénégal et Niger. Paris: Larose.

Delafosse, Maurice. 1924. Langues du Soudan et de la Guinée. In A. Meillet and M. Cohen (eds.), Les langues du monde, 737–845. Paris: Centre National de la Recherche Scientifique.

De Vaus, David A. 1986. Surveys in social research. Winchester, Mass.: Allen and Unwin.

Djité, Paulin G. 1988. Language attitudes in Abidjan: Implications for language planning in the Ivory Coast. Ph.D. dissertation. Georgetown University.

Dumestre, G. and G. L. A. Retord, 1981. Kó Dì? Cours de Dioula. Abidjan: Les Nouvelles Editions Africaines.

Edwards, John. 1985. Language, society and identity. Oxford: Basil Blackwell.

Fage, J. D. 1969. A history of West Africa: An introductory survey. London: Cambridge University Press.

Fasold, Ralph. 1984. The sociolinguistics of society. New York: Basil Blackwell.

Ferguson, C. A. 1959. Diglossia. Word 15:325–340.

Fishman, Joshua A. 1968. Nationality-nationalism and nation-nationism. In Joshua A. Fishman, Charles A. Ferguson, and Jyotirindra Das Gupta (eds.), Language problems of developing nations, 39–52. New York: John Wiley and Sons.

Fishman, Joshua A. 1969. Bilingual attitudes and behaviors. Language Sciences 5:5–11.

Fishman, Joshua A. 1972a. Domains and the relationship between micro and macro-sociolinguistics. In John J. Gumperz and Dell Hymes (eds.), Directions in sociolinguistics: The ethnography of communication, 435–453. New York: Holt, Rinehart and Winston.

Fishman, Joshua A. 1972b. Societal bilingualism: Stable and transitional. The sociology of language, 91–106. Rowley, Mass.: Newbury House.

Fishman, Joshua A. 1972c. The sociology of language, an interdisciplinary social sciency approach to language. In Joshua A. Fishman (ed.), Advances in the sociology of language 1:217–404. The Hague: Mouton.

Gal, Susan. 1978. Variation and change in patterns of speaking: Language shift in Austria. In D. Sankoff (ed.), Linguistic variation: Models and methods, 227–238. New York: Academic Press.

Greenberg, Joseph. 1970. The languages of Africa. Bloomington: Indiana University Press.

Griffeth, Robert R. 1971. The Dyula impact on the peoples of the West Volta region. In Charleton T. Hodge (ed.), Papers on the Manding. Bloomington: Indiana University Press.

Grimes, Barbara F., ed. 2000. Ethnologue: Languages of the world, tenth ed. Dallas: Wycliffe Bible Translators.

Grimes, Barbara F. 1985. Comprehension and language attitudes in relation to language choice for literature and education in pre-literate societies. Journal of Multilingual and Multicultural Development 6(2):165–81.

Grimes, Barbara F. 1987. How bilingual is bilingual? Notes on Linguistics 40a:34–54.

Grimes, Joseph E. 1989. Widening circles of communication. Proceedings of the International Language Assessment Conference of the Summer Institute of Linguistics, 252–263. Horsleys Green, England, May 24–31, 1989.

Grosjean, François. 1982. Life with two languages: An introduction to bilingualism. Cambridge, Mass.: Harvard University Press.

Gumperz, John J. 1962. Types of linguistic communities. Anthropological linguistics 4(1):28–40.

Gumperz, John J. 1971. The speech community. In Anwar S. Dil (ed.), Language and social groups: Essays by John J. Gumperz, 114–280. Stanford, Cal.: Stanford University Press.

Gumperz, John J. 1976. Social network and language shift. In J. Cook-Gumperz and John J. Gumperz (eds.), Papers on Language and Context 46. Berkeley: Language Behavior Research Laboratory, University of California.

Hartell, Rhonda, ed. n.d. Language surveys in Burkina Faso. ms.

Hays, W. L. 1988. Statistics. New York: Holt, Rinehart and Winston.

Heine, Bernd. 1970. Status and use of African lingua francas. New York: Humanities Press.

Hudson, R. A. 1980. Sociolinguistics. Cambridge: Cambridge University Press.

Huttar, George, ed. 1982. Sociolinguistic survey conference proceedings. Notes on Linguistics (Special publication 2).

Hymes, Dell. 1967. Linguistic problems in defining the concept of "Tribe". In John Baugh and Joel Sherzer (eds.) Language in use, 7–27. Englewood Cliffs, N.J.: Prentice Hall.

Hymes, Dell. 1971. Pidginization and creolization of languages. London: Cambridge University Press.

Hymes, Dell. 1972. Models of the interaction of language and social life. In John Gumperz and Dell Hymes (eds.), Directions in sociolinguistics:

The ethnography of communication, 35–71. New York: Holt, Rinehart and Winston.

Institut Géographique du Burkina. 1988. Burkina Faso: Carte linguistique. Ouagadougou: IGB.

Institut National de la Statistíque et de la Deomgraphie. 1986. Recensement général de la population: résultats provisoires. Ougadougou: INSD.

Jeune Afrique. 1975. Atlas de la Haute Volta. Paris: Editions Jeune Afrique.

Kanyoro, Musimbi. 1989. The Abaluyia of Kenya: One people, one language. In Ted G. Bergman (ed.), Round table on assuring the feasibility of standardization within dialect chains, 87–107. Nairobi: Summer Institute of Linguistics.

Karam, Francis X. 1979. Processes of increasing mutual intelligibility between language varieties. International Journal of the Sociology of Language 22:115–137.

Ki-Zerbo, Joseph. 1972. Histoire de l'Afrique noire d'hier ĩ demain. Paris: Hatier.

Labouret, H. 1925. Les bandes de Samori dans la Haute Côte d'Ivoire, la Côte de l'Or et le pays Lobi: L'expansion anglaise sur la Volta Noire. Renseignements Coloniaux (supplément de l'Afrique Française, août 1925) 8:341–355.

Labouret, H. 1931. Les tribus du rameau Lobi. Paris: Institut d'Ethnologie.

Labouret, H. 1958. Nouvelles notes sur les tribus du rameau Lobi: Leurs migrations, leur évolution, leurs parlers et ceux de leurs voisins. Mémoires de l'Institut Français d'Afrique Noire n° 54. Dakar: I.F.A.N.

Labov, William. 1966. The social stratification of English in New York City. Washington, D.C.: Center for Applied Linguistics.

Labov, William. 1972a. Sociolinguistic patterns. Philadelphia: University of Pennsylvania Press.

Labov, William. 1972b. Some principles of linguistic methodology. Language in Society 1:97–120.

Labov, William. 1972c. The isolation of contextual styles. In William Labov (ed.), Sociolinguistic patterns, 70–109. Philadelphia: University of Pennsylvania Press.

Lafage, Suzanne. n.d. Opération 47.08.07: Etude sociolinguistique du français de Côte d'Ivoire. Photocopy of research proposal.

Lafage, Suzanne. 1979. Esquisse d'un cadre de référence pragmatique pour une analyse sociolinguistique en contexte africain. In Gabriel Manessy and Paul Wald (eds.), Plurilinguisme: Normes, situations, stratégies, 41–60. Paris: L'Harmattan.

Lafage, Suzanne. 1986. Outline of a practical frame of reference for a sociolinguistic analysis in an African context. In George Huttar and

Kenneth Gregerson (eds.), Pragmatics in non-western perspective, 143–159. Dallas: Summer Institute of Linguistics and University of Texas at Arlington.

Lambert, Wallace E., R. C. Hodgson, R. C. Gardner, and S. Fillenbaum. 1960. Evaluational reactions to spoken languages. Journal of Abnormal and Social Psychology 60(1):44–51.

Lavergne de Tressan, M. 1953. Inventaire linguistique de l'Afrique Occidentale Française et du Togo. Mémoires de l'Institut Français d'Afrique Noire n° 30. Dakar: IFAN.

Lewis, E. Glyn. 1985. Types of bilingual communities. In James E. Alatis and John J. Staczek (eds.), Perspectives on bilingualism and bilingual education, 49–64. Washington, D.C.: Georgetown University Press.

Lowe, Jr., Pardee and Charles W. Stansfield, eds. 1988. Second language proficiency assessment: Current issues. Englewood Cliffs, N.J.: Prentice Hall Regents.

Mackey, William F. 1968. The description of bilingualism. In Joshua A. Fishman (ed.), Readings in the sociology of language, 554–584. The Hague: Mouton.

Manessy, Gabriel. 1963. Rapport sur les langues voltaïques. Actes du second colloque international de linguistique africaine, 242. Dakar.

Manessy, Gabriel. 1977. Processes of pidginization in African languages. In Albert Valdman (ed.), Pidgin and creole linguistics, 129–149. Bloomington: Indiana University Press.

Manessy, Gabriel. 1981. Les langues voltaïques. Les langues dans le monde ancien et moderne, 103–110. Paris: Editions du C.N.R.S.

Mansour, G. 1980. The dynamics of multilingualism: The case of Senegal. Journal of Multilingual and Multicultural Development 1:273–293.

Mgbo-Elue, C. N. 1988. Social psychological and linguistic impediments to the acquisition of a second Nigerian language among Yoruba and Ibo. In W. Gudykunst (ed.), Language and ethnic identity, 153–161. Philadelphia: Multilingual Matters.

Mkilifi, Abdulaziz. 1978. Triglossia and Swahili-English bilingualism in Tanzania. In Joshua L. Fishman (ed.), Advances in the study of societal multilingualism, 129–149. The Hague: Mouton.

Naden, Anthony. 1989. Gur. In John Bendor-Samuel and Rhonda Hartell, (eds.), The Niger-Congo languages: A classification and description of Africa's largest language family, p. 140–168. Lanham, Md.: University Press of America.

Nida, Eugene A. and Harold W. Fehderau. 1970. Indigenous pidgins and koinés. International Journal of American Linguistics 36:146–155.

Osgood, Charles E., George J. Suci, and Percy H. Tannenbaum. 1957. The measurement of meaning. Urbana: University of Illinois Press.

Ouedraogo, Mathieu R. 1983. An analysis of some factors that affect curriculum implementation in Upper Volta. African studies in curriculum development and evaluation, 130. Nairobi: African Curriculum Organization.

Père, Madeleine. 1982. Les deux bouches: Les sociétés du "rameau lobi" entre la tradition et le changement. Thèse pour le Doctorat ès Lettres et Sciences Humaines. Université de Pantheon-Sorbonne, Paris.

Père, Madeleine. 1987. Interview. April 24, 1987. Radio Gaoua. Gaoua, Burkina Faso.

Père, Madeleine. to appear. Les gans de Loropéni ou des akan au Burkina Faso?

Parenko, Paley and R. P. J. Hébert. 1962. Une famille ethnique: Les gan, les padoro, les dorobé, les komono. Bulletin de l'Institut Français d'Afrique Noire n° 24, sér. B (3–4):414–448.

Partmann, Gayle Holley. 1973. Le dioula véhiculaire en Côte d'Ivoire: Etude comparative des jeunes locuteurs primaires et secondaires du dioula. Ph. D. dissertation. Stanford University.

Person, Yves. 1968. Samori: Une révolution djula, 3 vols. Dakar: Mémoire de l'Institut Français d'Afrique Noire n° 80.

Polomé, Edgar C. 1982. Rural versus urban multilingualism in Tanzania: An outline. International Journal of the Sociology of Language 34:167–181.

Population Reference Bureau. 2000. 2000 world population data sheet. Washington, D.C. (http://www.prb.org/pubs/wpds2000_SubSaharan Africa.html)

Prost, André. 1972. Le dogose ou langue des dogobe ou doghossié. Publications du Département de Linguistique Générale et de Langues Négro-Africaines, Faculté des Lettres et Sciences Humaines, 19. Dakar: Université de Dakar.

Quakenbush, John Stephen. 1986. Language use and proficiency in a multilingual setting: A sociolinguistic survey of Agutaynen speakers in Palawan, Philippines. Ph.D. dissertation. Georgetown University.

Raj Dua, Hans. 1981. Dimensions of speech community. International Journal of the Sociology of Language 32:85–119.

Ring, James Andrew. 1987. Planning for literacy: A sociolinguistic survey of multilingualism in Ghana. Ph.D. dissertation. Georgetown University.

Saah, Kofi K. 1986. Language use and attitudes in Ghana. Anthropological Linguistics 28(3):367–377.

Sanders, Arden G. 1977. Guidelines for conducting a lexicostatistic survey in Papua New Guinea. Language variation and survey techniques. Workpapers in Papua New Guinea languages, 21:21–41. Ukarumpa, Papua New Guinea: Summer Institute of Linguistics.

Savonnet, G. 1963. Quelques notes sur les gan et sur le rituel d'intronisation de leur chef. Etudes Voltaïques 4:125–132.

Sawilowsky, Shlomo S. 1990. Nonparametric tests of interaction in experimental design. Review of Educational Research 60:91–126.

Schmidt, Melinda. 1986. Personal letter to Mady Vaillant on the 17th of December. Tougbo, Côte d'Ivoire.

Schuerkens, Ulrike. 1983. Le rôle du français dans un pays en voie de développement, le Sénégal. Langage et l'Homme 52:67–73.

Scotton, Carol Myers. 1977. Linguistic performances as subjective measures: Some findings and implications. Studies in African Linguistics supplement 7:199–210.

Scotton, Carol Myers. 1982. Learning lingua francas and socioeconomic integration: Evidence from Africa. In Cooper, 63–94.

Shavelson, Richard J. 1981. Statistical reasoning for the behavioral sciences. Boston: Allyn and Bacon.

Showalter, Catherine. 1990. Measuring prominence in Kaanse, a tonal language of Burkina Faso. Paper presented at the pre-session on African linguistics at the Georgetown University Round Table on Languages and Linguistics (GURT). To appear.

Showalter, Stuart D. n.d. The Bambadion enigma. ms.

Sidibe, M. 1927. Contribution à l'étude de l'histoire de la region de Bdo-Dioulasso (Haute Volta). Bulletin de l'enseignement de l'AOF 64:54–71.

Simons, Gary F. 1983. Language variation and limits to communication. Dallas: Summer Institute of Linguistics.

Solomiac, Paul. 1983. Rapport d'enquête dogosé, gbadogo, komono. ms. Ouagadougou: SIL.

Summer Institute of Linguistics (SIL). 1987. The SIL second language oral proficiency evaluation (SLOPE). Notes on Linguistics 40a:3–33.

Tabouret-Keller, A. 1968. Sociological factors of language maintenance and language shift: A methodological approach based on European and African examples. In Joshua A. Fishman, Charles A. Ferguson, and Jyotirindra Das Gupta (eds.), Language problems of developing nations, 107–18. New York: John Wiley and Sons.

Tauxier, L. 1921. Noir de Bondoukou. Paris: Leroux.

Tauxier, L. 1931. Les dorhosié et dorhosié-finng du cercle de Bobo-Dioulasso (Soudan Français). Journal de la Société des Africanistes 1(1):61–110.

Tiendrebeogo, Gérard. 1983. Langues et groupes ethniques de Haute Volta. Abidjan: Agence de Coopération Culturelle et Technique/Institut de Linguistique Appliquée.
Tiendrebeogo, Gérard and Zakaria Yago. 1983. Situation des langues parlées en Haute Volta. Abidjan: Agence de Coopération Culturelle et Technique/Institut de Linguistique Appliquée.
Vaillant, Madeleine. 1967. Esquisse grammaticale du lobiri parlé dans la fraction septentrionale de la tribu lobi. Documents linguistiques, 10. Dakar: Université de Dakar.
Vaillant, Madeleine. n.d. Esquisse de phonologie Kásɛ. ms.
Weinreich, Uriel. 1953. Languages in contact. The Hague: Mouton.
Wolff, Hans. 1959. Intelligibility and inter-ethnic attitudes. Anthropological Linguistics 1(3):34–41.
Wolff, Hans. 1967. Language, ethnic identity and social change in southern Nigeria. Anthropological Linguistics 9(1):18–25.
Yanco, Jennifer J. 1983. Language attitudes and bilingualism in Niamey, Niger. Africana 14(1):1–9.

www.ingramcontent.com/pod-product-compliance
Lightning Source LLC
Chambersburg PA
CBHW050136240426
43673CB00043B/1692